Clovercroft Chronicles, 1314-1893

For my dearly loved great-granddaughter,
Mary Garrett Branson,
a well-spring of joy and hope in my heart,
this first anniversary of her birth, the
twenty fifth day of the First month, 1897.

" The beloved of the Lord
shall dwell in safety
by Him."

CLOVERCROFT CHRONICLES,

1314—1893.

BY

MARY RHOADS HAINES.

" I cannot but remember such things were,
That were most precious to me "

Printed for Private Circulation

PRESS OF J. B. LIPPINCOTT COMPANY,

PHILADELPHIA.

.TO MY

FAITHFUL AND BELOVED SON-IN-LAW AND DAUGHTER,

JOHN BIDDLE GARRETT
AND
HANNAH RHOADS GARRETT,

AND MY GRANDDAUGHTERS,

MARY RHOADS GARRETT
AND
FRANCES BIDDLE GARRETT,

THIS BOOK IS AFFECTIONATELY INSCRIBED

PREFACE.

To record some traditions and recollections that would pass away with myself, now the eldest in my generation, I began to write these chronicles.

Intended chiefly for the family of Clovercroft, and especially for my only child, who was deprived of the care of a most loving and honorable father when little more than ten months old, I hope they may not be without interest to some others of kindred descent.

I have carefully endeavored, so far as practicable with the resources that were at my command, to be accurate. From original records, certificates, and other manuscripts in my possession much has been drawn that is entirely reliable: to say that no mistakes have been made in any of the oldest dates and names would be presuming, but I have verified them as nearly as I can by collating with accounts to which I have had access.

It is my desire that the record here presented of many Christian men and women, whose aim it was "to do justly, and to love mercy, and to walk humbly with their God," may be an encouragement and a stimulus to their descendants to prefer and persevere in the paths of righteousness and peace, under the leadership of the heavenly Shepherd, our Lord Jesus Christ.

Like ourselves, our ancestors partook of the common lot of humanity. Life—with its joys and sorrows, its toils and trials, its prosperity and its successes—was much the same as that we

5

have experienced   They did not aspire to worldly greatness and renown, yet had their noble ambitions, and, while keeping "a conscience void of offence toward God, and toward men," they were blessed with competence, domestic happiness, and the power to help and comfort their fellow-men.

MARY RHOADS HAINES.

CLOVERCROFT, ROSEMONT, MONTGOMERY COUNTY,
    PENNSYLVANIA, Second month, 1893

CONTENTS.

8 *CONTENTS.*

CLOVERCROFT CHRONICLES,

1314-1893.

CHAPTER I.

EARLY RECORDS OF THE HAINES FAMILY.

THE earliest records of the family to which I have access are contained in a manuscript book presented to my sister, Sarah Ellis Haines, by James Starr Lippincott, Second month 15, 1879.

He refers to his authorities in the following paragraph

"Compiled from the collections of Dr. George Haines; The History of the Friendship Mill, near Medford, Burlington County, New Jersey; The Records of the Monthly Meetings of Friends of Delaware County, Chester County, and Lycoming County, Pennsylvania, and from private memoranda by J S L.

"The descendants of Richard Haines, or Haynes, of the village of 'Ainho, or Aynho-on-the-Hill,' in the county of Northampton, England, through his sons John, Richard, William, Thomas, and Joseph, are very numerous in the States of New Jersey and Pennsylvania

"The village of Aynho is a large, respectable collection of houses, and derives its name from a powerful spring, called the town well, which issues from below the rock upon which the village stands   The original name was Avon-ho, meaning well-head, or fountain, which usage has softened into Aynho. . . .

"Several families of the name of Haines now reside in Oxfordshire and Northamptonshire, in the vicinity of Aynho.   Samuel

Haynes formerly resided at Brackley, Northampton, whose
only daughter and heiress, Charlotte Catharine Ann, married,
January 14, 1783, General John William Egerton, seventh Earl
of Bridgewater, son of the Right Reverend John, Lord Bishop
of Durham," and brother of the eighth Earl of Bridgewater, who
left funds for treatises " On the power, wisdom, and goodness of
God as manifest in the Creation "

" The surname Haynes, or Haines, is probably derived from
Aynho, as above   The earliest information I have been able to
obtain respecting the advent of the Haines family to America
is from memoranda taken from the mouth of John Haines, of
Lumberton, a grandson of Richard Haines, one of the first
settlers, and who had known in his boyhood the three younger
of the pioneers "

RICHARD HAINES,

of Aynho, Northamptonshire, England, lived in the latter part
of the seventeenth century   His wife's name is believed to
have been Margaret   Their eldest son, John, was the first of
the family to come to America, and then sent an invitation to
his parents and brothers to follow him   Richard and Margaret
Haines and their four younger sons—Richard, William, Thomas,
and Joseph—accordingly embarked, but in the slow voyage of
those days the father died on the sea

JOHN AND ESTHER HAINES

John Haines had probably brought his wife, Esther Borton,
with him from England   Tradition says that his first home
was a cave on the banks of the Rancocus, not distant from a
small tribe of Indians known as the Cotoxen.

John Haines appears to have been a man of energy and
executive ability   In 1683, probably soon after his arrival, he
bought six hundred acres of land in Goshen, Chester County,
Pennsylvania, of Edward Jones and others   Of Isaac Norris
and David Lloyd he purchased several hundred acres more,
and in 1710, of Thomas Mercer, of Aynho-on-the-Hill, another tract.   He had two hundred acres on the Rancocus, and
was joint proprietor with his brother Richard, son Jonathan,
and others of two thousand one hundred and ninety acres,

upon which was located the Friendship Mill, on a branch of
the Rancocus   After the survey was made they bought the
Indian title and received deeds from the chief We-Sosig

John and Esther Haines had six sons and seven daughters,
most of whom reached maturity   Esther Haines deceased in
1719, and from the testimony of Friends appears to have been
an earnest Christian.

In 1722 John Haines married Hannah Wood, daughter of
John Whitall   He deceased in 1728, and Friends recorded
that " he was an appointed elder and a zealous man "

ISAAC AND KATHARINE HAINES.

Isaac Haines was the third son of John and Esther Haines,
and removed from Gloucester County, New Jersey, to Pennsylvania, bearing a certificate from the Monthly Meeting of Friends
there dated Second month 8, 1714   Early in the same year he
married Katharine David, a young Friend from Wales   They
became members of Goshen Monthly Meeting in 1722, when
it was set apart from that of Chester.   They probably settled
on the one hundred and fifty acres afterwards left to him by
his father's will.

Isaac and Katharine Haines had six daughters and four sons,
all of whom married, with possibly one exception.

The date of Katharine Haines's decease does not appear;
that of Isaac Haines is 1757, when he was aged seventy-seven

ISAAC AND MARY COX HAINES.

Isaac Haines, Jr., eldest son of Isaac and Katharine Haines,
was born 10th of Eighth month, 1718   On the 5th of Eighth
month, 1744, he married Mary, daughter of Lawrence and
Ellen Cox, of Willistown, Chester County, Pennsylvania.

Their children were:

Jane, who deceased aged 23 years	Jacob, who deceased aged 86 years
Ellen, who deceased aged 90 years.	JESSE, who deceased aged 100 years, less
Elisha, who deceased aged 81 years.	six days
Caleb, who deceased aged 93 years	William, who deceased aged 2 years
Isaac, who deceased aged 87 years	John, who deceased aged 67 years
Martha, who deceased aged 20 years	

Isaac Haines died of influenza in 1790, aged seventy-two years; his wife, Mary Cox Haines, deceased in 1773, aged forty-six years

Thus far I have drawn chiefly from the book by J S Lippincott   From this period onward there are numerous family records and personal recollections as reliable sources of information.

CHAPTER II

JESSE AND RACHEL HAINES.

JESSE HAINES was born in Chester County, Pennsylvania, on the 14th of Ninth month, 1756.   His home was near the "Turk's Head," now the town of West Chester   Although his parents were members of the religious Society of Friends, they were not regular in attending meetings for worship, and probably allowed too much liberty in their children   Having a cheerful and social disposition, Jesse Haines engaged with animation in youthful pleasures, pursuing them even on the First day of the week, yet often feeling dissatisfied on retiring from his companions, who were more fitted to amuse than to instruct.

On one occasion they proposed a nutting excursion on a First day, when Jesse Haines remarked, "Let us consider whether it will be right to go"   One of the company said, "Oh, no; that will not do   If we stop to consider the subject we shall not go"   Our grandfather was so impressed that the plan was relinquished, and from that time he was so fully convinced that he had been spending that day of the week improperly that he endeavored to prevail on his comrades to give up these gatherings for pleasure and attend meetings for worship, which he began to do, and found them to be seasons of spiritual refreshment.

The Holy Spirit so operated upon his heart as to induce him to withdraw from unprofitable company, showing him the exceeding sinfulness of sin and his need of a Saviour. As he listened to the heavenly voice he was led to inquire what the Lord would have him to do, and in simple faith he obeyed.

His faithfulness was often put to the test. During the Revolution he suffered repeatedly on account of his testimony against war ; much less, however, than might have been his experience had he gone into the war. At the age of eighteen he was called out to serve in the army; he objected, and the officers took all his money, his watch, and his best clothing. Again he was called out, and as he declined to engage in war they took him to Chester, intending to put him in prison. There a person told him that he would pay the fine for him, but our grandfather informed him that he could not accept his liberty on those terms ; this displeased the man who offered the kindness, and he said then he would have to go to the jail. However, an officer told him he might return to his home this time, but for what reason he was liberated he never knew.

At another time he was taken prisoner on his way to Philadelphia, while the British army had possession of that city. His brother Caleb had left home with the intention of joining the British, and grandfather, hearing of it, followed him, hoping to overtake him and prevail upon him not to enlist.* When near Springfield Meeting-house, in Delaware County, he was stopped by an American guard and asked where he was going. He gave a candid reply, on which he was arrested and placed as prisoner for the cold night in a small room without fire, or food, or a chair to sit upon. In the same room there were two other prisoners, who had been taken as they were going to Philadelphia with provisions for the English. For this they were taken into the garden and severely beaten, and their shoes exchanged for old ones much worn, but our grandfather was not disturbed. The next day he was taken to Providence, an adjoining township, where they detained him for some days. Becoming somewhat acquainted with one of the guard, our grandfather told him that he could take him to the house of his cousin, Thomas Evans, and get a good supper for them

* Caleb Haines did enlist in the British army, and was quartermaster under Tarleton.

both if he were willing to accompany him, to which the guard replied, " We will go " They went accordingly and enjoyed the repast. On their way back our grandfather told the guard his story in full, and said that if he could see General Greene he thought he could obtain a release The guard replied that General Greene was not in that vicinity, but he would speak to General Wayne for him. The day following General Wayne sent for him, and after some conversation informed him that he was at liberty to go home, but added, " The next time we find you going to Philadelphia while the British have possession there, we will shoot you."

Near the close of the war he was again drafted, and for his refusal to fight was sentenced to one year's imprisonment in Chester At first the jailer was severe with him, but became kind and sympathizing and allowed him to teach his children, and obtained books for him to read from a library. His health failed under the confinement in prison, and at the end of three months, by the entreaty of Friends of Chester Monthly Meeting, the officers of the American army released him and he resumed his school in Middletown, Delaware County His fondness for reading and study induced him to spend some of the evening hours in the quiet of his school-house. Some young men of the neighborhood, more addicted to fun than to literary pursuits, tried to frighten him from his seclusion One of them came crawling in one evening enveloped in the skin of an ox, with its horns and tail Seeing his victim walk quietly from his seat to the stove and take the poker to drive out the beast, he made a hasty retreat, and the school-master was thenceforth left alone in his glory to pursue his studies at leisure

In the early part of his life Jesse Haines frequently thought of engaging in some more lucrative business than teaching, but the admonition presented to his mind was, " Seekest thou great things for thyself? Seek them not;" and he felt best satisfied to continue in that employment. His Lord had also other work for him, and in obedience to the call he became a preacher of the gospel and was recorded a minister by his Monthly Meeting when he was about thirty years of age.

Kind and affable in disposition, he was much beloved by his pupils, and frequently joined them in their sports, while in the school-room they were steadily led on in their studies. He often spoke to them on religious subjects, giving them good advice, and exhorting them to love and obey their Heavenly Father.

On the Sixth day of Tenth month, 1785, at a meeting of Friends in Middletown, Delaware County, Jesse Haines and Rachel Otley were married. She was the only daughter of James and Ann Otley. The Otleys probably came to Pennsylvania from Otley, a market-town and parish in the West Riding of Yorkshire, beautifully situated in the valley of the Wharfe.

Descended from English ancestry, Jesse and Rachel Haines were actuated through life by the resolute and persevering spirit that characterized their forefathers, and were remarkable for their independence, integrity, and earnest Christianity. Their only daughter, Mary, and five sons, JACOB, Reuben, Jesse Peirce, William, and Thomas, all of whom lived to advanced age, were trained in similar habits and dispositions, and in their turn made strong impressions on their respective neighborhoods.

Some time previous to the summer of 1788, Jesse Haines removed with his family from Middletown to Wilmington, Delaware, taking charge of a Friends' school in that city and residing there several years.

During this period the fine region between the North and West Branches of the Susquehanna River was being rapidly settled by an intelligent and enterprising population, and offered many advantages to those who had families of boys growing around them. Observing this, Jesse and Rachel Haines thought it right to avail themselves of the opening and directed their steps at first to Columbia County, not far from Catawissa, where he pursued his previous occupation. For the first six months there was no meeting for worship near them, and Jesse Haines frequently walked to Muncy, a distance of twenty miles, on Seventh day afternoon, lodging at the house of his friend William Ellis, and attending the meeting there next morning. William Ellis generally took his guest some miles on his homeward way,

both of them enjoying those opportunities foi piofitable conversation

Attracted, as weie many others, by the noble forest-trees and
fine grass-lands north of the Alleghany range, in 1802 Jesse
Haines purchased a tract in the Elklands   Here were room
and occupation for his active boys, but circumstances occurred
that led to another removal in the course of a few years   Jesse
Haines combined physical with mental energy, and never hesitated in the path of duty to use the powers bestowed upon him.
The Monthly Meeting to which he belonged was held a pait
of the year at a distance of thirty miles, and at other times of
fifty miles, from his residence, and to this he would walk when
it was more convenient for him to do so than to ride

He was something of a hunter and angler, but only indulged
in such ciafts as a means of adding to the family comfort   Going
out one winter day he shot a deer, but saw, as it bounded
away, that the wound was not fatal   Unwilling that it should
linger in pain, he followed it through the wood till he lost his
way, and, night coming on before he could regain the right
path, he was obliged to keep in motion on account of the cold
until daylight, when the sound of neighbors coming to his
assistance drew him towards his own home, around which he
had been walking in the darkness at no great distance   But
the frost had done its work, and his feet were so injured by it
that afterwards he was never able for those long pedestrian
tours that were once so easy to him

A little incident in connection with those journeys to his
Monthly Meetings may be mentioned, although it is probably
of later date   In crossing the hills between Muncy and Fishing
Creeks on hot summer days, it was refreshing to partake of the
peaches from an orchard on one of the slopes   However freely
the owner gave permission, Jesse Haines saw another way for
the traveller's benefit, and with his own hands planted trees
along the road that in due time offered their luscious fruit to
the passer-by

Restricted by the injury received from the frost in the active
duties demanded by his highland farm, and the sons being
desirous of enlarged opportunities for learning, the family re-

turned for a few years to the southern counties of the State, and then finally settled in Muncy Valley.

Our grandfather was faithful to his calling as a minister of the gospel in his own meetings, and at different times travelled extensively in Pennsylvania, Delaware, Maryland, and Virginia In 1816 and 1817 he spent nearly a year in visiting the meetings and many families in New England, Canada, and the western part of New York In these religious labors he was cordially united with by Friends at home and accompanied by some congenial elder, and they were often given returning minutes by the meetings to which they came expressive of the value of their services and of the good influence of their exaample He had a peculiar gift for visiting families, and was repeatedly engaged in doing so within his own Monthly Meeting The last service of this kind was performed in his ninety-fifth year, when he frequently pressed upon the members the duty and privilege of worshipping our Father in heaven and of regularly attending religious meetings

Rachel Haines was a valued elder in our church and faithful in a loving exercise of her gift As wife, mother, and friend she was true and helpful, her home always well-ordered, neat, and beautifully clean, her hospitable table, though plain, was furnished with skill and care, and when her husband laid aside his vocation as teacher and occupied himself with gardening, reading, and meditation, their abode was patriarchal in its comfort, simplicity, and pleasantness

Catharine Ecroyd often recalled the motherly interest Rachel Haines had shown in her spiritual welfare When Henry Ecroyd, soon after his marriage, came to live near Jesse and Rachel Haines, the young wife sometimes felt the cares of a farm-house rather engrossing, and would omit attendance at the mid-week meeting for worship Whenever she did so she was sure to have a call from Rachel Haines in the afternoon, making kind inquiries as to their health and comfort, till, in the end, to spare her aged friend the uphill walk, Catharine Ecroyd was as regularly in her seat at the meeting-house as possible, and became overseer herself when the preceding generation passed from earth.

In 1834 Rachel Haines, then in her seventy-ninth year, was taken ill with paralysis, and being no longer able to attend to the care of her household, her eldest son, Jacob Haines, my father-in-law, invited his parents to his home, where they were honored and cared for with the greatest tenderness till the close of their earthly career For three months the venerable mother lingered on the shores of time, and then peacefully departed to enter on her heavenly inheritance, while for her faithful husband there were yet more than twenty years in reserve of active exercise in Christian faith and patience.

He was very regular in his habits and remarkably temperate in all things, which no doubt contributed greatly to the sound, healthy state of his mind and body. Through life he greatly enjoyed perusing the works of good authors, and, possessing a retentive memory and a contemplative mind, he profited by his reading and accumulated a large store of useful information He used to encourage his grandchildren to read carefully, and to take time to understand and reflect upon the subjects engaging their attention, quoting the lines,—

> " Knowledge and Wisdom, far from being one,
> Have ofttimes no connection Knowledge dwells
> In heads replete with thoughts of other men,
> Wisdom in minds attentive to their own "

For many years he read the Bible through annually, and besides spent several hours each day in reading such parts as he particularly enjoyed ; and appeared to be as familiar with the Bible characters as if he had lived with them and had known their thoughts and feelings

He derived much pleasure from good poetry, and hymns especially, often committing them to memory, even during the latter years of his life, and repeating them to his grandchildren With these resources, and his habitual communion with his Lord, the lengthened evening of his day was rendered pleasant, and he was made a partaker of joys far greater than this world can bestow

His conversation was highly interesting and instructive, and frequently enlivened by a touch of native humor I recollect one evening when some quotation occurred to his mind, and he wished to recall the name of the author. To assist him my father-in-law began to give him the names of some of our best English writers in prose and verse. As each one was named he gave a brief, clear criticism of his works, and his son, seeing how it stirred his memory, led him on, always with the same lucid result, till he stopped from fear of fatiguing him.

Our grandfather never lost his interest and pleasure in the society and improvement of young people and little children. When my little daughter would be playing near him he watched her with a smile, and occasionally a laugh, at her merry frolics. Calling her to him one day, when her attention was fixed, he said, " My dear, I wish to give thee a little piece of philosophy : Always wear a pleasant countenance." Speaking to her on another occasion, as she stood before him in a listening attitude with her hands behind her, he told of his having seen George Washington on horseback at the head of his troops in Philadelphia.

Feeling himself restricted to great simplicity in his dress and mode of living, Jesse Haines did not apply the same limits in judging others. He told me that he early learned a lesson in this respect. He and my great-grandfather, George Ashbridge, at one time belonged to the same Monthly Meeting, of which George Ashbridge was at that time the clerk. Jesse Haines, in those early days of his Christian course, had believed it right to lay aside some of the superfluities in which he had indulged, and seeing George Ashbridge in his handsome suit of fine broadcloth and polished shoes with silver buckles, he was disposed to judge his elder brother in the faith rather harshly ; but he soon found, as he attended to the still small voice, that he was in a wrong spirit, and that what might be required of him in some of those minor matters was no criterion by which others were to be tried.

With perfect loyalty to the religious society of which he was a member, and endeavoring to strengthen it on the true foundation and enlarge its prosperity, he was far removed from sectarian bigotry. Regularly attending all his religious meetings when physically able to do so, he was often earnestly and

affectionately engaged in directing those present to turn to the
Lord, to seek and serve Him, assuring them that in doing so
the Holy Spirit would lead them in paths of pleasantness and
peace For several years he was prevented by the long journey
from attending the Yearly Meeting in Philadelphia, but he kept
a lively interest in its proceedings, and very earnest were his
desires that the peaceable spirit of Jesus should prevail in all its
deliberations

The following is part of a sermon preached by our grandfather on the 20th of First month, 1850, when he was in his
ninety-fourth year   The substance and words are nearly
correct, as far as they go, but I could not recall some con-
necting sentences

"'Fear not, little flock, it is your Father's good pleasure to
give you the kingdom.' This was encouragement given to
His followers by the Lamb, when He had taken upon Himself
the form of human nature. I believe He hath a little flock
among the nations at this time who, whatever their name of
religion or way of worship may be, are concerned to attend to
the unfoldings of the light of Truth in their hearts, and I
believe there are in this assembly many who are desirous to be
of this number and to be counted as children of the Lord's
family   .

"It is a progressive work, and as we are diligent we will
progress from one stage to another, from that of a child to
that of a young man, a strong man, and to that of fathers and
mothers in the church

"Some who have been willing to bow unto their Lord and
enter into covenant with Him may at times think it no longer
necessary to maintain the watch so closely, but beware of this
Satanic subtlety, for it is only while we persevere, in lowliness
watching unto prayer, that we are preserved from temptation

"The way pointed out by the Divine Light is opposed to the
natural mind, and hence the unwillingness of some to walk
therein. It is a blessed thing for the young to become acquainted with this Light, and not through unwatchfulness
betray their Divine Master by frivolity or any conversation
inconsistent with a pure mind

". . . Blessed are they who maintain a watch unto prayer. These are the loyal stock, and are sometimes, while passing through this habitable world, fed with dainties from the holy table such as the worldly-minded have no conception of. . . .

"It is a high and holy way: may you with me and I with you be qualified to walk circumspectly therein while in the body, and when separated therefrom be found worthy to unite with cherubim and seraphim, and the spirits of just men made perfect, in ascribing honor and praise to the Lord of light, life, and glory."

In writing to one of his sons, he remarked, "I am now in my ninety-fifth year, and have heard of all my brothers being entombed, though when young I was of a more tender constitution than any of them. It has often been marvellous in my view that I am continued thus long in the body. One thing, however, I desire,—that I may still be willing to live or die at His pleasure. I feel renewed desires for your well-being every way, which you know can only be effected by attending to the means mercifully provided for our redemption and salvation."

After returning from meeting, one day, he said to our dear father that he had never been more sensible of the excellency of our manner of worship than in the silent meeting that day, adding, "I do not remember ever to have had a more comfortable meeting." At another time he said, "I have lately been looking over my long life and have found in it many things faulty, but I have a well-grounded hope that through the mercy of God in Christ Jesus I shall be accepted in the Lord."

His adoption of the doctrines and testimonies of Friends, because he believed them to be in accordance with the Holy Scriptures, did not prevent his enjoyment of the company and conversation of other religious persons, and we have heard him remark, "I am no sectarian; I can give the right hand of fellowship to all who look for salvation through the offering and atonement of our Saviour."

This fundamental doctrine of Christianity was ever dear to his heart, and once he said, "My mind has at times been prayerfully exercised on behalf of the dear youth among those who are separated from us: I have a hope there will be raised

among them a proportion who will think for themselves, and
under the Divine anointing the eye of the mind will be opened
to acknowledge the several offices of our Blessed Redeemer
as couched in Holy Writ"

He was confined chiefly to one room for about three months,
and when entering it for the last time he said, "I am comforted
with the promise, 'As thy day so shall thy strength be'" He
often spoke of the mercies and blessings bestowed upon him,
and once remarked, "Children, my situation may appear pitiable
to you, yet I do not wish to change it with that of any mortal.
I have comforts and enjoyments that others are not aware of"
This was not spoken in any feeling of boasting, but of Christian
humility and confidence in the Lord

On the 29th of the Sixth month he remarked, "There are
many ups and downs in this life, but if we only seek the pearl
of great price all will be well   It is said in the Scriptures that
when the merchantman had found one pearl of great price, he
went and sold all that he had and bought it, sold all that was
in the way of obtaining this pearl"

The physician coming in, asked how he felt   After a little
pause he replied, "I feel one day nearer death's door, and am
well satisfied it is so. I desire to be patient, but am not as
much so as I ought to be   I am reduced outwardly as a little
child and desire to be so inwardly"

At another time our dear grandfather mentioned that for a
few of the past days he had felt depressed; that for several
months previous he had been favored with a great flow of love
to his dear Redeemer, when his occupation had been more that
of praise than of prayer, feeling as if he were in a state of
acceptance, his sins washed away through the atonement of
Christ, but that lately his had been a season of trial.   Yet he
sincerely desired to be as willing to follow Christ to Golgotha
as to the Mount (of transfiguration)   that when it is the blessed
Master's will to chasten us in this way we should receive it as
dutiful children, remembering that whom the Lord loveth He
chasteneth, and that we should be willing to adopt the language
of David, "Thy rod and thy staff they comfort me"   "Yes,"
he again observed, "we should be as willing to receive the rod

as the staff, if the Lord sees meet to administer the rod. Hard things are good for us when sent by our Heavenly Father and borne in a proper state of mind, serving to show us our weakness, make us humble, and bring our wills into subjection to the Divine will. To make the way hard for ourselves is a very different thing: we must not expect the same good to follow from that.

"If I have ever done any good, the praise and glory are all due to Christ: the evil has proceeded from myself and the enemy, and I have often felt that I could truly adopt the words of the publican, 'God be merciful to me a sinner.'" Speaking of the past, he said his mind had often been filled and flowing with love to the Saviour; at other times he felt poor and cold, but when that was the case he endeavored to hold on and abide in the patience, and a change always came, and he would be restored to a sense of the nearness of his Lord, and that he frequently spent many hours of the night in prayer and praise.

Near the end of the summer of 1856 my little daughter and I arrived at Wolf Run. The dear grandfather welcomed us as usual, and understood all about our coming by rail, and the telegrams that had passed between us on account of his increasing feebleness. He seemed to have no suffering, and enjoyed listening to his faithful and attentive daughter-in-law as she sat by his bedside and read to him from some favorite book. When obliged to lay it down she would name the page to him, and he could always direct her to it, even when several hours must elapse before she could resume her reading.

One morning, after she entered his room to inquire how he had passed the night, he spoke to her very affectionately of his wife, of his having been very sensible of the nearness of her spirit and the pleasantness of their communion.

Three young men* from Philadelphia were at Wolf Run a few days. When about to return home they went into our grandfather's room to take leave of him. He asked them to sit down and then addressed them, beginning with this passage, "It

---

* They were William Evans, J. Wistar Evans, and Joseph W. Stokes. The last two were early called away from this world, as I believe, to their mansions in heaven.

is better to trust in the Lord than to put confidence in man . it is better to trust in the Lord than to put confidence in princes " After sitting awhile in silence he said, " May grace, mercy, and peace rest upon you ! This little season of silence with you has been very agreeable to me " He then bade them farewell

A few days before his decease he remarked, " I have been engaged in prayer to my Heavenly Father for myself, my children, my grandchildren, my society, and the family of man the world over, and am now ready in the Lord's time to depart "

Observing that he was increasingly helpless, he said, " Now I can do nothing but praise the Deity " He remained in a most peaceful state of mind, desiring to wait patiently for the summons, and looking forward to a glorious eternity with our Lord and Saviour, who had drawn him by His love in his youth, been with him to direct and cheer in the active part of life, and in the evening of his day had filled his mind with the consolations of the gospel

He did not appear to have any disease, but gradually failed in strength, and quietly ceased to breathe on the 8th of Ninth month, 1856

[In the foregoing account of our grandfather, Jesse Haines, I have drawn very freely from a memoir by my dear sister, Sarah E Haines, who has generously given me all the help she could —M R H]

CHAPTER III

THOMAS ELLIS, OF WALES AND PROVINCE OF PENNSYLVANIA— ELLIS AND LYDIA ELLIS—BENJAMIN AND ANN ELLIS

I REGRET that I have no access to the earliest records of the Ellis family, which are probably still extant in Wales, whence they migrated in the seventeenth century The Welsh belong to the Celtic branch of the great Aryan or Indo-Germanic race, and their language is one of the most ancient now spoken in Europe

With their hereditary characteristic of attachment to the past and its traditions, they still call their country Cymry.* "Their name, their language, and their honor they have preserved to this day as memories of the past." Authentic records in my possession trace the Ellis family through eight successive generations. The first in this line of which I have any account is Thomas Ellis, who was born in Merionethshire, Wales, about the year 1635.

In the history of Delaware County, Pennsylvania, by Dr. George Smith, it is stated that—

"Thomas Ellis was one of the most eminent of the Welsh settlers. He came from Pembrokeshire, and arrived here with his second wife Ellen and family, and settled on one of the two large tracts of land which he purchased and located in Haverford."

Besides the above-mentioned tracts of land, Thomas Ellis bought another of Richard Davies, "a purchaser of five thousand acres of unlocated land from William Penn," of which six hundred and twenty-five acres were sold to "Lewis Owen, Rowland Owen, Ellis Morris, and Ellis Pugh, who, in turn, conveyed it to Thomas Ellis, of Iscregan, in the county of Merioneth, gentleman, for £9. 17s. 2d." This conveyance was dated June 30, 1683.

There is also a "patent" to Thomas Ellis & Company for seven hundred and ninety-one acres on Mill Creek. In right of his purchase made in Wales, Thomas Ellis took up six hundred acres of land in Merion Township, adjoining one of the same extent belonging to Rowland Ellis. From his will it appears that he held above fifteen hundred acres of land near Philadelphia, besides city lots.

From the autobiography of Richard Davies, in the thirteenth volume of "Friends' Library," edited by William and Thomas Evans, and the twenty-seventh volume of "The Friend," pages 179, 180, 188, some particulars of Thomas Ellis's life and character in his native country are given here.

Richard Davies, in his account of some imprisonments for conscience' sake in Wales, goes on to say, "A little after this,

* Pronounced Kimry.

Thomas Ellis, called a deacon in the Independent congregation, was convinced a man of great esteem among them, and so he was also afterwards amongst us

" He came to my house to visit the prisoners, his former fellow church members, and showed me a letter that came to him from their minister, Vavasor Powell,* lamenting the deplorable condition and danger they were in at that time, saying that the Christians were in great danger to be split between two rocks, —viz, the world and Q (meaning by Q the Quakers), but the worst, said he, is Q But the Lord had opened Thomas Ellis's understanding and given him a sight of their decay and formalities Some years before, the Lord did break in among them to the convincing of many of them, for Thomas told me that there came two women Friends among them in the time of their breaking of bread (I suppose it was before I came from London), and when they had the motion of truth upon them they opened their mouths in the name of the Lord, in much fear and humility, so that the Independent elders stood still and gave the women leave to speak what they had to say to the people, then the professors went on with their business, and after some time the Friends spoke again, and then they commanded them to be taken away, but no one was very ready to do it Then their minister, Vavasor Powell, called, ' Brother Ellis, take them away ' Thomas Ellis told me that he remembered Christ was not hasty in passing sentence upon the woman that the Jews brought before him, but he stooped down and wrote with his finger upon the ground as though he heard them not. So, Thomas Ellis told me, he was not willing to take them away till they had fully cleared themselves of what was upon them to deliver among them, but at last they called to him again and bid him take them away Then he rose from among the company and went to them, and desired them to go with him to the next room, for he had something to say to them, and the Friends went readily with him Then he told them on this wise ' Friends, you see how we are met together here, we are like the prodigal who was spending his portion, and we have a little yet unspent And when we have spent all we must return

* See Allibone's Dictionary of Authors

to our Heavenly Father and come to you and your way.' The Friends went away well satisfied. I have made much inquiry who these Friends were and from whence they came, but could not certainly learn who they were. As for our friend Thomas Ellis, the Lord blessed him and poured his Spirit upon him and gave him part of the ministry, and he became a faithful labourer and serviceable man among us; and at length he was made a prisoner here at Welch-Pool."

About this time the fanatical John Perrot caused some disturbance among Friends in Wales. Before his errors were fully manifested, Thomas Ellis was somewhat deceived by John Perrot's seeming humility and profession of great spirituality, but soon saw and acknowledged his mistake, and "was sweetly restored again to his former love and integrity, to the great comfort of himself and brethren."

* "In the Sixth month, 1660, he with a number of others were arrested at a religious meeting, and, with much abuse, were driven twenty miles on foot to a town called Bala, where, for the conscientious refusal to swear, they were put in fetters and sent twelve miles further to prison. In this prison they were kept about fifteen weeks, during which time they suffered much abuse and hard usage.

"In the next year he with six other Friends were again arrested, and for refusing to take the oath of allegiance were committed to prison, where they were kept fifteen weeks. Being brought before the Quarter Sessions, and offering to make public declaration of their fidelity to the king in place of the oath, they were discharged. Twice again during this year they were arrested, and the last time they were confined in a hole in which the marshal had been accustomed to keep his hogs. They were much exposed to the weather, in time of rain not being able to find dry spots to lie down on, and this, together with the noise of the swine, who at night clustered round their usual lodging-place, prevented the prisoners getting much rest. They were kept in this pig-pen for ten weeks and then were removed to another prison, where they for a time did not receive proper nourishment, and had to sleep upon the bare floor because they

* " The Friend."

were not willing to submit to the illegal and exorbitant demands of the gaoler However, in time, their patience proving more than a match for his cruelty, he became much softened towards them and treated them with some degree of humanity This imprisonment was one of many weeks' continuance.

"In the year 1662, for a tithe valued at £1 10s, he had fifty-one loads of rye, oats, and barley, worth £10, taken from him. Thus was he schooled in persecution, which, say his friends in their memorial, he bore patiently Glad he was that the Lord counted him worthy to suffer for His name's sake, and for the testimony He gave him to bear for His Truth "

Richard Davies relates that about 1668, " There being a meeting of Friends gathered at Aberystwith, in Cardiganshire, most of them were sent to prison to Cardigan, and our friend Thomas Ellis was taken prisoner with them Having the sufferings of these young convinced Friends under consideration, I found much love in my heart towards them, even so as to go to the magistrates of the county, to offer myself a prisoner instead of my friend and brother Thomas Ellis, and some others, that they might go home and visit their families I acquainted my wife of my exercise, which came pretty close to her; but she likewise in love, after a little consideration, gave me up for that service So in a few days I took my journey, and went first to Thomas Ellis's house, to visit his wife and family before I went further, his house being about twenty-four miles from Welch-Pool, and not far out of my way towards Cardiganshire There I very unexpectedly met Thomas Ellis himself at home, he told me they were all discharged out of prison Thus I saw it was the good will and pleasure of my heavenly Father to accept of my free-will offering instead of the deed, and my friend Thomas Ellis and his wife were sensible of my love and kindness to them therein

"And now my service being farther for Pembrokeshire, Thomas Ellis was willing to accompany me in my journey, and we went to Aberystwith, to visit those Friends there, where we had a pretty large meeting the First day in the morning, and there came one Thomas Price, brother to Sir Richard Price, of Gogorddan, who took us all prisoners and committed us to the town prison. That evening we had a meeting in the house where we were prisoners. Many of the town's people, some of them persons of account, were at the meeting that evening. I declared the word of the Lord to them and showed them the way to the kingdom of heaven. A sweet, comfortable meeting we had, and great satisfaction it was to them that were there.

"That night a weighty consideration came upon me about those young convinced Friends that were so lately discharged of their imprisonment, because they were like to go so quickly to prison again. So I asked counsel of the Lord what we might do for, and in behalf of, these young and tender Friends ; and being under great exercise in my spirit, earnestly praying to God that He might make some way for their enlargement that time, it came into my mind to write to the chief-magistrate, Sir Richard Price, and give him an account of my journey so far, and that my friend Thomas Ellis and myself intending for Pembrokeshire, and resting with our friends, and having a meeting with them that day, were taken prisoners by his brother Thomas Price ; and, if it was his pleasure to send us to prison to Cardigan, that he would be so kind as to leave his neighbours at home, and accept of my friend Thomas Ellis and me as prisoners instead of them all. To this effect I wrote to him and sent it next morning, but he sent me no answer. But the high-constable came to us and told us we must all prepare to go to Cardigan town, where the county jail was kept. So Friends freely and heartily prepared themselves to go.

"When the time of our going was come, they tenderly taking leave of their wives, children, and neighbours (for some of their neighbours came a little way to see them out of town), the constable stopped and bid all go home, except Thomas Ellis and me ; for it seems the high-constable had private orders not to go with them, but to do as I desired in my letter. Thus the Lord did try those tender Friends, and also deliver them.

"The constable had instructions to bring us to the quarter-sessions, then held at Llandebar, and not to Cardigan. When we came there, the justices being on the bench, we were had before them : some of them were formerly acquainted with Thomas Ellis, he having been in authority, and, according to

his place, somewhat sharp against offenders   The justices were
very moderate to him, but the clerk of the peace was very
peevish and froward. I asked the justices whether that man
that questioned my friend was a justice of the peace, they told
me he was not   Then I told them we were not bound to answer
him, but, if they would give me leave, I would give them a just
account of my business in that county and upon what account
we were sent there before them, and they desired me to speak on
I told them I was at my own house, with my wife and family,
in Welch-Pool, in Montgomeryshire, and hearing that my friend
Thomas Ellis, and other of my friends, were in prison in this
County of Cardigan for a considerable time, it was with me to
come to the magistrates of this county to offer myself a prisoner, that my friend Thomas Ellis and the rest of them might
go for a little while to visit their families   In order thereunto I
came as far as my friend Thomas Ellis's house, where I found
him at home with his wife and family, and they being discharged of their imprisonment, I had a further concern upon
me to go to Pembrokeshire; my friend Thomas Ellis, not being
willing that I should go alone, accompanied me

  " We came to Aberystwith, to rest there the first day of the
week, and had a meeting with our friends, so were taken prisoners, and sent here to you, and now desire to know your pleasure   The justices answered, it was great love indeed that
caused me to come to offer myself a prisoner upon such an
account, and they were sorry that Sir Richard Price gave us that
trouble to send us there. and so they discharged us   And the
court being silent I had an opportunity to declare the word of
the Lord among them   Very still and attentive they were, as
if I had been in a meeting   I commended their great moderation, and in the love of God we parted with them   The deputy-
sheriff and the high-constable that brought us there, came out
of the court and treated us very civilly, and would have bestowed on us the best that the town could afford, but we were
sparing of taking anything of them.

  " I was informed that the deputy-sheriff and the high-constable were convinced, and very loving to Friends all along
I know not of any that were imprisoned in that county after-

wards. The Lord was with us, and He had a regard to the integrity of our hearts, and He alone pleaded our cause, and was with us in our services

" Then we took horse and left the town, and went towards Pembrokeshire till we came to Cardigan, about twenty four miles. We met with some hardships on the way, having little or no refreshment till we came here, where we had very good entertainment for ourselves and horses, and from thence we had a Friend for our guide towards Poutchison in Pembrokeshire, but we were benighted, and it rained, our guide lost his way and we wandered up and down among the peat or turf-pits, and other dangerous places, but the Lord preserved us out of them all.

" At length we came to Poutchison, but it being dark, we did not know the house where our friend, that we intended to go to, lived, but I spoke to our guide to see where the steeple-house door was, and he brought us to it, then I told them the Friends' house was opposite to it, for I remembered when I had a meeting there, my back was against the wall of the house and my face towards the steeple-house door So we went forwards and found the house I desired Thomas Ellis to call and tell them, that there were some Friends who had lost their way, and desired to have lodging there that night. They being in bed answered, they thought that no good Friends were out at that time of night Thomas Ellis reasoned a little with them, but still they were not willing to rise and let us in. At last I called to the Friend, whose name was Thomas Simmons, and to his wife, and desired them to rise and let us come in He asked me who was there ? I told him in Welch, Richard Davies was there, What, said he, Richard Davies of Welch-Pool ? I told, I was the man Thereupon the tender-loving Friends hastily came down and let us into their house, and we were satisfied in the love of God This was the first journey that Thomas Ellis made to Pembrokeshire since he was convinced

" Hence we went to Haverfordwest, and so through all the meetings in that county till we came to Poutchison again, and had a meeting there, where there came many Friends both

Welch and English, so that the house could not contain us, and we had the meeting out of doors in the street, and I declared the word of the Lord to them, both in Welch and English

"As we came to Pembrokeshire, we went to a Baptist's house and the woman of the house being loving and tender, promised we should have a meeting among the Baptists there We also appointed a meeting at Newcastle, in Carmarthenshire Peregrine Musgrave, James Lewis and several other Friends accompanied us to the meeting at Newcastle The magistrates of the town were very civil, and several of them came to the meeting The weight and service of the meeting lay chiefly upon me, for though our friend Thomas Ellis was reckoned a deacon, and an eminent preacher among the Independents, yet his mouth was but very little as yet opened by way of testimony among Friends He was an understanding man in the things of God, and was not hasty to offer his offering till he found a very weighty concern upon him. As I was declaring to the people in the Welch language, I stood opposite to a great window that opened to the street, and there was an evil-minded man in the street, that had a long fowling-piece, who put the mouth of it through the window and swore, that if I would speak another word I was a dead man But blessed be God, I was kept in that which was above the fear of man, and the Lord kept me in dominion over all There were two women sitting in the window, and the mouth of the gun came between them both, one of them, seeing the gun turned her back upon it, and said in Welch, when the man threatened as before, I will die myself first And there was one in this meeting went to this man and took the gun away from him, and that wicked man came into the meeting and was pretty quiet then The Lord's good presence was with us, and a good meeting we had, and I may say, They that trust in the Lord, are as Mount Zion, that cannot be moved And as it was said of old, As the hills were round about Jerusalem, so is the Lord round about His people, to be a present help to them in every needful time

"Here Pembrokeshire Friends and we parted, and it being

somewhat late, the meeting having held long, we travelled all night over some doleful hills, intending to be at the Baptist meeting next day which we had appointed, as before mentioned. It was by computation about twenty-four miles. In this time we had little refreshment for ourselves or horses, but when we came there we had no meeting. The woman of the house said that the magistrates had heard of it and charged them we should have no meeting there. So the slavish fear of man came over them. The woman seemed to be sorrowful and would have given us some victuals, but I told her we did not travel so hard to come there for her meat and drink, but in the love of God for the good of their souls.

"So here my friend and companion Thomas Ellis and I parted; he went homewards and I went that night to William ap Pugh's house, a poor Friend, who had a considerable company of small children."

"In the year 1677 our friend John Burnyeat came to give us a visit in Wales, and had a meeting at Machynlleth, in Montgomeryshire, where appeared an informer, Oliver Maurice, of Drain Llwdion, in Merionethshire, and caused a disturbance, and went afterwards to William Pugh, of Mathafern, near Machynlleth, a justice of the peace for this county. He was one of them that had his commission when David Maurice* was turned out, as before related, who granted him a warrant; and himself, together with his bailiff and a constable, meeting John Burnyeat and Thomas Ellis upon the road, stopped them and seized their horses, with their saddles and bridles, so that they were constrained to travel on foot. John Burnyeat's mare died within an hour and a half after seizure, and Thomas Ellis's horse died in the informer's hands in a half year's time; in which also a distemper infected most of his cattle, whereby he suffered very great loss. The said justice likewise fined several other Friends at the same time, though they lived in another county. Thomas Ellis despatched a messenger to me at Welch-Pool, being about twenty-two miles. The next day, the lord Powis being at home in his castle of Powis, I went to him and acquainted him thereof, and he was very sorry. I desired of

* A persecuting informer.

him that he would grant me that favor to make use of his name, that he had heard such and such things concerning the before-said justice. 'Not only so,' said he, 'but let Mr Edmund Lloyd' (this was a neighbouring justice and no persecutor) 'write to him and tell him that I am angry with him for such proceedings.' So I went to my friend, that other justice, and got him to write a few lines to the said William Pugh He wrote effectually to him and I sent it away by night, by which means the rest of the fines were stopped

"After this I went to London to the Yearly Meeting (1677), and continued there some time, in and about the city, and so came leisurely down through several meetings, visiting Friends

"A while after I came home Thomas Ellis and James Halliday came to our town I told James it was well done of him to give us a visit in these parts of Wales They said they came to visit us against their wills I asked them whether they were prisoners they said they were, and soon after came other Friends with them I took them along with me to my house to refresh themselves. They told me James Halliday came from London to South Wales, intending to take shipping there for Ireland, to be at the half-year's meeting, but the wind proving contrary, he was necessitated to come for North Wales to Holyhead, and having a meeting in this county, near Llanydlos, they were taken prisoners and fined by Evan Glyn, a justice of the peace, and sent here. I was very much concerned for James Halliday, that he should be stopped in these parts and hindered of his service So next morning about two of the clock, I took horse and went to this justice's father-in-law, Justice Devereux, and found him at a village, three miles from Welch-Pool He asked me what was the matter. I told him that his son-in-law, Glyn, had committed some of our friends to prison to Welch-Pool and fined them also, and I told him I thought, by the law, that no man was to suffer twice for the same supposed transgression He gave his son hard language, and desired me to see some way to get them off I went to a neighbouring justice and got James Halliday a discharge, and brought it with me that morning So we hastened

him away with a guide towards Holyhead, and I was informed
he had a good and quick passage, and got in time to the half-
year's meeting in Ireland, as he intended

"For Thomas Ellis and the rest of the Friends the jailer
took our words that they should be forthcoming at the next
quarter sessions, at which time Charles Lloyd and myself
attended the court, and went to the clerk of the peace and
desired him to call our friends first, which he did   The Friends
being all at the bar, no prosecutor appearing against them
(Justice Glyn not being then come to town), they were soon
discharged without demanding any fees, and after Friends had
refreshed themselves in town they went homewards, some of
them towards Radnorshire, and those that went towards Llanydlos met Justice Glyn, who had committed them, going towards
the quarter sessions   He spoke to them, and they told him
they were discharged   He seemed not to be sorry for it, for he
was not a persecutor at the bottom "   1139000

Early in the year 1681 Thomas Ellis was in London, as
appears by a letter from John ap Thomas to his wife, dated
"London, 28th of Third month, 1681," informing her of his
arrival there   He goes on to say, "And Thomas Ellis likewise
came the same day, and, as the Lord may order and make
way, we both intend to set out together the same time likewise
(to wit), the next Second day

"The Lord's presence and appearance among His people
here at this time hath been beyond expression, and the number
increasing likewise from year to year, as doth the power and
presence of the Lord in and among the precious ones of Zion "

In the same year Richard Davies went to the Yearly Meeting in London, in reference to which he writes in his narrative,—

"Persecution was very severe upon Friends in the city, and
elsewhere in those parts; at which meeting it lay upon my
mind to move for a Yearly Meeting in Wales, and after some
consideration about it, it was left to Friends in Wales to appoint
their first Yearly Meeting, as in the wisdom of God they should
see meet at their half-year's meeting, held at Swanzey, the 28th
of the Seventh month   An account of which my friend
Thomas Ellis sent me to London, as followeth.

"'DEAR FRIEND, R DAVIES,—In the love of God is my remembrance of thee at this time, with many others of the like minded, in and about the city, and especially those who from the beginning have been and still are most exercised under the glorious weight of the care and concerns of the church of Christ, the remembrance of whom hath divers times, and especially of late, as at this present, wrought both eyes to tears, and hearts to tenderness   Although I was disappointed in my expectations of seeing thee here, at this half-year's meeting, yet thy letter to John ap John, coming so seasonably, did so answer for thee, that it was both joy and refreshment to many of us We had a full meeting of Friends from most parts of Wales, many having come upon the account of the yearly meeting, which was concluded to be at Haverfordwest, the second day of the week, called Easter-week, for the following year.

"'Here were E Edwards, John ap John, W Players, Francis Lea, Philip Leonard, and Richard Walter, who had testimonies; and many other Friends besides from other remote parts, all zealous for the yearly meeting   We had meetings here the three last days   Thy friend and brother,
"'THOMAS ELLIS
"'SWANZEY, the 28th of the Seventh month, 1681'"

Materials from which to draw a picture of Thomas Ellis's domestic life are scanty, but clear inferences from facts in our possession enable us to form some correct ideas of it

Numerous testimonies represent his whole life as singularly pure and upright   his disposition was amiable and affectionate, his temperament firm in adherence to just principles, his social position was good, and his circumstances appear to have been easy

As justice in the courts of his native county, and as deacon and preacher among the Independents in his early prime, he held the confidence of his countrymen   We have not obtained the Christian name of his first wife, nor the date of their marriage; the latter was probably prior to 1657 or 1658, and seems to have been every way suitable. They had four children. two sons,—Elliss and Humphrey, and two daughters,—Bridgart and Ellinor

Comfortably settled amidst the picturesque hills and vales of his native land, enjoying the esteem of his friends and neighbors, his home warmed by the love of a faithful wife, and brightened by the charms of their young children, life must have shone with a pleasing and hopeful aspect   But change is inseparable from mortal existence , it comes from within and without , and when Thomas Ellis was convinced that his Lord was leading him into closer communion with Himself, and a nearer walk with the blessed Saviour, he was not " disobedient to the heavenly vision," but cheerfully followed in the path open before him, however it might expose him to loss of property and painful imprisonments   Whether the severity of his sufferings and long enforced absences from home bore too hardly upon a loving wife we cannot tell , but before many years she was taken from her husband and children to a haven where " no storms ever beat on the glittering strand "

His time was now frequently given to missionary journeys among Friends and others, when he was at liberty, and he grew in power and efficiency as a minister of the gospel of Christ Jesus   For a while he resided in Pembrokeshire, and a strong attachment bound him and Friends there together, as many among them expressed in their certificate on his removal

In the latter part of Thomas Ellis's residence in his native country he married the second time   His wife was Ellin (Rees ?), and they had one daughter named Rachel

Many Friends were looking towards the newly-acquired Province of Pennsylvania as a refuge from the persecutions to which they were subject in their native land, and among them the attention of Thomas Ellis turned in the same direction

In 1682 he made preparations for bringing his family to America ; and early in the following year, 1683, came over with his wife and two sons,—Elliss and Humphrey , and three daughters,—Bridgart, Ellinor, and the youngest, Rachel

Out of several large tracts of land that he had purchased in the new province he chose for his residence one of those located in the township of Haverford-West, which had been named after the capital of Pembrokeshire   The Friends he left expressed their love and esteem in the following certificate, which is copied from the records of Radnor Monthly Meeting, Penn-sylvania

"A Testimony from ye County of Pembrock in South Wales Concerning oʳ Deare frind and

" BROTHER THOMAS ELLISS.

" WHFRLAS, We are given to undᵉʳstand that oᵉʳ deare frind Thomas Ellis, wife, and family, doe intend to remove themselves for Penn-Sylvania in America, he Being a man that for many yeares have Traveled amongst vs And for some time Resident in these Parts we thought it oᵉʳ duty to give this oᵉʳ Testemony in his Behalfe

" Our deare friend is a man of a Tender Sperit and often Broken before the Lord, the sence of the power of an endless life being upon him · his testemony for the Lord and his trueth hath been very weighty to the reaching the Consciences of many, his labour in the Lord hath been very effectuall being endued wᵗʰ an Ex-celent gift in opening of deepe devine misteryes And as to the Innocency of his Conversation in general (wᶜʰ is the most evident token of trueth and Sincerity) we have this to say we know few like him, for in that God hath made him an adorn-ing to the doctrine of the Gosbell. neither can we omitt mentioning his deepe Travel care and desiers for the prosperitie of the trueth, his Labour in the Lord hath not been in vaine, he is owned by vs to be a selfe denying man truely Sent of God & deligently seeking the good of all his Imprisonments hath been many and difficult wᵗʰ spoyling of goods upon trueth's accompts All wᶜʰ was borne by him in that patience wᶜʰ is the gift of God for the satisfaction of those whom it may or shall concern, we have hereunto subscribed oᵉʳ names at oᵉʳ Monthly meeting at Redstone in the aforsᵈ county of Pembrock the Second day of ye Seaventh month 1683

EDWARD LORD	LEWIS JAMFS
JOHN POYER	JAMES LEWIS
JOHN BOURGE	RICHARD WHIFL
JAMES THOMAS	DAVID JOHN
WILLIAM JENKINS	DAVID REES
EVAN BOWEN	PEREGRINE MUSGRAVE "

We must recollect that the early settlers in Pennsylvania who came from Wales were accustomed to speak and write in the Welsh language, which may excuse the want of good syntax or elegance in their use of English, which was also understood and spoken by most of them

Their hopefulness and gratitude on gaining a refuge from the bitter persecutions they were subject to in their native land are quaintly expressed, after the manner of the Welsh bards, by Thomas Ellis, "Who immediately after his arrival here com-posed, in British language, the following 'Song of Rejoycing,'

which was turned into English [probably to its disadvantage]
by his ffriend, John Humphrey".

> " Pennsylvania, an habitation
> With certain, sure, and clear foundation,
> Where the dawning of the day
> Expels the thick, dark night away

> " Lord, give us here a place to feed
> And pass our life among Thy seed,
> That in our bounds true love and peace
> From age to age may never cease

> " Then shall the trees and fields increase,
> Heaven and earth proclaim Thy peace,
> That we and they forever, Lord,
> Show forth Thy praise with one accord "

Thomas Ellis was one of William Penn's commissioners
Although his principal residence was in the country, " he spent
much time in Philadelphia, where he held public trusts under
the government" " July 28th 1687 Thomas Ellis was commis-
sioned Registrar General for the Province, and held the office"
till his decease His deputy was David Lloyd

Faithful to his calling as a minister of the gospel, he still
travelled in that service. About 1685 he visited Friends in his
native country, and " many were glad to see his face once more,
that they might be helped on their way by the power that
accompanied him " Early in 1688 he had liberty given by his
meetings at home to visit the meetings and Friends in New
England, accompanied by Samuel Jennings

Worn with suffering for conscience' sake in Wales, he did not
long survive to enjoy peace and freedom in the land of his
adoption Having been faithful unto death, he received the
crown of life in the Eleventh month, 1688, and his body was
interred in the burial-ground at Haverford meeting-house on
the eighth day of the same

Again Radnor Monthly Meeting recorded a testimony to his
well-spent life, from the minutes of which the following is copied

" The Testimony of Hugh Roberts and John Bevan for their
antient and well-esteemed friend

"THOMAS ELLIS

"He was a man yt was Religious and had a zeal for good before he was convinced of God's trueth, he walked amongst them yt was called independents, & was counted by them to be a godly gifted man, & about ye year 1660 he was convinced of the blessed trueth, and when ye Lord in his great love reached unto him, & opened his understanding to see the way of peace and salvation he did not long consult with flesh and blood but gave himself up in obedience to the Lord's will and testimony for his blessed trueth for which he was an early sufferer both in body & estate, wch he bore patiently, and glad he was yt ye Lord counted him worthy to suffer for 's name sake & for the Testimony he gave him to bear for his trueth; soe he came to see yt his sufferings and outward losses was not to be compared to ye gain and inward comfort yt ye Lord God had brought him unto soe he growed in the trueth, & ye Lord was pleased to bestow on him a large gift in the ministry, unto wch he like the good steward diligently improved & gave himself up to visit the churches throu 's native country Wales, & his ministry was very effectual to the convincing of many & for those yt were convinced by him & others his godly care was very much to water & nourish them yt they might grow in grace & in ye wisdom yt come from above, and it is evident unto many yt are yet alive in ye body yt his labo{rs} hath been blessed, & we may truely say of him as Paul said of Timothy that we had amongst us noe man (in those days) like minded, for 's Godly care was very much for the growth of trueth amongst us And was given very much to travell and visitt o{r} meetings in all Wales

"Though 's body is removed from us yett yt life & power yt attended and supported him in all his service and labours is still amongst us, blessed be ye name of the Lord who is carying on 's great work through them yt are faithfull, & truly their names are worthy to be kept on record for the encouragement & benefitt of those yt are yett unborn

"About the beginning of the year 1683 he with many more had it in their hearts to come for this country, & his service amongst us in o{r} first setling here was of Benefitt & advantage

to us, and in the year 1685 he was drawn to visitt ffriends &
acquaintance in his native country, wch accordingly he did, and
good service he had in many places there, & many did rejoice
to see his face once more y^t they might be helped in their way
by ye power y^t was upon him, and after some time he returned
here to his family again & was of good service, concerning w^{ch}
we do not say much because it is well known to most of us. Soe
in ye year 1688 he departed this life in peace and was buried at
ye burying place near the meetting house in Hav^{r}ford the 8th
day of the 11th mo of the said year

" HUGH ROBERTS
" JOHN BEVAN "

Thomas Ellis's will is dated the first day of Eleventh month,
1688   After making ample provision for his wife, he bequeathed
lands to his children in Merion, Haverford-West, city of Philadelphia, and in "dyffryn Mawr" (Great Valley)   His personal
estate was divided among his two sons and two of his daughters,
the other daughter having land only left by will to her

What relationship existed between Thomas Ellis and Rowland
Ellis, of Bryn-Mawr, is uncertain   By members of Thomas
Ellis's family Rowland Ellis is mentioned as a friend and cousin,
and there appears to have been somewhat intimate intercourse
between them

ELLIS AND LYDIA ELLIS

The eldest son of Thomas Ellis and his first wife was born
in Wales about the year 1659   He came with his father in
1683 and settled on part of the large purchase made by him in
Haverford Township, Delaware County, Pennsylvania

He married Lydia Humphrey, eldest child of Samuel and
Elizabeth Humphrey, the 19th day of the Sixth month, 1685,
at the house of William Howell, in Haverford

Of Lydia Humphrey's parents there is the following record
"Samuel Humphrey and Elizabeth Rees were married before
two Justices of the peace, named Morris Wynn and Robert
Owen, of Dole Serrey on ye 20th Day of Aprill 1658, and resided in the parish of Llangelynin in the county of Merioneth,

where were born their children, LYDIA, Daniel, Benjamin, Joseph, Rebecca, Ann, and Gobeitha The father died 17th of Seventh month 1677, and was buried at Bryn Tallwyn, aged 71 (?) years and nine months The mother and her children came over in 1683, excepting the son Daniel, who had preceded the rest about twelve months"

Ellis and Lydia Ellis had ten children Of these, Rachel, Thomas, and William (?) died unmarried Elizabeth married Rees Price, Bridget married John David, the name of Joseph's wife is unknown; Evan married Sarah Yarnall, BENJAMIN married Ann Swaffer, Rebecca married Richard George, of Radnor; whether John married is not stated

It is recorded of Ellis Ellis that "He was a Friend, and a good citizen" "He made his will the 13th of Sixth month 1705, which was proven April 6, 1706 He directed that 150 acres of his land be sold to pay debts, and the remainder, 275 acres, he gave to his eldest son Thomas, who was to pay £80 to the other children, and reserving a life interest therein to their mother Towards repairing the burial place at Haverford, 30 shillings Wife, executrix and well-beloved friends Rowland Ellis, John Richard, Rees [blank] and Benjamin Humphrey to be guardians of the children

"Witnesses, Rowland Ellis, Humphrey Ellis, Benjamin Humphrey"

His children were all minors at the time of his decease, some of them under four years of age

Some handsome legacies fell to the portion of Elizabeth Ellis and Rachel Ellis—one hundred acres of land each—by the will of Ellis Hughes, of Easttown, dated 11th of First month, 1715

After the decease of her husband, Ellis Ellis, Lydia Ellis appears to have resided in Easttown, and the above-named Ellis Hughes left to her two hundred and fifty acres "in lieu and consideration of her great care and pains taken for me upon my sick Bed, also two cows and yearling calf, my horse Jack, &c" "To friend John Ellis the remainder of my land (40 acres), whom I appoint executor, and my friends Benjamin Humphrey and Rowland Ellis Jun' to be overseers.

"Witnesses, Rowland Ellis and Thomas Ellis"

For more than thirty-six yeais of widowhood, Lydia Ellis "kept the noiseless tenor of her way" in the performance of those daily duties and ministrations of love that befit the faithful mother, friend, and neighbor Near the close of her eighty-fourth year her last will was written, in which she mentions her "Daughter Rebecca George and her children Lydia and Ellis and 'other' sons, daughter Bridget David and her children, daughter Elizabeth Price, deceased, and her sons and daughter; son Joseph's children, son Benjamin's children, son Evan Ellis, and nurse Susanna Shelton"

This will is dated November 25, 1742, and before another month was completed Lydia Ellis had passed away from earth

BENJAMIN AND ANN ELLIS.

Benjamin was the ninth child of Ellis and Lydia Ellis, and was born at Haverford the 8th of Eighth month, 1701.

In 1726 Benjamin Ellis bought of the heirs of Ellis Hughes two hundred acres of land* in Easttown Township, which was probably his residence from that time, retaining his right of membership among Friends of Haverford Meeting, although, as being more convenient, he might attend worship at Radnor.

Benjamin Ellis was not so absorbed in the care of his estate as to become indifferent to society, and having arrived at the mature age of thirty-three, decided to bid farewell to life as a bachelor The virtues of Ann Swaffer, a lady several years his junior, attracted him, and the offer of his heart and hand was accepted in good faith, and their marriage was accomplished on the 1st of Third month, 1735

It is said that the family of Ann Swaffer had been driven from England to the Netherlands in a time of religious perse-cution, which is believed to be true They probably returned to their native country with other refugees when the storm abated, as William Swaffer, the father of Ann, came to Pennsylvania from Newton, in Cheshire, England, about 1684 He married . in the Sixth month, 1694, Mary Caudwell,† of Ridley, at a

---

* For which he gave one hundred and twenty pounds

† Now spelled Caldwell I well remember when Caldwell was pronounced Caudwell in Delaware County

meeting held in the house of Walter Faucet, at Ridley William Swaffer was an active member and overseer of Chester Monthly Meeting He deceased 17th of Second month, 1720.

Of William Swaffer's daughter, Ann Ellis, it is on record that "She was a pious, exemplary woman all her days." As her home before marriage was in Nether Providence, Chester Monthly Meeting gave her a certificate to Haverford, but in the First month, 1741–42, at Goshen Monthly Meeting, "Benjamin Ellis produced a certificate for himself and wife, Ann, from Haverford, 'to introduce them into fellowship with you, the reasons given they can more conveniently attend the meeting at Newtown than Radnor, being nearer and a better road,'" etc Signed by Edward Williams and thirteen women Friends

Benjamin and Ann Ellis had four daughters and three sons Rebecca married Henry Reynolds, and they went to Wilmington, Delaware Mary married Thomas Tucker, some, if not all, of whose children lived in Philadelphia, and the sons were among the first manufacturers of china in this country Ellis was complained of for fighting in a public-house, and made an acknowledgment to his Meeting, which was accepted, he afterwards went to Deer Creek, Maryland, to reside Hannah married Abraham Davis and went with her husband to Fairfax, Virginia Rachel lived unmarried Of WILLIAM, who married Mercy Cox, more will be related The youngest, Thomas, whose life was marred by drinking to excess, died unmarried

Benjamin Ellis deceased in 1753. His will is dated the 5th of Third month in that year, and was proven 20th of the same. The will is substantially as follows

"To wife Ann Ellis my plantation where I now live (Easttown), with all my other lands and Tennaments, and as much of the stock and implements of husbandry as my other executors, hereafter named, shall think sufficient to carry on the Business of the Plantation, she maintaining my children until son Ellis attains the age of twenty-one years · after which she shall have the use of the stone end of the dwelling, some part of the Seller under the kitchen, with some meadow near the dwelling, firewood, feather bed and furniture, warming pan, case of drawers, large pine chest, side saddle, a young pacing mare, and one milch cow

" To son William Ellis a piece of Land to be taken off my Messuage or Tenament where I now live (survey given), containing twenty-nine acres, adjoining lands of Thomas McKean and Francis Wayne

" To eldest son Ellis Ellis the remainder of land, buildings, and appurtenances on the north side of the Church road, subject to his mother's privileges and the payment of £25 to her

" To son Thomas Ellis my messuage and appurtenances on the south side of the Church road

" Sons Ellis and William are to have the use of the water between them to water their meadow

" To daughter Rebecca £25, a new case of drawers and side-saddle, and to my other three daughters, Mary, Hannah, and Rachel £20 each at eighteen or marriage

" My son Ellis is to school and maintain his brothers William and Thomas until they are fourteen years of age

" To John Brooks £6, to be paid by son Ellis within ten years after my decease; also a dun mare

" Executors, wife and friends Thomas Macy (Massey) and Thomas McKean (uncle of Governor McKean).

" Friends David Lawrence and Henry Lawrence, Junr, to be trustees Witnesses, William Silleker, Elizabeth Brooks, William Lewis "

Ann Ellis lived to see all her children arrive at mature age, surviving her husband twenty-four years She departed this life the 27th of Fourth month, 1777, aged sixty-nine

---

CHAPTER IV.

EARLY HISTORY OF THE COX FAMILY.

JOHN AND SARAH ALLERLY

I HAVE no access to the record of their birth, but they must have dated their nativity from about the middle or in the latter half of the seventeenth century. They lived in or very near London, England.

John Allerly was a brewer, and he and his wife were zealous members of the Church of England. He died suddenly of apoplexy. After rising from the tea-table and sitting down in an arm-chair, he exclaimed, " Lord, have mercy upon me!   My head!" and in a moment he was gone.

John and Sarah Allerly had three children,—MARY, Sarah, and Elizabeth. Elizabeth married John Gardiner. Mary married John Goldhawk, whom she survived some years, and afterwards married a gentleman of the name of Shirley.

JOHN AND MARY (ALLERLY) GOLDHAWK

owned property at Staines, but probably resided for a time at Eghamhithe, somewhat to the west of Staines, as their daughter MARY was born there. They were warmly attached to the Established Church, and the neighboring clergy were in the habit of dining at their house on the First day of the week. They appear to have lived in affluence, from the account given by their granddaughter, Mercy Ellis, to my sister-in-law, Mary E. Haines (afterwards Marshall). Mary Goldhawk was very particular in her housekeeping, testing the fidelity of her maids in their care of the rooms in her house by taking a fine pocket-handkerchief to ascertain whether any dust had been left on the furniture. Thirty pairs of fine linen sheets, the hems trimmed with handsome lace, formed part of the treasures of her linen-closet.

The second marriage seems to have been less happy than the first, Mr. Shirley's mental powers becoming confused, as was shown by having some fine trees on the estate cut down, and otherwise endangering his wife's property. When Mary Shirley, anxious for the safety of some valuable papers and deeds belonging to herself and her children, began to search for them, she ascertained that her daughter Mary, giving early proof of her ability in business affairs, had quietly conveyed them to her Grandfather Allerly's for security.

The dates of the birth and decease of John and Mary (Allerly) Goldhawk are not within my reach, but from known circumstances I infer that they were born late in the seventeenth century that John Goldhawk probably deceased prior to 1735, and his wife subsequent to 1750. No doubt the parish registers in England would supply the information correctly.

CHAPTER V

WILLIAM AND MARY (GOLDHAWK) COX, 1721–1790.

MARY GOLDHAWK, daughter of John and Mary (Allerly) Goldhawk, was born at Eghamhithe, near Staines, England, 1721. By her parents and grandparents she was educated in religious profession with the Church of England, and for some years in her maidenhood resided with her Grandfather and Grandmother Allerly in or very near London

Her mother, Mary Goldhawk, according to tradition, was a proud and haughty woman, and had her daughter trained in all the accomplishments in vogue at that time. She grew up a handsome and graceful woman, dressed with elegance, and mingled freely in fashionable society, partaking with zest in the amusements common to the circle in which she moved.

*At one time Mary Goldhawk heard there was to be a meeting of Friends held in the neighborhood, and she, with some others, in a spirit of frolic attended it It so happened that a minister there preached a powerful sermon on the parable of the sower. It affected her so greatly that she was almost impelled to cry aloud, "O Lord, of what soil is my soul composed?" The impression lasted, and for some time she attended secretly such Friends' meetings as were held there, for her mother, being a stanch member of the Established Church, held all dissenters in little esteem, most especially the despised Quakers Finally her daughter felt so fully persuaded of the truth as revealed to her that she acquainted her mother with the change in her religious views, arousing even more indignation than she had anticipated But she felt constrained to persevere, and we

* Much of what is stated from this point and on the following page is taken from a Baltimore manuscript, belonging to the family in Maryland

may imagine the mother's horror when she heard that her
daughter was likely to marry a Friend. This was too much,
the madness seemed too great, and she called her to a strict
account. "Are you going to marry this Quaker?" demanded
the mother, to which the daughter replied, "Yes, with thy consent, I am going to marry this Quaker, the Oxford graduate who
has taken first honors, and the handsomest man in the shire!"

This was more than the mother could endure, and she sternly
said that if disobedience should be carried that far her daughter
should never see her face again

After a long time of waiting, and finding it was in vain to
expect her consent, the young couple concluded to marry without it, and their wedding was consummated in 1743 For two
years the merchant and his winsome bride lived in the great
metropolis But their thoughts turned to the American colonies, and they decided to avail themselves of the freedom and
scope for enterprise offered on the western side of the Atlantic.

With the liberal assistance of his father, William Cox prepared for the voyage, and with his brave wife sailed from England in the Eighth month, 1745. No luxurious and stately
steamers in that day carried their thousands of passengers
from one populous city to another on opposite shores of the
Atlantic Ocean, and, instead of the few days now required,
the ship sailed slowly on, drifting so far to the south that op-
pressive heat added to the tedium of the passage, and nearly
four months elapsed before William and Mary Cox landed in
Maryland, Eleventh month, 1745

In thinking of the old home the fair emigrant had the comfort of knowing that her mother had become partially reconciled to her marriage, and of receiving from her during the
later years of her long life letters and regular remittances.
They chose for their allotment a portion of the picturesque
lands in Deer Creek, on the banks of the beautiful Susquehanna

A blessing rested on the skilful management of both husband and wife, and they appear to have been surrounded by
more than the comforts and conveniences of life, with hearts
ready to share their abundance with those less favored, and a
house wide open to hospitality

Prosperity and domestic happiness, as a large family of sons and daughters grew around them, did not absorb their attention and prevent those higher aspirations for spiritual life and progress that are paramount to all merely earthly considerations

William Cox was a Friend, and diligent in attending his meetings for worship His wife went with him, but her education and natural disposition allowed her to indulge in some things that were not in unison with his feelings The early death of one or more of their little children was loosening her hold on worldly pleasures : but she was not quite prepared to give them up, when an invitation came to a dancing-party in the neighborhood Travelling was chiefly accomplished at that time on horseback, and to reach the house of Jacob Giles, an English gentleman of some note in the vicinity, a stream of water had to be crossed Mary Cox still dressed handsomely and in the mode, and with her gown and laces for the ball folded and carried before her on the saddle, she mounted and rode off Owing to some accident in fording the creek, her clothing was plunged into the water Too spirited to turn back, she went on to the house of Jacob Giles, where she was welcomed and made as comfortable as circumstances would permit

The wardrobe of his mother was placed at her service , and, dressed in the slightly antique, yet rich and becoming, costume of the elderly lady, she descended, joined the guests, and was led out in the dance by the host himself, enjoying the festivities well on into the night

On her way home she felt very uncomfortable , thought how little happiness she gained by indulging in amusements which her husband could not approve, and made up her mind there and then that her feet should never again glide over the floor of a ball-room, keeping time with the music

Continuing to listen to the voice of the heavenly Shepherd in the obedience of faith, she became convinced that Christianity, as understood by Friends, agreed with the teaching of the Lord Jesus as it is given in the New Testament She united in membership with their religious society, and found in this connection additional sweetness in the marriage bond, when husband and

wife had but one interest in all that related to their temporal
and spiritual welfare

A memorial of Deer Creek Monthly Meeting respecting her
says, "About the thirty-ninth year of her age she was called
to the ministry, and for a number of years her words were few
and pathetic She, however, grew in her gift, and with the
concurrence of her friends visited many of the meetings in the
neighboring provinces"

The mother of four sons and five daughters, surrounded by
numerous negro servants, her husband engaged extensively in
business, and both of them given to hospitality, must have been
a woman of active mind and methodical habits to maintain a
well-ordered house Mary Cox was fitted by nature for her
position, and she used her powers with judgment and celerity,
whether the immediate objects in view were more especially
secular or spiritual

When the British army occupied Philadelphia, at the time of
the Revolutionary War, she went there to attend the Yearly
Meeting A visit to the city at such a time would naturally
excite suspicion in the minds of her countrymen, and as she
was on her way home she was arrested and carried before the
officers of the American army.

There she was strictly questioned and threatened with the
penalties of martial law, but as nothing could be proved against
her, she was released Before taking leave of them she asked
liberty to address them, which being granted, she told her
audience that it had been on her mind for some weeks to see
them and give them a gospel message She then preached the
doctrines of peace inculcated by our holy religion

Joshua Pusey and George Churchman were particular friends
of William and Mary Cox, and members of the same Quarterly
Meeting. My honored cousin, Hannah Gibbons, late in her long
life told me of the esteem her father, Joshua Pusey, had for them,
and how they were welcomed by her parents when they came
across the Susquehanna to attend the meetings held in their
vicinity William and Mary Cox used to come to their house on
horseback, next day take seats in Joshua Pusey's carriage, and
leave their steeds for the young people to mount and follow.

George Churchman's daughters, although greatly my seniors, were much beloved and reckoned among my best friends. From a letter written by me, while visiting in Philadelphia, dated "Union Street, First month 6th, 1852," I copy the following· After stating that the weather had been so stormy as to confine me to the house, it goes on to say, "Hannah and Margaret Churchman are here spending the day, having been sent in a carriage by the friends with whom they are staying a few days. If you know them at all, you know they are animated in conversation   Hannah looked at my little daughter and remarked there was none of the Evans or the Rhoads in her face, it was an Ellis countenance   She said that her father valued none of his friends more than William and Mary Cox, who often came to his house when attending meetings that were near it   She told me some anecdotes of Mary Cox which her father used to relate   She had a talent for business and would take an active part in it, and being besides a spiritually-minded woman, a black man who lived with her used to say, 'I never saw anything like missus, she can jump so quick from earth to heaven.'

"At one time, when she was crossing the ferry at Havre de Grace in a storm, the boatmen were much terrified and perplexed   She undertook the direction, ordering them to keep the boat's head to the wind   The passengers would call out, 'Mind the old lady! Mind what the old lady tells you!' And finally they landed in safety"

When far advanced in life and in impaired health, Mary Cox and her companion, Mary Husband, made a general visit to Friends in the lower parts of Maryland and Virginia   Subsequently she crossed the Alleghany Mountains, visiting the Friends in what was then considered "those remote parts, and having meetings there with those of other societies, where she was enabled to explain the principles of Christianity and tell to others what the Lord had done for her   At home, when scarcely able to get to her seat in her meetings, 'she frequently bore lively testimonies' and her manner was 'exemplary and teaching.'"

In the Sixth month, previous to her decease, she went to the Yearly Meeting in Baltimore, and afterwards attended a number of meetings in and near Pipe Creek and visited some of the families Owing to her infirm health this was accomplished with some difficulty, but she expressed her thankfulness for the ability given her to perform these acts of apprehended duty In a short time she was confined to her room by illness The closing story of her life can be best given in the words of the memorial of Deer Creek Monthly Meeting, before referred to It states that for a time she had some close searchings of heart, and "fervently prayed that she might be shown whether her sufferings were on her own account or on account of others, adding, if she could but find favor at last, and have without doubt, as heretofore, an evidence of eternal peace, she would be satisfied The next day she movingly broke forth with the following portion of Scripture, 'Comfort ye, comfort ye my people, saith your God Speak ye comfortably to Jerusalem, and cry unto her that her warfare is accomplished, that her iniquity is pardoned, for she hath received of the Lord's hand double for all her sins' And some time after further expressed that the Lord had happily sealed her peace, and in thankful praises she rejoiced therein and said, 'Oh, how sweet I feel! I feel perfectly easy Some poor souls are trying all their lives to get to heaven, and how hard they find it! while others are at ease and take little care about it,' adding, 'Whom the Lord loveth He chasteneth'

"On eating a little bread she said, 'How many poor, afflicted ones have I given bread to! I could not see them want while in my power to help, which is now a great comfort to me'

"On a number of Friends being present she said, 'This is a trying time, all things appear clear;' adding, 'We have been often favored to go together with that sweet, uniting power of Truth which was always precious to me.' At another time, after sitting in a solid frame of mind, she broke forth, saying, 'Oh, the love I feel that flows through Jesus Christ, which none can feel but those who believe in Him!'

"At another time, just before the close, being asked how she did, she answered, 'Just going to enter the promised land!' And to another, who asked if she were alarmed, she cheerfully answered, 'Nay, I feel that which triumphs over death, hell, and the grave' She dropped many more comfortable and edifying expressions not now particularly remembered.

"We have further to add that she was a loving and faithful wife, a tender parent, a sympathizing friend, and remarkably charitable to the poor.

"On the fifteenth day of the Eighth month, 1790, about nine in the evening, she quietly departed this life, without sigh or groan, aged about sixty-nine years, a minister about thirty years. On the seventeenth of the same was interred in Friends' burying-ground at Deer Creek, accompanied by a great company of Friends and others. after which a meeting was held and attended with stillness and gravity well becoming the solemnity of the occasion

"Read and approved at Deer Creek Monthly Meeting, held the 23d of Twelfth mo., 1790, and signed by order thereof by

"JOHN COX, Clerk,
"SARAH ELY, Clerk

"Read and approved at our Quarterly Meeting, held in Baltimore the 5th of the Second mo, 1791, and signed by order thereof by

"JOSEPH TOWNSEND, Clerk,
"MARY PRICE, Clerk"

WILLIAM COX

William Cox was the son of John Cox and his wife, Mary Banes Cox, and was born in Essex, England, in 1717 or 1718 His mother's family name was Banes John Cox was a man of considerable wealth, owned several mills, and was engaged in the shipping business,—sending vessels to Norway for deal boards His son William accompanied him on one of his voyages and brought home a handsome Norwegian pony

It appears that William Cox lived for some years as a merchant in London, where he was married to Mary Goldhawk, a young lady of strong mental endowments and fascinating accomplishments, in 1743.

In the Eighth month, 1745, they embarked for America The vessel sailed so far to the south that the pitch melted on deck, and, after a tedious voyage of nearly four months, they landed and settled at Deer Creek, Harford County, Maryland. Here they resided till the close of their life on earth, respected for their energy, activity, and success in temporal affairs, esteemed as exemplary and devout Christians, beloved and honored heads of a large family of children and numerous servants and dependents   At one time they held their servants as slaves, but they set them all free, and it is said that not one left their former master and mistress   William and Mary Cox labored diligently with Friends who were slaveholders to induce them to liberate their slaves.

The Monthly Meeting of Friends held at Deer Creek thought it right to record their testimony to the worth and usefulness of William Cox's character, from which the following extracts are taken

" He was a useful member in our meeting, having stood in the station of elder for years, diligent in attending meetings when at home, and remarkably attentive to the time appointed, exemplary and solid in his sitting, and a man of good understanding   As it is the end which crowns all, we have to believe that, in the latter part of his life especially, he was favored with a lively sense of Truth and its powerful operations, which refine and quicken in the best things, a sweetness and living savor attending his expressions in the time of his last illness, appearing remarkably concerned to leave his testimony for that simplicity which becomes the followers of Christ

" At one time, in the forepart of his sickness, he said nearly as follows. ' I have been much distressed for some time on account of the taxes demanded for the support of war   Those who gather tax have not lately applied to me for it, and I think it has been paid by a certain person,' whom he then named, and said, ' I have warned him to do so no more, and have desired my son not to grind wheat for him in the mill, apprehending he hath proposed to stop in that way what he has paid on my account   But I had rather suffer affliction with the people of God than enjoy the pleasures of these things for a season '

" At another time he broke forth in the following manner ·

'My heart mourns, all I have to desire is that my end may be peace and assurance forever. A few things lay heavily on my mind which I intend to do to-morrow, when I am better, and though I may be derided by some, let them mock and deride I believe my eternal peace is concerned in it' The next day, being easier, according to his expectation, he expressed to a friend at his bedside to this purpose 'I have soared too much above the pure witness in my own heart respecting little things'

"He then mentioned several things in his dress that he thought were too luxurious or superfluous, and the order he had given respecting them, to which the friend replied that she hoped he would now be easy, as he had borne his testimony if the tailor did not come to carry out his orders His answer was, 'No, no, we must be faithful in small things, for oh, there is nothing short of our coming up in a faithful discharge of duty, according to the sight afforded, will yield peace at such a time as this If I live I mean to enforce these things, and if I die I leave them as my testimony'

"Shortly after he said, 'Into the arms of thy mercy, O Lord, I commit my body, soul, and spirit!' Being favored with his understanding clear to the last, he was frequently heard in fervent supplication to the Almighty in the time of sickness, in which he lay somewhat more than two weeks, and quietly departed in great serenity of mind

"Signed by order, and on behalf of our Monthly Meeting of Deer Creek, held the first day of Eighth month, 1782

"John Wilson, Clerk"

The children of William and Mary Cox were, John, Sarah, William, Israel, James, Mary, Elizabeth, Mercy, and Rachel. Their daughter Mercy was married to William Ellis in 1785

William Ellis had a high regard for his wife's father, and added his testimony to that of the Monthly Meeting that he had copied into a book containing letters, remarks, etc, that had been collected by William Cox It is as follows

"As I have often believed there was something inviting to imitation in the portrait of an amiable character, I have been thoughtful of throwing together, for the future perusal of any relative or other, a few remarks on his, which in my view was embellished with many excellent qualities

" He was a man endowed with a strong natural capacity, which he had in early life been successful in considerably improving, wherein, as he became measurably qualified by the Truth, he was rendered very useful to the meeting he belonged to, and to us He acted as clerk from the time of its being established a Monthly Meeting until his death, which was upwards of twenty years, and in that station frequently manifested abilities surpassed by few

" His house might be truly said to be a stage of rest for weary travellers, for he received his friends with open arms, not with an ostentatious, but a generous hospitality, often having been heard to repeat, in familiar conversation with his family, the language of the poet,—

> " ' Without a vain, without a grudging heart,
> What Heaven has given I freely give a part '

" There was indeed a striking nobility of mind appearing in many parts of his conduct which was superior to the contracted feelings of narrow minds, wherein he could prefer the publick safety of a cause to any sinister or private bias, a virtue known only to such as have witnessed the cultivation and enlargement of the finer faculties of the human heart

" He had, to a considerable experience of life and manners, both in England and this country, added a valuable acquisition of useful knowledge from books, which, as he was favored with strong retentive faculties and a great share of pleasantry in conversation, rendered him a most agreeable companion

" Thus qualified, he was capable of entering into the tenderest sensations of the married state and partaking largely of domestic happiness, and to an affectionate wife and children his society had become almost inexpressibly dear And his servants both loved and feared him, for although there was a certain majestic firmness in his countenance and behaviour that had a tendency to keep both his children and servants at a degree of solemn and respectful distance, yet he appeared careful to qualify it with that proper share of affable tenderness which effectually secured him an uncommon share of the affections of both, few men appearing happier at home, although for a series of years deeply engaged in a wide field of business, wherein he manifested a great share of regular method, prudential economy, and persevering industry These, with the blessing of Providence, furnished him with a handsome competency, living and dying in reputation and esteem, not only in our Society, but in the community at large. All which he has now left for a more durable inheritance, and is landed, I trust, in the everlasting enclosures of a quiet habitation

"A degree of desire impresses my mind, while I write, that we to whom he was known may endeavor to walk in imitation of his virtues, and particularly that his offspring may be favored to fill their proper allotment through life with equal propriety, for although mankind are not all equally qualified, nor can consistent with harmony all fill the same stations, yet it is, or ought to be, the business of every person of common capacity to be useful to the age they live in, and to fulfil the religious, social, and relative duties of life with propriety and dignity, for

> "'Honour and fame from no condition rise,
> Act well your part, there all the honour lies'

And it is, generally speaking, from thus acting well our part that can arise through life a well-grounded expectation of its being closed with that welcome sentence of 'Well done, good and faithful servant'"

CHAPTER VI.

WILLIAM AND MERCY ELLIS

WILLIAM ELLIS, son of Benjamin and Ann Ellis of Easttown, Chester County, Pennsylvania, was born in 1751

He received a good education, and for a few years in early life engaged in teaching His school was in Harford County, Maryland, where he went to reside when about twenty-one,

5

having a certificate from Friends in Chester County to the
meeting at Deer Creek, dated 6th of Eleventh month, 1772
He remained there some years, but a more enterprising course
accorded with his disposition, and in 1777, near the time of his
mother's decease, he is said to be of Easttown   A few days
after her departure he sold his property there to Samuel Burge,
of Philadelphia, for one hundred and eighty-three pounds, as
shown by a deed dated April 2, 1777, conveying "Thirty-one
and a half acres and nineteen perches of land in Easttown,
which Benjamin Ellis, by will dated 1st of Third month 1753,
devised to his son William Ellis, party hereto "

   This sale was probably preparatory to his purchase of land in
the beautiful valley of Muncy, on the West Branch of the
Susquehanna River   Selecting a fine locality in that newly-
opened country, he built a house and planted a garden and
orchard, in the hope that here he might transplant the Rose of
Deer Creek

   Before his new home was completed, Indian tribes from the
western part of New York made a hostile incursion, bringing
destruction as they came   William Ellis caught a whisper of
their advancing raids, and immediately mounting his horse, rode
with all speed up the river as far as Jersey Shore, warning the
English settlers along its borders to fly to some place of safety
without delay   They crowded into a fort at Muncy, and when
they were sheltered there, William Ellis, not wishing to avail
himself of military protection, and having no one immediately
dependent upon him, was about to go down the Susquehanna
to his friends and family.   But the women and children whom
he had assisted in their escape from death or captivity came
to him with tears and entreaties, begging him to stay with
them as the one on whose foresight and wisdom they most
relied   He could not withstand their appeals, and remained
to give such aid as he could, thus subjecting himself to the
censure of his friends, who could not approve of his tarrying
in a fortified place   That he afterwards explained to their
satisfaction

   When the blast of war was blown over, and he returned to
his possessions, he found house, garden, and orchard destroyed.

Not discouraged by these disasters, he renewed his exertions to provide a home and a competency in the valley of his choice, and was aided in his enterprise by acting as surveyor of lands and as agent for Samuel Wallis and others, who were making extensive purchases in that part of the State

He now felt himself in a position to marry, and pressed his suit for the hand of Mercy Cox, who had long been the object of his admiration and love. Her family, living in comparative wealth and ease, had strenuously objected to their union in the prospect of the daughter and sister removing to a newly-settled country, where they supposed she might have many privations to endure Perseverance and his brightening prospects, however, won the day, and they were accordingly married with the consent of all concerned at Deer Creek Meeting of Friends on the 10th day of the Second month, 1785.

In after-days the young wife often alluded to the circumstances of their early attachment with a glad and thankful heart that they had been permitted to consummate their union, which to both of them was so full of blessing She was the eighth child and next to the youngest daughter of William and Mary Cox, of Harford County, Maryland, and was born in 1761 Under the wise and religious care of her excellent parents she was trained in the exercise of those faculties and dispositions that were so remarkably developed in her long and beautiful life

The home at Muncy was not quite ready to receive its future mistress, and to complete his preparations William Ellis was obliged to leave his bride for a few weeks in the paternal mansion, while he went northward At the house of his friend George Churchman, in East Nottingham, Third month 24th, he "forwards a line" to his "dearest earthly treasure" to tell her that he had a good passage across the river. Then came detentions, and from Philadelphia he writes in the Fourth month, sending by the hand of a friend, for there appears to have been no postal communication with Deer Creek at that time,—

"My dear Mercy,—I have written so lately, and so often,

that writing at this time seems useless   I am however led to
it from a pleasure I feel in talking to thee even in this way   I
am sorry I am so detained, yet, perhaps, it is right, the waters
have been very high, and the roads to the North west very
bad, but I expect they are now pretty good and I am anxious
to be gone that I may seem the nearer returning

"Ah, why did thou not write by Nancy Rigbie?   Perhaps
thou did not know of her coming in time enough   it was
indeed very grateful to me to find she had so lately talked to
thee, that my dear little Treasure was well.   Let the example
of my repeated writing excite my dear, amiable Companion to
like attention   I shall undoubtedly make my stay as short as
possible, yet the anxious hours of this stay may be sweetened
by often receiving letters from her, if those letters give an
account of her well fare

"I told Nancy Rigbie she must tell you how I talked about
you, and how much I love   She said I must write, but that
some of you know how much I love you   She told me thee
had fixed a day for my return, she could not tell me what day.
Don't get uneasy, my dear, as to a day, keep in resigned reliance on the providence of the Father of men

"I ask, sometimes, my own heart, when ruminating on these
things, is it possible my dear, generous Fan can wish earnestly
my return, whilst that return must be considered as the pro-
logue to the affecting scene of her departure from the beautiful
Banks of Deer Creek, and from, at least, the second tenderest
connections in life ? and have been answered by the sensations
I have felt, It is possible   If this should even be flattering
myself, perhaps, it's a pleasing delusion

"I want a long letter   How did thou feel after our departure
from Deer Creek ?   How soon did thy heart get lighter ?   Who
came to see thee, and what did they say ?   How come on
Brother Israel and his Eliza ?

> " Farewell, my Dear, may every rising day
> To thy dear bosom health and peace convey.

"WILLIAM ELLIS

"P.S —Give my affectionate love to our dear Mother · tell

her I called immediately on Caleb Lownes with her message
and he said he should govern himself accordingly Give my
love to thy connections, and brother Jonney and family in a
particular manner ; tell him I mean to write to him early from
Muncy "

All that summer his connection in business with others
obliged him to remain at Muncy, the prolonged separation from
his wife being cheered by frequent correspondence and brightened by hope. One more letter before he could leave to bring
her to the home he was making for her appears to close the
record of this solitary but active period

"MUNCY 9ᵗʰ mo 3ʳᵈ, 1785.

" MY VERY DEAR MERCY,—I have received thy two late very
acceptable favors, one by S Harris about four or five days
past, and the other by Benjamin Warner yesterday, and I thank
thee for thy care, thou Pattern of female excellence ! in thy attention to my wants respecting clothes, not that I was in any
great need of them, but nothing comes from thee but what
doubles its value to me.

" I know one of the weaknesses of my constitutional disposition lies in saying too much, yet if I had twice the command of language which has fallen to my share, I should not
be able to reach the amount of the many things I have to
say, or to describe the pointed feelings my heart is acquainted
with when I am writing to the excellent Reward of my seven
years' servitude Believest thou that I love thee above every
earthly object ? Yea, I know thou believest it ! How then,
may it be asked, is it possible for him to submit to such a
length of absence. I answer, I submit to it for that very
reason, to wit, because I thus love thee, and conceive my
leaving here at present would injure my interest more than
is consistent with an object I have sometimes held, and still
in measure hold in view, viz., to close a youth of labor with
an age of ease, whilst favored, if so supremely favored, with
the sweetness of thy conversation and the brightness of thy
example

> " Farewell my dear, my charming wife farewell,
> Whilst I the hours of tedious absence tell,
> Thy pleasing Image round my fancy plays
> In nightly slumbers and in waking days
> O, mayst thou witness Heaven's surrounding arm
> To shield thy precious life from every harm
>
>   " W E."

One more journey, shortly after the above date, and on his return his wishes were realized in having the company of his wife, who now bid adieu to Deer Creek. Their first residence at Muncy was only preparatory to a more desirable one, but William Ellis never allowed the hardships of a settler's life to press upon his wife, and, while his property and resources were steadily increasing in extent and value, there was much comfort and happiness within their reach, reconciling the separation from distant friends and relations, and counterbalancing the want of easy access to the luxuries and refinements of cities

The means of public worship in the way of their fathers was supplied as families of the same religious beliefs came to the valley, and a meeting for worship was established where all could unite in the same simple rites *

A warm feeling of neighborly interest led to the interchange of friendly offices, and the supply of domestic needs, received and returned in this way, carried with it a pleasure peculiar to itself

Children came to gladden the home: Mary, the eldest, a lovely girl, whose heart seemed early set on things above; William, ardent, impetuous, ambitious, and affectionate, RACHEL, fair and thoughtful, were born in this first homestead. The father was often called away by business or religious engagements, and, when the little Mary was scarcely four years old, wrote to his wife from Philadelphia in the Twelfth month, 1789

"When I shall leave here I cannot at present say, though I long sincerely to be done with this kind of separate life. I prize thy precious society at too high a rate to feel reconciled to such continual separations, the nature of my engagements seems, however, to require it at present, and I must labor, as

---

* See note at end of this chapter for the origin of Muncy Monthly Meeting of Friends

well as my dear Mercy, after a disposition of resignation to the
allotment which I hope may not last long   I have been thinking, my dear, that our little Molly ought by this time to know
how to spell pretty well, I wish thou wouldst be steady in
taking proper opportunities of learning her the letters and from
that to spell.   Tell her if she tries to learn like a good girl I
will buy her a pretty new book

"I was at meeting in the evening, it was much crowded, the
ministry rested chiefly with a European woman-Friend and was
indeed a heart searching testimony.   There are two of them
here, commonly called the Irish Friends   They are visiting
families in the middle district at present, and will, I suppose, go
through the city.   I saw Jacob Lindley in the street, he sent
his 'dear love to thy Mercy,' to use his own expression

"Be wise in all thy conduct, let the principles of Truth govern
thy spirit and practice, so shall safety surround thy footsteps,
and thy spirit land finally in peace and everlasting harmony
I am sensible in this I recommend what I never yet attained to
for any length of time together, but I believe it is attainable,
and we must never give over striving as our eternal all depends
on ultimate success."

Dear "little Molly" seems young to have it expected of her
to know how to read, but it was the constant aim of the loving
father to give his children every opportunity in his power to
provide for the full development and cultivation of their mental
and moral natures, and his efforts were largely successful.   If
somewhat of the tone of the mentor is mingled with the love
of the husband, we may excuse it on the ground of his being
ten years in advance of the age of his wife

From another letter, probably near the date of the preceding,
we catch a glimpse of his experiences in Philadelphia.

"Dined at Samuel Emlen's a few days since   He sent his
dear love to thee, and desired me to tell thee he wished grace,
mercy and peace to abound in thee, and that thou might take
heed to the principle, that in the room of the honorable mother
there might be the daughter coming up in beauty and usefulness.

"In the company of such good men and in attending meetings, I try to keep the Evil down, yet often find it a hard

combatant. I wish much for the quiet of thy society, and sometimes feel earnest desires for thy welfare and preservation as well as my own."

About this time he was building the Wolf Run house, which, with the exception of a few years, has been the family residence to the present time   Selecting a pleasant site on a hill sloping to the stream from which the house takes its name, near a group of noble white oaks, and commanding lovely views of the valley and river and mountain, he erected a substantial dwelling of stone taken from an opposite ridge   The proprietor of extensive tracts of arable land in the fertile valley, of pine forests among the hills, and an interest in valuable coal-mines, felt justified in bringing around his increasing household the refinements of life in addition to the comforts that they had always enjoyed

Liberality and taste combined to give space and attraction to the house, several cottages, for colored people employed on the premises, were built beyond the western wing, and the interior was suitably furnished   A gentleman from a Southern State, who was there on a visit, expressed his surprise, in a letter to one of his friends, at finding in a place so remote from cities wines as good and china as fine as he might expect on a table in the metropolis

This was not the abode of selfish indulgence.   The doors opened to the touch of the stranger, whatever might be his rank in the world, and in the days when public conveyances were unknown and immigrants were seeking their fortunes in newly-discovered regions of even these Eastern States, the stream of travel often passed through the valleys of the Susquehanna   Many a weary one, and even whole families, found food and shelter at the Wolf Run house, as a son testified when reviewing the scenes of his childhood from the midst of his busy professional life in Philadelphia

> " Those friendly halls no pilgrim sought in vain,
> At night, in tempest, or descending rain "

It appears from one of William Ellis's letters to his wife, in the autumn of 1792, that they had recently removed into their new house that year.

The number of colored people who appear to have been employed in the family is explained by the fact that some Friends in Philadelphia were at this period actively engaged in the interests of the colored race Pennsylvania had recently passed laws for the gradual abolition of slavery throughout the State, and these Friends thought that Muncy was a desirable place for a colony. Accordingly, a number of the African race were sent there, where homes and employment were provided for them The climate proved too severe for them, especially for those who came from the Southern States, and there has never been a large proportion of colored people resident in Lycoming County, although a warm feeling of kindness towards them has always existed there, and fugitive slaves were welcomed, sheltered, and assisted in reaching a place of safety Once a poor woman and her children, flying from slavery, took refuge at the Wolf Run house Confiding her sorrows to its mistress, she was terrified to learn that her nominal owners were near relatives of the family, and it required some tact and patience on the part of her new friends to restore her to a condition of trust and composure

To understand life on the West Branch at this time one must bear in mind the very different state of the country and means of travel from what is now existing. Much of Northwestern Pennsylvania and nearly all of Western New York was a wilderness, the newly-made roads over the mountains were scarcely adapted to any other mode of travelling than on horseback, so that days were often required in passing from one point to another, where hours are now sufficient

Some flashes of light from the past come to us through letters from William Ellis to his wife, when they were temporarily separated, revealing a little of the domestic life of the times and the tenor of their thoughts, which may be most clearly conveyed by portions of the letters themselves.

"PHILADELPHIA Fourth month 12th 1797

"I received, my dear Mercy, thine of 29th of last month this morning, and in the information of your reasonable health know I ought to be very thankful, and hope I am in some measure. What shall we render unto the Lord for all His benefits? What can we render? We can, as we feel a degree of the convicting power, with a measure of its own assistance, render a degree of obedience thereto, and this, I apprehend, would qualify at times for offering a tribute of praise   The greatest tribute of praise, and the offering of the greatest acceptance is obedience to the law in the mind, 'If ye love Me keep My commandments'

"Kiss the dear children for me and tell them their father loves them dearly, return my love also affectionately to sister, and Phebe,* and Henry and Martha Parker   No late accounts from William Savery and the other friends in Europe

" W. E "

" PHILADELPHIA · Fourth mo 18th 1797

"MY DEAR MERCY,—I returned last evening from an excursion of twenty-eight miles up the Delaware to see young Henry Drinker   I was induced to go by his Father's offer to give me a seat in his carriage   We called to see two Indian boys, who are placed with William Blakely, a Friend of Middletown meeting

"At the marriage of Thomas Harrison's son (his mother has been in Europe on a religious visit some years), who was this day married to a young woman of the name of Roberts at the North meeting, Nicholas Waln appeared in a testimony on the excellence and necessity of walking in the Truth, in a very unusually dignified manner, and in a supplication equally so   I never heard him better, if equally, covered with the Divine armour in my life. The testimonies of the Church were exalted to the Apostolic height of the new creature in Christ, and enforced to the necessity of not denying Him before men in dress and address, in the names of the days, months, &c, yet with great clearness and wisdom impressing the indispensable necessity of so witnessing the operation of the fire that burned in the bush and consumed it not, as to know a deliverance from the

---

* Phebe Randal, a young Friend who lived in their family assisting Mercy Ellis as an older daughter might   She afterwards married Henry Widdifield   They went to Canada to live, and were useful and valued Friends

body of sin and death, and being made free by the Truth operating in the heart, and laying the foundation there by the
washing of regeneration. W E "

"PHILADELPHIA. Second mo 20th 1798.

" I have just returned from a little excursion to Woodbury,
to Salem quarterly meeting held there, in company with our
precious friends Sarah Cresson and Rebecca Archer, and young
John Morton I went at the request of Sarah Cresson ; we only
however attended the quarterly meeting, youths' meeting there
was none held , we went up yesterday and returned to-day

" I saw Joshua Evans and John Simpson, both of whom expressed great love for thee. They think thou art much better
than I, indeed Joshua told me so once, but in that they and I
are of one opinion , yet, as John Salkill said to Thomas Chalk-
ley, I think thou hast not had as hard work to be good as I.

" I hope however, I do at times feel a disposition to leave
the things that are behind and press forward to the things
that are before I try to believe that there is a fountain
set open in Judah for the sons of Jacob to wash in, and I am
at times persuaded, that in the nature of things, we may be
cleansed from much as well as little, seeing it remains to be a
faithful saying that Jesus Christ came into the world to save
sinners, and that we are all, though not equally, children of
wrath. It must be by grace we are to be saved, and not of
ourselves , it is the gift of God, not by acts of righteousness
which we have done, but by His free mercy He saveth us by
the washing of regeneration, as saith the Apostle, and by the
renewing of the Holy Ghost Hence then it is truly ' Not of
him that willeth, nor of him that runneth, but of God that
sheweth mercy '

" Let thy spirit, when clothed with innocence and supplication, beg that I may be made partaker of this mercy, that the
Lord may create in me a clean heart, and renew a right spirit
within me, and that I may be brought, if it should even be
under the flaming sword, to partake of the Tree of Life Give
my love to the dear children.

" W. E "

William Ellis had one of those sensitive natures, inclined to doubt his own attainments, yet perseveringly pressing towards a high mark   That his friends had a different estimate of his progress in spiritual life is evident from their recognition of his gifts and recording him as an elder in the church

The Yearly Meeting of Philadelphia was for a time held in the autumn, but owing to repeated visitations of the yellow fever making it dangerous, and in some instances fatal, for Friends to meet in the city at that season of the year, it appears to have been adjourned to the Twelfth month in 1798, and finally changed to the spring, as related in the annexed letter

" PHILADELPHIA, Twelfth mo 15th 1798

" MY DEAR MERCY,—The yearly meeting has been large for the season and favored with great weight and solemnity, in which many living testimonies were borne, of which however at present I have not time to say much. Yet I can hardly avoid saying I believe it was found by many to be a time of searching of heart when in the opening of the state of society an examination was felt how far our individual conduct had been conformable to the standard of truth and righteousness

" The subject of what alteration, or whether any, should take place in the time of holding the yearly meeting was committed to a committee of sixty men and thirty women, who under all relative circumstances with great unanimity reported as their sense, that the third Second day of the week in the Fourth month would be the most suitable time   Which report was agreed to, and the general Spring meeting, of course, discontinued   of this the representatives were desired to inform the monthly and preparative meetings

" Our friends here are all in good health   I have heard of one solitary instance of the yellow fever, and only one

" Our dear Jacob Lindley* is here firm and unshaken in the faith, and very living in his testimonies, though to him, indeed, it may be said, the earth and the heavens have been shaken   .

" May our souls be quickened, my dearly beloved Mercy, to

* His wife, Hannah Lindley, died of the fever in the early part of Tenth month preceding

watch over ourselves and our little flock that we may by witnessing the availing operation of that grace that brings salvation, be enabled to guide and to command our house and our
children after us

" I find I cannot reach the monthly meeting, but don't intend
to stay above a week or ten days, if spared in health, of which
I enjoy a good share at present   My love affectionately to
sister and the dear children   Accept it thyself, untold, un-
counted, give it also to our beloved friends of our meeting as
occasion may occur   Affectionately thine

" W. E."

To Mary and Rachel Ellis, his daughters at Westtown
Boarding-School, he writes,—

" Muncy . Sixth mo 8ᵗʰ 1799

" DEAR LITTLE GIRLS,—I am about to accompany the letter
written you by your excellent mother with a few lines from
myself   And while I refer you to hers for information of our
journey home, and our present health, permit me to join my
desire to hers that you may live under the increasing influence
of love for and obedience to the principle of grace and truth in
your own hearts, and the wise counsel and directions of your
instructors, made wise by an adherence to this principle, and
quickened to an anxious concern for your right improvement
and true happiness in this world and that which is to come, and
under the influence of the spirit of love and kindness towards
one another as sisters and towards your lovely companions as
children of one family partaking jointly of the favors of the
day . .   Ah ! my dear Mary and Rachel may this care, this
day of uncommon favor not be lost upon you, but profiting
under so excellent and guarded an education, may you come
forth with hundreds of others, with your minds so matured
under right impressions that your conduct through life, under
merciful preservation may certify on behalf of the concern, and
on behalf of your beloved instructors that you have indeed
been taught in a school of wisdom.

" I think it likely some of the Friends of this meeting will be
down at the Eighth month Quarterly meeting and call to see

you Perhaps I may myself, but it is uncertain Accept my love and present it to your Superintendent and teachers Impressed with sincere desires for your health and preservation I remain your loving father,

"WILLIAM ELLIS"

An earnest and affectionate letter of the same date was written to his eldest son, William Cox Ellis, who was also a pupil at that time in the school at Westtown, urging him to use all the advantages he was favored with to the improvement of mind and manners and the confirmation of right principles Some self-denial on the part of parents and children was needed in those days to secure an education in schools so far from home The "little girls" and their brother travelled over the mountains on horseback, and Rachel, at eleven years of age, could not restrain her tears when setting off in that way from her comfortable home on a snowy day It was not till they reached their cousin Benjamin Tucker's, in Philadelphia, that they were supplied with a carriage to perform the remainder of the journey

"MUNCY Twelfth mo 25ᵗʰ 1799

"To MARY AND RACHEL,—We received yesterday our dear Rachel's letter of the 12th inst, in which she mentions having written before, lately, and something about William's writing But none has come lately to hand, that I remember, but this one, and with this, short as it is, we are much pleased, and we wish the writer's encouragement, and that our dear Mary and William may be also stirred up to industry in this respect We receive your letters with great satisfaction, and wish to contribute to yours by answering them and by sending you an account of our state of health and other familiar circumstances which may occur when writing

"Your dear little brother Benjamin and sisters Sarah and Anna are well, accept their love and your dear mother's If your visit to the city has not yet been paid I believe it will be best to leave it till the Yearly Meeting, at which time it is probable I may be there.

"It is drawing towards meeting time, which is now held on

Fourth days Accept my love, my dear children, and expression of strong desires for your preservation and safety From your affectionate father,

" WILLIAM ELLIS "

" MUNCY First mo 8th 1800

"We received, my dear children, the letters of our dear Mary and Rachel, dated from about the 4th to the 12th of last month, and were much pleased to hear of the continuation of your health and of our dear William's safe return, but should have been also pleased to have had a few lines from him

"While we would not wish to impose burdens on you by pressing you to write oftener than be made reasonably convenient, yet we think it right you should remember your letters from time to time yield us great satisfaction, as we know your own affectionate hearts will easily admit that we possess an anxious solicitude for your welfare every way We also on our part think it right to give you the comfort of hearing often from us, as convenience and opportunity permit. I have written to you once or twice since my return, and am favored to be able to inform you in this that we are still continued in health Your sisters and little brother are well he is a fine, rugged boy, but rather too driving in his disposition, has long run about, and now attempts talking

"Rachel says she would like to be at home about two weeks to see how we look, and we would like to have you at home about two weeks and see how you look and how correctly you behave, if it were near enough to make it reasonably convenient, yet we believe the sentiment of resignation expressed by Mary is on the best ground for you and us. We did not, however, understand Rachel as being restless in her situation, but only expressing the choice pleasantly . as such we accepted it and smiled at the idea, and were much pleased with her letter

"William may be informed the stock is well and the gray colts sometimes go in harness Accept the love of the family and mine very sincerely. Much desiring your preservation in innocence and safety, I remain your affectionate father,

" WILLIAM ELLIS "

In one of his letters he alludes to the good accounts of the conduct of his children at the school, and expresses the joy that it gave their parents to receive such testimonials. He then adds, " We are pleased to have had H Hartshorne under our roof with other friends. We know how kind and attentive his worthy parents have been to you, and to other dear children separated from their parents and under their care"

Leaving home to attend the Yearly Meeting in Philadelphia, William Ellis wrote to his wife,—

"MAIDEN CREEK Third mo. 25th, 1800

" MY DEARLY BELOVED MERCY,—I have reached this place in good health, and yesterday we rested, and paid a visit to James Starr Jr and Francis Parvin. James is married to our cousin Nelly Davis

" James Ecroyd and J Widdifield went on yesterday morning, we expect to go to Thomas Lightfoot's this afternoon, stay to meeting to-morrow and then proceed to the City

" Now thou hast a detail of our route, permit me, for a moment, to turn my pen to a subject that, but for the peculiarity of its nature, would long ere this have been worn threadbare, and tell thee how increasingly I love thee Ah, my Matty, how we have been blest in the society of each other with the good things of this life and the manna of this world Do thou pray, whose mind is formed for prayer, whilst I also endeavor to join thee in my way, that we may be increasingly qualified for, and favored to partake of, the manna of the soul anew every morning

" Take care of the fires, take care of the children, take care of the servants, wash the saints' feet, lodge strangers, and cultivate the spirit of love

" Give my love, joined with cousin Ann Tucker's, who is now here, to Sister, to the dear children and Phebe, and remember me with great regard to all our family Accept my love without money or price from thy own affectionate

" WILLIAM ELLIS "

"POTTSGROVE, Third mo 27th, 1800

" MY BELOVED MERCY,—We attended the monthly meeting at Maiden Creek and came on in the afternoon to Benjamin

Wright's, and this forenoon to this place   Our dear friends are as well as usual   Martha Rutter better   Our dear Ruthanna and cousin are now sitting by me conversing about meetings &c, and we have had some pleasant conversation about our mutual friend Jacob Lindley,* who left here but a little before we got here   I don't apprehend, however, there is anything so very hastily like to take place   But I am willing however soon, as I look upon so great a proportion of what is called happiness in this life to depend on and be promoted by the society of those we love

"Take care of thyself and the children, and command, like Abraham, thy house after thee

" May thy spirit partake from day to day of the Spirit of Consolation as times of refreshment from the Divine presence.

" Thine affectionately,
" WILLIAM ELLIS "

In the latter part of this year, 1800, he accompanied his friend, Jesse Haines, on a visit of gospel love to the Friends of the western parts of Pennsylvania, Virginia, and some other places near the borders of his own State   The following letter was probably written in the autumn, but the exact date is wanting.

" REDSTONE at Jonas Kattle's

"My DEAR MERCY,—We are here enjoying good health, and our horses appear well, but they are both lazy and dull hackneys   Last evening Friends here laid out the route that we are to pursue in this quarterly meeting, and it is truly an extensive one, as it is composed of very distant meetings, amounting in the whole to four hundred miles' riding   This, however, includes the Friends over the Ohio at Wheeling   We got to a preparative meeting here at Providence, the day after our arrival and attended the monthly meeting at the same place the next day. My companion appeared comfortably in the first, but was silent in the second   To-day is the quarterly meeting at Redstone, where we were yesterday at their First-day meeting, and the Select meeting the day before. Yesterday Jesse

---

* He and Ruthanna Rutter were afterwards married

6

was large and weighty (in the ministry) Our dear old mother, Hannah Reeves, was also there . she appeais to have been laigely and acceptably engaged in these paits

"There appears to be a large body of solid Friends in this countiy, and it is the most extensive and iichest looking country that ever I have seen I am sometimes induced almost to lament the situation of numbers of collections of Friends, who, when they have been on the wing have settled down on rough lands in rough countries, while by going out this way they might have possessed such rich inheritances for themselves and their childi en

"I have seen the wonderful boy seveial times, but have not asked him any questions as I wish to be cautious of manifesting any idle curiosity about the business, while our pursuits ought to be, and I trust are, of more serious importance

"My beloved companion desires his love be given to his wife and children, and they informed he is very well, but thinks he cannot wite this morning as the time is short.

"I must hasten to a close as I want to write a few lines to the dear children at school Accept my dear love abundantly and affectionately and distribute it to the dear children and to William veiy especially. Tell him it is his father's desire and request that he will tiy all he can to be a comfoit to his dear mother and be a satisfaction to all around him My love also to Sister and Phebe and to all the family Again accept my love and believe me very affectionately, Thine,

"WILLIAM ELLIS"

"WINCHESTER Twelfth mo 30th, 1800.

"MY DEAR MERCY,—I have industriously written from time to time informing of our being favoied with health I still have it in my power to continue this favorable account . we have been slightly indisposed with colds, but are now bravely

"Friends are veiy kind to us Aftei attending, as I now expect, Crooked-Run and Hopewell monthly meetings, which come in a few days, we shall set off towards James River settlement of Fiiends This, I expect, will be the furthest side of the route, but it will be likely to take a good while there as well as on the route towards home through Fairfax, Pipe-creek, Baltimore, &c , &c , so that I do not see any prospect of getting home soon We have been at a number of meetings here, but the power has been less felt than over the mountains, yet not to be complained of, and it is to be hoped will rise again · indeed I have no doubt of it. .

" I am in measure, I trust, in my way labouring to leave the things which are behind, and to feel for a power to enable me to pursue those things which are before, and if strength enough is obtained to preserve on the right foundation against which the counsels of the dark power, it is said, shall not be able to prevail, it will be cause of great thankfulness But mark, I am not presuming on it, but pray thou for it.

" How do you come on in your little meetings on First-days and on Fourth-days ? As I sit in meetings I sometimes try to take a view of you, but can't see you as plainly as the Red-stone boy is supposed to do in the case of distant objects. Accept my love unfeignedly, affectionately, my dear, lovely Mercy.

"W Ellis "

The " Redstone boy" alluded to in the foregoing letters was Eli Yarnall, a remarkable person He possessed a mysterious faculty for seeing places, persons, and occurrences at great distances from him and with which he had no previous acquaintance. If the testimony to this were not so reliable and well known I would not think it worth mentioning It was first observed by his mother when he was a little child She noticed one day that he was laughing, appearing to be excessively amused, and asked him what was the cause of it He replied that he saw a jug rolling down hill and his father running after it His father at that time was away from home, probably gone for domestic supplies, and far enough beyond ordinary powers of vision The fact was confirmed on the father's return

Among other instances of this peculiar gift may be given that of two Friends, ministers from Europe, who were at Eli Yarnall's home in the course of their religious labors in this country In answer to their questions the boy described with accuracy their families, one in England, the other in France, and how they were at the time, also some particulars relating to the English residence that were entirely different from anything he had ever seen in his own country The Friends thought that some things he told were mistakes, but on corresponding with their families they had all particulars confirmed. I have understood that when the boy had done what he knew to be wrong the faculty was obscured for a time, and when grown up it disappeared, as he was not faithful to his best convictions

Minutes from the meetings visited in this journey were given to William Ellis and Jesse Haines, expressive of the value of their labors among the Friends composing them, and of their unity and love.

In 1801 his children Mary and Rachel were still at school at Westtown While away from home himself, apparently on business of his own, he wrote to them from Lancaster

"LANCASTER Sixth mo 22nd, 1801

"You are, my dear children, fast advancing towards an age that awakens in the minds of your parents additional degrees of care and anxiety to those that have long occupied them in watching over your more infantile years and I know you will agree with me, that more care and caution are also needful and will be expected on your part, both in proportion to your advancing years and the very improving society with which you have been for some length of time favored. We are comforted in believing that a good degree of this care is opening on your understanding, which, if you are happily preserved in the due exercise of, under the influence of light and grace, your paths may, I trust, be kept free from many snares and consequent thorns that are, alas! too often attendant on the footsteps of unguarded mortals.

"It is an excellent thing to set off rightly, and I acknowledge, I consider the opportunities put in your power at Westtown as highly calculated to give you this advantage, it being admitted on all hands, that the company we keep and the books we are familiar with go great lengths, especially in early life, in

giving a bent to our taste and manners Of what vast importance then, that at this time of life every improper example and
every improper sentiment should be kept out of sight and out
of hearing , that the heart being kept clean by the fear of the
Lord, may become increasingly acquainted with His law and
feel increasing power to yield obedience to it, and thus to choose
the ' Lord for its portion and the God of Israel for the lot of its
inheritance ' Innocence is a sure protection, and as through
the gentle, the effectual redeeming power this ground of standing is witnessed, a degree of humble confidence will be felt at
times to adopt a language like this of David in his twenty-
third Psalm

> " ' The Lord my pasture shall prepare,
> And feed me with a Shepherd's care ,
> His presence shall my wants supply,
> And guard me with a watchful eye
> My noonday walks He shall attend,
> And all my midnight hours defend '

"You are very tenderly mentioned in a letter I received early
in this month from a very valuable friend of the City, who saw
you at the School and conversed with you May you long
continue to enjoy the love of your friends and the friends of
Truth We received Mary's letter about the 5th inst , and
Rachel's as I was coming from home, both by post, the first
dated Fifth mo 14th, with dear Rebecca's note of love at the
bottom Tell her her love is a cordial to our hearts, desire her
to accept ours in gospel measure , we love her very sincerely
and wish, how much ! our daughters may be like her Present
our love also very affectionately to all your other Mistresses
and your very worthy Superintendents

"William Cox is very well and your little brothers and
sisters William is busy farming your dear Mother was well
and your Aunt, and all the rest when I left home, Sixth day last
The cough has left me and I am favored also with good health.

"I returned lately from Milesburg on Bald Eagle, having
gone that far with Elias Hicks* and his companion on their

---

* Elias Hicks was a popular preacher in the Society of Friends, but became
clouded in his views and finally adopted Unitarian sentiments

way to Redstone   We have also had Joseph Potts and companion, thus we are continually visited by the servants who
are sent out to invite to 'The Supper,' to wit, to an attention to
the principle of light and life in our own hearts, to an inward
communion with the Seed, and participation of the Bread of life,
in feeling the Divine power gradually increasing to the overcom-
ing of the powers and propensities of our nature   May it be our
experience and yours

"I observe in Rachel's letter to her aunt an expression of a
disposition to come home at the expiration of your three
months, if we are willing.   If you are serious in wishing to
come home we shall certainly be willing to indulge it   Accept
your dear mother's love and mine, renewedly and affectionately
Write us more especially about coming home that I may know
how to act

"I remain, dear girls, your affectionate father,

"WILLIAM ELLIS."

"LANCASTER   Second mo 3rd, 1803

"MY DEAR MERCY,—I received a letter from my friend, John
Adlum, by the bearer of this, Abel Marple, with whom J A.
appears to be going into an extensive Susquehanna trade.   He
appears like a very respectable man, and for that as well as for
the sake of his respectable partner, please treat him with all the
attention and respect that can be furnished in our homespun
way.

"I believe I will take the stage [coach] from here as the
weather seems boisterous and I must try to go in to-morrow
night.   My writing on business at present seems but of little
use and I will not take up thy time, nor mine with it

"I have so long, when addressing my dear Mercy, indulged
myself with the softer and tenderer themes of love and friendship, that should my letters, now in the advanced period of life
that I have been permitted to reach, slide into the appearance
of indifference, it would be an appearance that the state of my
heart would not justify.   Permit me then once more to repeat
how much I love thee, how much I consider it a favor to be
intrusted with the charge of such an excellent treasure; with

the intimate society and increased friendship of so excellent a woman, and my children with so excellent a mother. I strongly desire they may inherit thy virtues Give my love to them one by one, desire William to do all he can for the prosecution of the feeding, keeping every thing in order, and that he will persevere steadily in the school

"We need the preserving Power continually around us at home and abroad may we be favored to witness it as a hedge, —as walls for a sure defence

"Give my love to sister and Phebe, E Kitely, M Parker, and remember me very respectfully to the other members of our own family, and believe me thy affectionate

"WILLIAM ELLIS"

In the repeated references to his son William's giving his attention to farming affairs, and the prospect of his inheriting extensive landed property, it appears to have been the father's wish that he should give his chief care in business to agriculture This, however, did not coincide with the natural bent of the eldest son, who subsequently studied law, became an eloquent pleader, and entered on a political career The next letter is addressed to him

"PHILADELPHIA Second mo 16th, 1803
"WILLIAM COX ELLIS

"DEAR SON,—I have conversed with John Cox on the subject of thy going to the Burlington School. He did not appear to disapprove of it, but said he would give me his sentiments fully on the subject, but we did not meet again before he left town except in public meetings I have written · to him and expect his answer Dear Alexander Wilson, who is also interested for thy welfare, thinks it will be as well, perhaps, as anywhere else, but we all think it has its share of dangers, indeed, so has every situation in life

"I am, through mercy, in pretty good health, still have some remains of a cold which I suppose I a little added to by yielding to E Garrigues' kind and pressing invitation to go out to see his family at Kingsessing on Seventh-day afternoon On First-day evening I came in through heavy rain . .

" I several times saw, heard, and was in company with the great Richard Jordan : he was at Darby on First-day, and I left him at E Garrigues' in the afternoon   Among the many ministers of the Gospel in our Society, I think he stands in the first rank, but the office of all outward ministry is to call and direct the mind of man and woman to the operation and ministration of the principle of Truth or grace in the heart, and my mind is in mercy, at times, made as solid in our own little meeting at Muncy as here   This principle or Witness in the mind is felt very strong and clear in early life before there has been any strong habits of disobedience or long trifling with its dictates slidden into, through the deceitfulness of sin   Thou hast often felt it, dear William, very strong and clear   I hope thou hast often yielded, and often will yield to it

" I hope thou art, my dear son, doing all in thy power to assist thy dear mother in preserving the order and industry of that large family   Accept my love, and believe me with affectionate care for thy right improvement, thy friend and father,

"WILLIAM ELLIS"

The following appears to have been written on the same sheet of paper as the above

" MY DEAR MERCY,—I have said so much to William Cox that I have but little room left except I write on the other side

" I dined with our dear Martha Routh day before yesterday She charged me with her love for thee and to say that it would be very pleasant to see thee at the Yearly Meeting   How is dear Henry ?   Yesterday, or to-day, is post-day and I have yet received no letter except by Silas

" Perhaps in a week or ten days I may be able to leave the city   Our friends are all well, Sarah Cresson [included].   They all love thee very much, and, if they knew thee as well as I do, they would love thee more   Surely it was a day of great favor when thou, my dear Mercy, wast intrusted to my care.   I may and can with great cordiality subscribe to Solomon's declaration, and, perhaps, with more affirmative though less negative experience on the subject, that ' The price of a virtuous woman

is above rubies, and that she is a crown to her husband,' and
that, the good old woman said in her testimony, 'You know,
friends, is above the head'

"Please give my love to sister, the dear children and Phebe,
and remember me with great kindness to Biddy and to all the
domestics. Accept my love largely and believe me thy

"Affectionate husband,   WILLIAM ELLIS."

In closing a letter written in Philadelphia, Second month 19,
1805, he says, "How is dear little Henry? Not a word has
been mentioned about him, how are sister, and the rest of the
flock? If I write to William I must close First let me, however, say our precious female Friends are at the Grove quarter
Ann appeared at the marriage of J Warder last Fifth-day almost
like an earthly female angel. There is something very extraordinary in her gift of the ministry, one expression glows out
of another very much resembling, perhaps quite equal to, Sarah
Grubb's Letters. I suppose they will again be in town this
week. Now shall I indulge myself with a few sentiments of
love at the bottom of this long letter? Accept then, thou sum
of all earthly truth, thou greatest earthly treasure of my life,
my love unfeigned and unchanged and express a proportion of
it to Sister and the dear children Say a great many tender
and agreeable things to them from me and believe me

"Thine,   WILLIAM ELLIS"

"PHILADELPHIA Third mo 5th, 1805

"MY DEAR MERCY,—I have just received thy acceptable
favor of the 28th ultimo, and am pleased with thy attention in
the information given in the minutia

"I dined yesterday at Samuel Fisher's in Front street, and
his wife desired her love to thee, so have Rebecca Jones, the
old Queen, and many others

"Our old friend Joseph Ogden is deceased some months
since, and our truly valuable friend Henry Drinker has been
very ill for some time past, but is now believed to be mending
and likely to get up again. Yet there is some doubt even in

the mind of the physicians as he is far advanced in life and his constitution much impaired.

"The Friends have just returned from Canada,* but I have not yet had an opportunity of inquiring of Jonathan Evans any particulars.

"I was in company with dear Ann and Mary since my last: they are indeed very amiable women, and so is my dear Mercy It seems hard that after waiting near seven years for the possession of thy society I should be doomed to give up so large a part of it. But I yield submissively to the dispensations of Providence, they have been very favorable, beyond my deserts and beyond my expectations

"I am sorry to hear of sister's indisposition, give my love to her, say a great many things to dear little Henry and the other dear children Tell Rachel exert every hour of time and every power of her mind to forward her French now in the society of our beloved friend I will bring her French books with me Young minds should be stored with knowledge and leave the uses which may be made of it to the occurrences of life.

"But I must attend to different engagements which are on my hands. Adieu, my dear Mercy. Thine affectionately,

"WILLIAM ELLIS"

"PHILADELPHIA Fourth mo 22nd, 1806

"MY DEAR MERCY,—I received yesterday evening thine of the 17th. There is indeed something very accommodating and very satisfactory in thus conversing weekly with thee when one hundred and fifty miles distant

"I received from the son of Evan Thomas our beloved Mary Mifflin's letter a day or two after their arrival, at the close of which are these expressions. 'My love most affectionately salutes thee and thy wife as one, hoping without doubting that you are so Oh! what a blessing!'

"We are all in health except our son William who is recovering fast, but he has had a pretty smart attack of inflammatory

---

* A deputation sent by Philadelphia Yearly Meeting They were gone three months, and in returning came down the Hudson River on the ice in a sleigh I have heard my mother speak of it, her father being one of them

rheumatism, and having been bled pretty freely is of course much weakened S Marriot has been faithfully attending to him and is so still Whether he will be able to ride home at the close of the meeting with us I cannot say I fully believe he is fairly and fully recovering and wish thee therefore not to let in apprehensions that things are worse than they are stated

"It is possible the dispensation may be of lasting use to him. When alone with him one day he told me he had had a sense of the mercy of the Divine Power, and a hope that if he were taken he might be saved by it. . . .

"But poor fellow! there is not much stability about him He is soon on and soon off, and I suppose he inherits from me, for thou knowest, my beloved and preciously valued Mercy, that much of this instability is interwoven with my nature, and Peale, the great limner, says the wax fitted on my face would fit on his, there is such a perfect likeness My paper is full, accept my love most affectionately and tenderly, and present it to Sister and the dear children Thine,
                              " WILLIAM ELLIS."

Again he underrates himself in tenderness for his son

Instability could not have been one of his characteristics, as his course through life was always onward and upward, and when a worthy object was his pursuit he kept on till it was attained, and his efforts were remarkably crowned with success.

There is no portrait of him, but his son William, who was thought by Peale to resemble him so closely, was a strikingly handsome man, and I have heard my mother, who knew him as a friend of her father, speak of him as being in personal appearance, in dress and manners, a true gentleman

From the correspondence it appears that William Cox did not recover his strength so as to return to Muncy with his father. Probably he left Philadelphia and stopped at a friend's house near Reading, as the next letters are addressed to Mercy Ellis, who had gone to be with their son till he should be able to continue the journey home

" MUNCY Sixth mo 19th, 1806

" MY DEAR MERCY,—I received last evening thine of the 17th by Cesar, who arrived about bed time. I am very anxious for poor, dear William, and very desirous we might be favored once more all to be together under our own roof Yet I expect his weakness will not permit his attempting to come very soon

"Dr. Rose regrets much he had not known where William was, that he might have called to see him as he came by Reading. Tell him to keep in good heart I had a severe and long spell of illness about his time of life, a stranger in a strange land, where I had no mother to comfort me, and no special friends to sympathise with me and assiduously attend to my wants, none, however, except such as were made so by short acquaintance Half a crown a day was my income, and this of course was stopped when my hand was stopped and my arm unstrung for labor Present my love cordially to William and Susan Marriot Accept it affectionately thyself, and the expression of my desire that you may be preserved by the Divine Providence and sustained by the Divine Power

                                        "W. E"

                                "Muncy Seventh mo 6th, 1806

"It is, my beloved Mercy, a harvest morning, and while the hands are gathering in the yard, eating bread and butter in the store room, or grinding their scythes, I embrace a few minutes to write my weekly intelligencer We are still favored with a good share of health Aunt has got tolerably well again and is very useful. Rachel keeps very well, but she is very busy She has, however, a great deal of composure in her composition notwithstanding her auburn locks would indicate a good deal of fire. Among the rest of her offices she is my chief butler. Biddy I expect is chief baker

"Little Henry is not quite so brisk at times, or does not eat so much, or something, Aunt tells us of when we get round the table The other little fellows are very well Benjamin has at times raked steadily in the clover field, and yesterday helped carry sheaves in all day He is quite a worker and a very fine boy, but Charles is a fine boy too

"Our precious Sarah has a pet robin which sometimes flies away and excites her anxiety Cousin Martha is well, and is a fine, plump, hearty girl

"I hope you are preserved in health and that our dear William Cox is steadily recovering   Aunt desires her love to you all.   Please to accept Rachel's and mine and present it warmly to William and Susanna, and the valuable and beloved family where you reside

"Accept the oft-repeated declaration of it again thyself and believe me thine affectionately

"WILLIAM ELLIS"

The illness of this beloved eldest son was not the only sorrow that the affectionate parents had been called upon to bear with Christian fortitude.   Two boys and one daughter deceased in early infancy,—Rebecca, John Cox, and Charles, and their lovely eldest daughter Mary had been called away from her earthly to a heavenly home, in 1802, at the age of seventeen years

From some memoranda left by her mother I take the following·   "Mary Ellis was among the number of those precious young persons who 'Remember their Creator in the days of their youth,' and by so doing she was prepared through the visitations of heavenly love, early to become a partaker with the saints in light   She had been at Westtown school and returned but a few weeks when she was taken ill with the measles, which continued three weeks and terminated her youthful career

"She had a sense that her change was near, and supplicated that the Lord would strengthen her, for she was well assured that no one could do the work of her soul's salvation for her   Her secret cry was that she might be in possession of Divine grace, and lying still, several persons being present, she bore testimony to the blessed truth as it is in Jesus, and expressed that she had been resigned to the cross . .

"The promise recorded in the Scriptures of Truth was fulfilled in her experience, 'They that seek Me early shall find Me,' for truly she found Him whom her soul loved to be strength in weakness, riches in poverty, and a very present help in every time of trouble

"When at meetings for worship she was an example of a

solid, weighty deportment She did not when in health neglect
the heavenly call to 'Come, taste, and see that the Lord is
good,' and that He is a rich 'Rewarder of them that diligently
seek Him'"   . .

She "was early called from time to enter an awful eternity,
but to the believer in Jesus it is a glorious entrance, even a
union with the company of redeemed spirits whose robes have
been washed and made white in the blood of the Lamb immac-
ulate "

These trials, while keenly felt by William Ellis, did not lessen
his gratitude and thankfulness to the Giver of every good and
perfect gift for the many blessings that still surrounded him, nor
prevent a diligent attention to the duties that day by day came
to his hand. Not only were the welfare of his own family and
the right conduct of his household, a generous exercise of hospitality, and care of the poor, the objects of his concern, his
thoughts and his help were given to public interests

He assisted liberally in providing a place for public worship
and a burial-ground for Friends, and in 1797 a plot containing
three acres, on a pleasant eminence, was purchased, on which
an ample and substantial house was erected in 1799 For a
school he gave large and convenient grounds in one of the
finest locations on his own estate,—a school that has been abundantly blessed to many in that part of the country But his
active, useful, and honorable life was nearing the close of its
earthly career

Not many weeks after writing the preceding letter, dated
Seventh month 6, 1806, he was taken seriously ill A crisis
came and hope of his recovery was nearly extinguished, when
suddenly he seemed to be relieved of the pressure of disease,
and his wife and children, anxiously watching beside him, were
cheered with thoughts of his restoration to health But his
strength was too much exhausted for him to rally completely,
and it gradually waned till he passed beyond their loving care
His son, Dr Benjamin Ellis, in "A Tribute of Affection" to his
parents, expressed the feelings of the bereaved family

> " How oft I've sought the shadowy walks alone,
> Since this cold world has marked me for her own,

And poured in solitude the stream of grief
O'er thy career, so honored, but so brief
Thy life consumed amid the toils of time,
Thy name untarnished with the soil of crime,
Remains a treasure which thy children hold
More dear, more precious than unbounded gold
'Twas not thy lot of opulence possest
On the soft couch of indolence to rest,
To quaff the cup prepared by other hands,
Or reap the fruit of patrimonial lands
Thy knowledge flowed from no time-honored dome,
Where sacred science fixed her classic home,
In sylvan scenes with grace and beauty fraught,
Thy soul received the elements of thought,
And books and men, as Time pursued his flight,
Impressed their lore, their wisdom, and their light
First of the few, whose spirits dared invade
The boundless solitude of Nature's shade,
Where Susquehanna rolls her silver flood
Bosomed in trees thy humble cottage * stood,
And every year beheld the forests bow,
And solemn deserts own the conquering plough,
Till e'en those wilds have blossomed like the rose,
And smiled the land of promise and repose
Then wast thou summoned by that fearful voice
Which leaves to pilgrim man no power of choice
Well might the people tremble at the doom
Of vigorous manhood sentenced to the tomb,
And worth and virtue from their country riven
To wear a glorious diadem in heaven
My honored Father ! All who knew thee loved,
For all thy pure integrity had proved,
And the sweet valley, where thy ashes rest,
By many a deed of thine is still imprest,
And still thy honest fame by those is spread
Whose manly tears for thee and thine were shed
But the small band that round thy pillow knelt
The deepest anguish, darkest ruin felt
They watched each moment as it stole thy breath,
Till hope sank prostrate in the blow of death "

Among the tokens of affectionate sympathy that assured
Mercy Ellis of the love of her friends and their share in the

---

* The first home he made there, it will be remembered, was destroyed by the
Indians   Then another cottage was built, and in 1791 or 1792 the Wolf Run house
was completed

sorrow that had fallen upon her, I will take a few words of Henry Drinker's He was the intimate friend of both husband and wife . " In revolving in my mind my knowledge of the dear deceased in acquaintance and intercourse with him for many past years, and freshly remembering his upright walking and religious integrity, I believe that dear William is happily landed where the wicked cease from troubling and the weary are at rest."

But no one could have shown a deeper sympathy with the widowed mother than the son, whose " Tribute of Affection" goes on,—

> " My tender Mother ! in that hour was rent
> All the bright prospects which the world had lent
> A thunder-cloud in terror crossed thy path,
> And thou wast widowed by the tempest's wrath
> Then on thy house misfortune's shadow fell
> And bright-eyed gladness bade a long farewell
> The gloom of sadness pressed upon thy heart,
> And tears of sorrow would unbidden start
> As on thy orphaned band thou turned an eye
> And knew their Sire had passed into the sky
> Yet strong in very gentleness thy mind
> Rose from this ruin to thy lot resigned,
> And thy meek spirit unsubdued remained,
> God was thy anchor and thy soul sustained,
> He bade the stormy elements be calm;
> And healed thy wounds with Gilead's soothing balm
>   *   *   *   *   *   *
> As Time who brings his pleasures and his pains,
> His griefs and joys, his losses and his gains,
> Pursued on soundless wing his even way,
> Thy woes, my Mother, felt his soothing sway
> Maternal love that slumber never knew,
> Thy heart from its deep sorrows kindly drew
> Thy children, budding like the flowers of spring,
> For shelter sought beneath thy fostering wing,
> And shelter found, such as is rarely known
> By orphans rudely on the wide world thrown
> That debt remains unpaid and ever must,
> Till we are summoned to the silent dust ;
> For filial love exhaustless in the heart,
> Though strong its stream, can but requite in part
> The boundless sympathy, the anxious fears,
> The nights of watching, and the hours of tears,

Which for our sake our peerless Mother knew
As round the hearth to manhood's strength we grew
She taught our tottering steps to print the ground,
, Attuned the ear to language and to sound,
Gazed on our infant faces while we slept,
And o'er the fatherless in silence wept,
Our kind protectress in those flowery years
When childhood danced amid its smiles and tears,
When life was brilliant as a morning dream,
And hope was lovely as the rainbow's gleam,
And like that fleeting, glorious arch on high,
Embraced the earth, the ocean, and the sky
Yes, in those golden days, too bright to last,
Which lent their loveliness to all the past,
Thou wast the guardian spirit hovering near,
To check the transport, and to wipe the tear,
To teach with gentle art the infant thought
That every pleasure would be dearly bought,
That passion s flame was but the meteor wild
Which led to ruin the bewildered child,
That virtue only shed that perfect light
Which banished sorrow s cloud and error's night
It was thy aim, my Mother, to impress
Those hallowed truths, and with those truths to bless,
To lead thy offspring from the world's deceit,
And kindly house them in a safe retreat
For all thy love, which never knew decay,
Accept the homage of this humble lay,
Accept my gratitude, which shall remain
While my heart palpitates to joy or pain
And all the children that to thee belong
Will breathe an echo to this feeble song,
Will join with me in deep and fervent prayer
That thou mayst still be heaven's peculiar care.
May every blessing with thy years increase,
To smooth thy pathway and augment thy peace;
The richest boon that teeming earth bestows,
The blushing fruits with which her bosom glows,
And hearts that beat in unison with thine,
Who own one Lord, and worship at His shrine,
With firm allegiance advocate His cause,
Proclaim His glory, and obey His laws
And as the shadows of thy years extend,
May light celestial with those shadows blend
Till Death has rent what we so dearly prize,
And thou art summoned to thy home, the skies "

7

Left sole head of a large household, including four sons and three daughters and a number of domestics and dependants, the eldest child still in his minority, there was no time for the indulgence of selfish sorrow Mercy Ellis was enabled by the power and presence of the Lord Jesus to take up the duties that devolved upon her, and relying on the promise then sealed upon her spirit, "I will never leave thee, nor forsake thee," she cast her burden on the heavenly Shepherd and walked steadily forward in her solitary pilgrimage

There was no want of outward means for temporal support Won for them by the enterprise and energy of him whose loving care had extended to their future, ample resources were provided for herself, and for each child, in the fertile lands of their beautiful valley, and in valuable tracts among the hills, rich in coal and forest trees

The spirit of liberality and generous hospitality continued to be the rule in the domestic management, but it was joined to a wise economy that prevented wastefulness and insured sufficiency The parental care in the religious training of Mercy Ellis, the seed sown in her youthful heart and received into good ground, were now bearing fair and abundant fruit In early life she gave herself to the Lord Jesus, and by the transforming power of Divine grace was created anew in Him In the obedience of faith she dedicated the prime of her days and the vigor of her physical and mental powers to the service of her Redeemer

Impressed with the belief that some parts of her dress were superfluous, she laid them aside and felt strengthened in such little acts of obedience, and without doubt the simplicity of her neat and becoming costume gave her opportunities for more frequently relieving the wants of others

Her watchful demeanor and conversation were adorned with those Christian graces which made her a bright example of meekness and humility, and of that Divine charity which suffereth long and is kind, which seeketh not her own, is not easily provoked, and thinketh no evil, and which, while it glows with especial warmth towards the household of faith, embraces within its influence the whole family of man

Although of a delicate frame and accustomed to many in-
dulgences previous to her removal from Maryland to the newly-
opened country of Lycoming County, Pennsylvania, she was
cheerful and contented, considering the want of a meeting for
public worship the greatest of all the privations that she and
her husband had to encounter   The Monthly Meeting to which
they belonged was at that period about one hundred miles distant, and to this she went several times on horseback over a
range of rugged mountains

After meetings were established near to them she was diligent and earnest in attending them and careful to take her
children, often remarking late in life on the solid comfort and
instruction she was permitted to experience in those small yet
solemn gatherings

Believing that her Divine Master was calling her to the
ministry of the gospel, she entered upon the work about the
thirty-ninth year of her age.   Taught in the school of Christ
to distinguish the voice of the Good Shepherd from that of the
stranger, she was careful to wait for His renewed putting forth
and then simply to follow His leading, by which her communi-
cations were made lively and impressive, ministering grace to
the hearer and tending to the building up of the church   Her
first religious engagement with a minute was to the families of
her own and a neighboring Monthly Meeting.

Subsequently she was several times engaged in religious
labors in the city of Philadelphia, in the State of New York,
and in Canada   Although she had a family of children around
her, several of whom were small, she was willing to surrender
all at the call of her Lord, and to run in the way of His requiring, not doubting that He who put her forth would open
the way and watch over those she left behind

In her service there was nothing constrained and unnatural.
One illustration occurs to my memory   A valued friend and
minister was her companion when travelling in Western New
York, whose life had been rather circumscribed, rendering her
fearful of having her thoughts turned aside from their immediate
mission   On arriving at the vicinity of Niagara Falls, E M
declined looking at that grand display of Almighty power and

goodness, while our dear grandmother enjoyed viewing it and felt her mind and heart enlarged by such a vision of beauty and magnificence.

Previous to the marriage of her eldest son she made arrangements for leaving to him the occupancy of the Wolf Run house and its premises, building for herself and the other members of her household a new dwelling, named " The Cottage," situated on an eminence near the old home, overlooking some of the loveliest scenery in the vicinity and flanked by a beautiful piece of woodland.

There she continued to reside the remainder of her days, carrying into it all the warmth and love and charitableness that had characterized the former home

Her deep interest in the religious and literary education of children did not abate as her own outgrew the years for youthful training   A school under the care of Friends was contiguous to her, and she extended the hospitality of her house to many who were remote from suitable schools, or who from other causes claimed her sympathy and aid   She also promoted the opening of a school on First days for Biblical instruction, and when an ardent young Friend, Rebecca Singer,* felt it to be a religious duty to devote herself for a time to teaching at Muncy, our Grandmother Ellis proffered her a home in " The Cottage," which was cheerfully accepted

To the poor and those in affliction, whether of body or mind, she was a tender and sympathizing friend, frequently engaged in searching out objects of charity, and prompt in her endeavors to afford them timely and suitable relief.   Should a poor man lose his cow, one from her own herd would, probably, be sent to take its place.

In making a gift to any of her friends she was careful to have it of good quality, whatever its kind, saying that one should never present a mean offering

It was one of her special delights to entertain ministers of the

* Rebecca Singer was afterwards the energetic Christian minister and philanthropist of New York City, well known as Rebecca Collins   More than threescore years of loving labor were fulfilled by her, and as late as 1890 she visited Friends in Canada   She was called to her reward in 1892

gospel, or others engaged in religious service, not only attending to their comfort while under her roof, but anticipating their
wants, if they were going into neighborhoods where accommo-
dations might be scanty, and providing them with such portable
articles as they were likely to be in need of as they went
forward   Many a weary traveller found refreshment in " The
Cottage," many an ambassador of the gospel from distant lands
was cordially welcomed there, enjoying religious fellowship and
social converse, in return cheering the life and giving added
courage to the heart of its mistress

Two elders of Muncy Meeting occupied a humble dwelling
near to that of Mercy Ellis   When the wife became a widow,
already far advanced in years, and with little means for her
support, Mercy Ellis took her to her own house, appropriated
to her private use a large and pleasant apartment, and shared
with her from that time her house, her table, and the use of
her carriage, leaving her as a legacy to her children, who
carefully watched over her declining years and supplied all her
needs.

In the earlier years of Mercy Ellis's married life Friends had
not seen the danger of keeping wine and beer on their tables
and sideboards, but when she was convinced that the custom
put temptations in the way of the unwary that might lead them
astray, she abandoned it

For the suppression of intemperance and the iniquitous
practice of converting the gifts of a bountiful Providence into
liquid poison, as she often termed it, she labored much both
publicly and in private   She repeatedly visited those not in
profession with Friends, who were engaged in distilling,
endeavoring in love to dissuade them from an employment so
unrighteous and so destructive of the comfort and happiness of
their fellow-men

One so governed by love could not have enemies ; but if she
learned that any one, through misapprehension or any other
cause, had let in feelings of coldness or estrangement towards
her, she quickly made them a visit, and by her frankness and
good-will dispelled the cloud in the mind of her neighbor or
acquaintance.

The natural vivacity and cheerfulness of her disposition, tempered by trials, and joined to an uncommon sweetness and tenderness of spirit, made her company peculiarly attractive and teaching, while her kind and maternal interest in young persons secured her a large place in their affection   Affable and affectionate, courteous and kind to all, she was greatly esteemed and beloved by a large circle of friends and acquaintance

In the society of her children and grandchildren she was permitted to enjoy largely the fruits of her maternal care and vigilance.

William Cox Ellis, already alluded to, married Rebecca Morris, daughter of Benjamin Morris, an accomplished young lady, and it was said that when the youthful bridegroom led her from the marriage altar they were the handsomest couple in Lycoming County   William Cox Ellis's natural tendencies drew him to the pursuits of law and political affairs, and he became an eloquent advocate and a member of Congress.   He was a man of quick impulses and warm affections, in social life a brilliant conversationist, in religious connection a zealous member of the Episcopal Church   Four sons and four daughters inherited the personal beauty of the parents, who lived to celebrate the sixtieth anniversary of their wedding, and were scarcely parted by death, so nearly did one follow the other

RACHEL, as may be seen in the memoirs of the Haines family, married Jacob Haines   Their lives were lovely exemplifications of the one hundred and twenty-eighth Psalm   Eight children gladdened their hearts and walked in the ways of wisdom, and to them was principally given the privilege of ministering to the honored mother in her later years.

Anna—lively, energetic, capable, and loving—married Samuel Morris, of Wellsborough, who was well known as a member of Congress and county judge   They lived handsomely at Wellsborough, connected themselves with the Episcopal Church at that place, and trained up a large family of sons and daughters who have honorably occupied positions of trust and importance   The eldest son, William Ellis Morris, was a successful and widely-useful civil engineer, another son, Benjamin Wistar Morris, is at this time bishop of Oregon

Sarah Ellis, the fifth daughter, lived to her twenty-fourth year She seems to have been one formed for a purer region than earth,—so lovely in person, mind, and heart, a sweet, trusting child of the blessed Saviour, giving and receiving happiness in all her surroundings.

The fourth son, Dr Benjamin Ellis, has already been referred to His career, "so honored, yet so brief," was one of which any mother might be proud, were pride allowable in any circumstances He married Amy Yarnall, daughter of Ellis Yarnall, a lady every way fitted to insure the highest domestic happiness Their home was in Philadelphia

A second time the name of Charles was bestowed on one of the sons, the first having been transplanted in his infancy to the heavenly city, and when a fifth boy was added to the domestic circle he was called by the name already dear to the mother Charles Ellis lived in Philadelphia ; as a successful pharmacist he developed the science and art of pharmacy and won his way to wealth and influence He continued in religious communion with the church of his forefathers, and was highly esteemed by his fellow-members for his steadfastness, the purity of his life, and the controlling charitableness of his spirit. He was an active philanthropist, attractive and pleasing in person, in manners gracefully courteous and kind He married Deborah Tyson, of Baltimore, who was beloved for her amiability, but was early removed by death, leaving a son and an infant daughter to the care of their excellent father

Some years after he married Mary L Morris, a woman of noble traits of character, remarkably faithful to her family and friends. She survived him several years They had one daughter, Nancy Morris, beautiful in person, warm in her affections, quick in acquiring knowledge, intelligent in the use of it, and gifted for success in social life She married William M Ellicott, Jr, of Baltimore

All Mercy Ellis's children, to the third generation, were at home in her house, always welcomed there with the genial warmth of a mother's love, and their interests cherished in her

unselfish heart, while the memory of her husband, and the four
who had preceded him in reaching the heavenly mansions,
bound her more firmly to the skies

One more, the youngest, remains to be noticed,—the Henry
often alluded to in his father's letters as the delicate child   He
grew to manhood and turned his attention to the law, and
united himself to the Presbyterian Church in Williamsport
His abilities were above the common order , his knowledge and
judgment in his profession were highly valued, and, from his
superior literary culture, he was an interesting and improving
companion   He married a lady who was heiress of considerable
property in Williamsport, where they resided.   One son, a boy
of noble promise and of a pure Christian life, died in early
youth from an attack of scarlet fever   Four daughters survive
them, two of them married and living in handsome homes, one
in Philadelphia, the other in Williamsport, where an unmarried
sister also resides

To aid and solace our dear grandmother in the decline of her
physical vigor, one of my sisters-in-law generally formed a part
of her household   Even " little Tachie" could assist in making
tea, and by her budding business faculties help to counter-
balance the autocracy of Biddy, the kitchen department's long-
reigning Irish queen, and keep a wholesome guard over the
increasing streams of bounty flowing from the establishment.
But it was Mary, the eldest, who attended and ministered to the
last

To me it was a great pleasure to visit her, and very instructive to see such gratitude and cheerfulness undimmed by the
infirmities of age   She never seemed to allow herself any in-
dulgences on the plea of advanced years, always sitting very
erectly, the tones of her voice animated, her hands employed
in knitting when not otherwise occupied, and demanding no
especial deference while gracefully maintaining the dignity of
her position

The neatly-kept premises in summer, in cooler weather the
open fire on the parlor hearth, and sunshine falling on the floors
through windows framing in far-reaching landscapes, gave an
air of refinement to the simplicity of her well-furnished apart-

ments In one of my visits to her—I think it was the last—she was particularly interesting, in the course of conversation repeating with much animation a part of Addison's hymn, and emphasizing the stanza,—

> ' Ten thousand thousand precious gifts
>   My daily thanks employ,
>   Nor is the least a cheerful heart
>   That tastes those gifts with joy "

Her labors of love within the compass of her own Meeting were abundant, and she was deeply concerned for the spiritual welfare of its members, warning, exhorting, reproving with all long-suffering and tenderness, desiring that all might be gathered into the fold of Christ Several times she visited the families of her Monthly Meeting, which, owing to their great distance from one another, required much travelling and involved a large share of bodily fatigue

To attend the meetings of which she was a member, whether at Muncy, Fishing Creek, Elklands, or the Quarterly and Yearly Meetings held in Philadelphia, never seemed to be a question in her mind. Duly were preparations made, and, health permitting, she would patiently set off in her carriage, be the distance one short mile, the twenty or the thirty, or for the four days' journey over the mountains to the city

In the spring of 1831 a lovely granddaughter was lying very ill, apparently near the close of her young life on earth It was painful to Mercy Ellis to leave home under the circumstances, but, looking to Him who had so graciously been her unerring guide heretofore, she felt best satisfied to proceed as usual

She arrived in Philadelphia, attended some of the sessions of the Yearly Meeting, and was suddenly called to the bedside of her gifted and beloved son, Dr Benjamin Ellis, who was rapidly sinking under an attack of scarlet fever No message could have reached her in time had she remained at home, and the comfort of a mother's love would not have soothed the last hours of one so dear.

Her last journey to Philadelphia was made in her seventy-seventh year. In her eighty-fifth, she and her aged friend

Jesse Haines visited the families of Muncy Monthly Meeting together, accompanied by their son and daughter, Jacob and Rachel E. Haines. She expressed a belief that it was the last opportunity of the kind she should have with her friends, and earnestly encouraged the young and middle-aged to make their calling and election sure while strength was given them

At Greenwood, on one occasion, when a family convened for a religious meeting with these faithful ministers, Mercy Ellis addressed a person in deep distress in words of tender sympathy and encouragement, and that was all she had to say   Her daughter, knowing there was no one in the family to whom such an address could be applicable, was much perplexed and anxious. But her mind was relieved and her faith confirmed on learning, after the family had dispersed, that while they were sitting together a young widow had come in, silently and unseen, and had taken a seat in an adjoining room, where she could distinctly hear the loving message

Mercy Ellis was able to attend meetings for worship till about two weeks before her decease   Although her bodily strength had much failed, her mind was clear and vigorous, and she was frequently engaged in the ministry with a freshness and unction that evinced greenness in old age and her continual care to dwell near the Divine Fountain   Her last public engagement was in solemn, fervent prayer for the " little meeting in this part of the Lord's heritage "

In the course of their religious labors in this country, Benjamin Seebohm and Robert Lindsay came to Muncy and were at her house   As they were sitting quietly together, Benjamin Seebohm expressed his belief that the happy period of her release from mortality was at hand   Alluding to it afterwards, she remarked that it was, indeed, as good news from a far country, and that through the mercy of her God and Saviour her end would be peace

Her spirit seemed clothed with peaceful quiet, calmly awaiting the summons as one whose day's work was done   She had prayed that she might, if it were consistent with the Divine Will, put off mortality without much suffering, and her prayer was mercifully answered

She was taken ill the eighth day of the Second month, 1848 Her mind was clear and calm, and her dependence was upon the Lord in the blessed assurance that her sins were washed away in His precious blood, and a mansion prepared for her in His heavenly kingdom

She was reminded of the promise made to her in a time of great affliction (before alluded to) She replied, " Yes! and His promises are Yea and amen forever." She desired the family to be called in to see her end, which was emphatically peaceful, and she gently departed on the afternoon of the ninth, having nearly completed her eighty-seventh year

Muncy Monthly Meeting was set off from Catawissa Monthly Meeting in 1799 William Ellis was the first clerk, and his opening minute was adopted It states the object of meetings for discipline to be, " That needful attention be given to the various circumstances and situations of our members, that their necessities may be duly inspected and relieved, and that Friends be encouraged in orderly and circumspect walking, and that when deviations appear they may be admonished and labored with in the spirit of meekness and wisdom " Friends were earnestly and affectionately desired to seek watchfully and diligently for the qualifying virtue of Truth to enable them to discharge every duty

The early minutes of that meeting show great care, labor, and love, in endeavoring to reclaim those who were tempted to countenance military measures, partake of spirituous liquors, or fall into other errors incident to exposure in frontier life.

William Ellis left by will one hundred pounds to be held in trust by Muncy Meeting, to assist in schooling children of Friends or others who were in straitened circumstances.

CHAPTER VII

JACOB AND RACHEL ELLIS HAINES

JACOB HAINES, eldest son of Jesse and Rachel Otley Haines, was born in Wilmington, Delaware, the sixth day of Seventh month, 1788

From early boyhood he was thoughtful, earnest, industrious, overlooking his own ease or advantage when he could be helpful to his parents or others, and untiring in efforts to improve in learning, manners, and moral attributes

While the family resided in the Elklands, and particularly after the injury by exposure to cold that prevented his father for a year from taking an active part in business, Jacob Haines was very energetic in clearing and cultivating their land, planting fruit-trees, making sugar from the groves of native maples, and in other ways providing for domestic comfort   At this time the children of the household pursued their studies when at leisure, and in the evenings under the care of their father.   The older ones united with some of their neighbors in forming a small social circle for the study of poetry, committing it to memory and reciting at their meetings.   Our father's only sister, Mary, took great pleasure in these exercises, and, as books were comparatively rare in that vicinity, frequently called upon her brother to transcribe choice selections for her   His only objection to it was that what he once wrote down he could not forget, and he feared his memory might be overcrowded

Some of their supplies had to be brought over the mountains from Muncy   On one such expedition our father had gone in a sleigh and stopped at the home of Mercy Ellis Before his business was completed the snow rapidly melted, and Mercy Ellis remarked to him that he had better change his mode of conveyance, to which he replied, " If there is not a spoonful of snow left, I intend to return as I came." This little proof of perseverance made an impression on the future mother-in-law

It was probably the last winter of their life in the Elklands that our father and two neighbor lads attended a school in Muncy, coming over the mountains, sometimes afoot, early in the week, and going back to their homes on Seventh-day afternoons Returning one extremely cold day on foot, John Huckle, one of the youths, was so overpowered by the cold that he begged his companions to go on and allow him to sit down and go to sleep Knowing this would be death, they supported and urged him to keep pace with them till they came to Bear Creek, carrying him over as they forded it, and then setting him on his feet again and keeping him in motion till they reached the friendly shelter of a house, where they were warmed and refreshed so that they could finish their journey of thirty miles Late in our father's life John Huckle came to see him, and with much feeling related the above circumstance to his daughter, expressing his belief that to him he owed his escape from an untimely death

About the nineteenth year of his age Jacob Haines was pursuing his studies under the teaching of a well-known mathematician of that day, Enoch Lewis, in Chester County, and passed several years after that as student and instructor

Youthful as he was for such an undertaking, he opened a school in Philadelphia for the daughters of the wealthier class of citizens This was successful till a serious attack of typhoid fever obliged him to give up all employment for several months * On recovering his health he accepted a position as teacher in Friends' Boarding-School at Westtown

While there he completed one of the happiest events of his life in his marriage with Rachel Ellis, daughter of William and Mercy Ellis, of Muncy, in the Tenth month, 1815. She had been the object of his especial regard from the age of thirteen, when he had first observed her as she moved about her father's house, and his youthful admiration and devotion only increased

* During that illness his friend Thomas Kimber was most faithful in his care and assistance

with time as the nearly half-century of their wedded life on earth rolled on   The attentions and courtesy of a young lover only became more and more habitual and beautiful.

He was a man of fine physique and great strength, of undaunted courage, and his sympathies were wide and warm.

In 1823 with his wife and three children he removed from Westtown to Muncy, Lycoming County.   Their first residence was a farm belonging to his wife, but an opportunity soon occurred for him to purchase the paternal dwelling of the Ellis family with its ample acres   Of this he gladly availed himself, and the Wolf Run house became the happy home of his family, as it continues to be to the present day, in the possession of two of his daughters,—Sarah E. and Rebecca E Haines

To provide for the comfort of those dependent upon him, and promote in every way their best interests for time and eternity, to develop the resources of his own county and benefit his fellow-men, his time and energies were freely given

The home on Wolf Run was the centre of a lovely hospitality, a refuge for the afflicted, and particularly so for the fugitive slave   Many of the latter class were sent on by Micajah Speakman, of Chester County   When they presented a paper with our father's address and signed " Humanity," it was understood where they came from and what was desired, and aid was furnished at once   If they were women and children flying from slavery, our father sent them forward in some conveyance over the mountain to John Hill, thence they were taken to Marshall Battin, in the Elklands, who helped them onward to Joseph Jones, of Penn Yan, New York, and he saw them safely placed beyond the grasp of their pursuers across the Canadian border.   Our father acted from a settled conviction that slavery is contrary to the law of God, and that it was his duty to aid all whom he could in their attempts to escape it

Tall, erect in person, with a heart unacquainted with fear, and a countenance in which were mingled firmness of purpose and kindness of disposition, he seemed naturally fitted to be the friend of the distressed and the oppressed

He had a keen enjoyment in the society of his relatives and

friends, and his uniform cheerfulness, genial temper, and richly-stored mind gave equal pleasure in return

His patriotic spirit led him to promote all public improvements, always assisting to the extent of his means in defraying expenses necessarily connected with them In addition to the care of his farm, he was often occupied with surveying and conveyancing for several years after removing to Muncy "The Lycoming County Mutual Insurance Company" was almost a creation of his own, and while under the supervision of himself and some of its founders was financially successful and widely useful During the construction of the Philadelphia and Erie Railroad through that part of the country he was commissioner for the award of damages on the property through which it passed, for which he was well qualified by knowledge acquired in previous lines of business

The last engagement of this kind was in acting as vice-president of the Catawissa Railroad while it was being made through the mountain region to Williamsport Like many such enterprises, it had a struggle for existence at first, and, convinced of its importance to the welfare of the region over which it passed, he aided it in a time of difficulty by endorsing for a sum of money which the company was unable to redeem. But all obligations were scrupulously met, and in a few years our father had the satisfaction of knowing that every dollar had been fully paid, while the homestead remained intact and the family comfort had been maintained

The cause of education was dear to his heart, and did not cease to enlist his efforts in its advancement when his own children were provided for and their training had received his earnest attention A good school under the care of Friends was vigorously supported, and when some children who were too far away to be benefited by it, and had no other means of receiving proper instruction, were brought to his notice, they were taken into his house and sent to this school

Firmly established in the principles of Christianity as revealed in the Bible and unfolded in his own soul by the Holy Spirit, his course was undeviating A Friend by conviction as well as by early education, he was regular in attendance on Divine

worship, in his family daily, and in the meetings for the public
twice in the week, never allowing business or difficulties to prevent when he was within reach of such opportunities   As
overseer he watched affectionately the flock committed to his
charge, being careful to carry out the discipline exercised by
the Monthly Meeting in the spirit of love, and with the view of
edification and of restoration if any went astray   Several times
in the year he was in the habit of going with some of his family
nearly two hundred miles to attend their Quarterly and Yearly
Meetings in Philadelphia   These journeys were made in the
family carriage, occupying several days, until the completion of
railroads offered a speedier mode of transit   But there was
always pleasure as well as profit mingled with the exertion
necessary for such expeditions   Nature in its various aspects
was observed, picturesque scenery dwelt upon with delight,
conversation was not only lively, but instructive and tending to
subjects for profitable reflection, and visits, cheering and bene-
ficial on both sides, were made to friends who resided on the
routes

While adhering strictly in his belief, manner, and habits to
the teaching of the religious society to which he belonged, he
was always liberal in views and feelings, and ready to recognize
all that is good and holy in others, whatever their profession as
to religion might be

His hopes for the church and his country rested on his belief that sooner or later the doctrines and precepts of the
New Testament would become engrafted in the hearts of the
people

His devotion to the happiness of his family and ever fresh
delight in domestic intercourse were reciprocated by their
warmest affection and unremitting attentions

By the removal to a better inheritance of his eldest and
dearly-loved son in 1846, of a charming and lovely daughter
a few years later, and of the beloved wife in 1862, his heart was
pierced with the keenest sorrow.   But the Saviour on whom he
leaned did not fail him in the time of sorest need, and it was
instructive to see his Christian resignation and his care that
grief for the departed should not lessen his regard for the

happiness of those remaining with him, or check the flow of gratitude and thanksgiving to the Author of all his blessings

After completing his seventy-third year slight attacks of paralysis undermined his physical vigor, but for nearly six years more his family were favored with his bright example of cheerful submission to the Divine will, the strong, energetic man yielding without a murmur to the restrictions of enfeebled health His mind was filled with love, and in recounting his blessings he numbered among them this season of quiet retirement from care. He continued to enjoy the society of his friends, sometimes remarking, "I always loved the society of my friends, but now it is increasingly precious to me" The reading of the Holy Scriptures and other religious books was a great source of help and comfort to him, while his entire dependence and all his hopes were placed in the merits and the mercy of his Lord and Saviour

During the last few weeks of increasing illness he was surrounded by his watchful and loving children, and faithfully waited upon by Henry Harris, a powerful colored man whom he had been the means of rescuing from prison and establishing in a useful and happy course of life Gradually growing weaker, he fell asleep in Jesus on the morning of the 27th of First month, 1866

Rachel Ellis Haines, daughter of William and Mercy Ellis, was born at Muncy the 25th day of Eleventh month, 1788. From childhood she was remarkably correct and steady in her deportment, although her beautifully fair complexion and brilliant color seemed to indicate an ardent temperament

When about seventeen her father, in writing to her mother, who was away from home in consequence of the illness of their eldest son, says, "Rachel keeps very well, but she is kept very busy She has, however, a great deal of composure in her composition, notwithstanding her auburn locks would indicate a good deal of fire Among the rest of her offices she is my chief butler, Biddy I expect is chief baker."

Her tastes were literary, and she had an excellent and accurate memory, habits of observation and reflection, and a sound judgment

8

Her character corresponded well with Solomon's portrait of
a virtuous woman, when we view the ideal as transferred to a
time nearly three thousand years later than the one in which
it was drawn

As she unconsciously won the heart of her future husband
almost in her childhood, she as unconsciously held sway over
him to the close of their long companionship on earth   She
was always the faithful friend to whom he looked for counsel
and support, his untiring helper in temporal affairs and spiritual
duties, and the light of his home   In turn she received from
him chivalrous courtesy and devotion and all the freshness of
youthful love, deepening with the flow of time

By the wise training of her children and her unfaltering
maternal love, she insured their tenderest affection and reverent
regard   To her father-in-law, who from his eightieth to his one
hundredth year lived under the same roof, she was more than a
daughter   Her seat at table was between him and her husband,
and both there and at all other times every little want or inclination was attended to with unselfish punctuality

Her heart was ever open to minister to the wants of the poor
and suffering, and her interest in the cause of the slave was un-
ceasing   When "Uncle Tom's Cabin" was first published as a
serial in *The National Era*, she was absorbed in its pictures of life
in a slave-holding country, never suspecting it was anything but
a veritable history, as it was in fact a perfectly true representa-
tion of those times   As it was not her practice to indulge in
reading fiction, her daughters amused themselves at her expense,
calling the work "Mother's Novel."

At different times she received into her household boys
who, from one cause or another, needed the care and help of
a wise friend, and the years of patient labor bestowed upon
them were well repaid by their orderly and upright conduct in
after-life

John Wesley, on being asked what he should do to-day, were
he sure that he should die to-morrow, replied, "I should do exactly that which I now intend to do"   So it was with her, there
was no necessity to alter her daily routine in anticipation of the
call to give up her stewardship

The last morning of her continuance with us, she rose as usual It was the First day of the week, the 12th of First month, 1862 My father-in-law's health had begun to fail, and that day he did not seem to be well enough to leave the house She said to her daughters, " I will not go to meeting to-day. I wish to stay at home with your father ," which she did, and read to him most of the time while they were gone. Her son Jesse and his wife came from the meeting to dine at Wolf Run After breakfast she filled a basket with clothing, etc , and sent it off by a boy for an old Englishwoman who had served in her house, and was then a sort of retainer on their bounty When they rose from the table after dinner she gave attention to her son and his wife, who were about to leave for their home at Montoursville, and seeing that they were well protected for their long, cold drive, she bade them farewell

That winter she frequently retired to her own room for times of quiet thought, and, as was her custom, she now went up again Her husband and their daughters Mary, Sarah, and Rebecca were still sitting in the comfortable dining-room when she came down-stairs and opened the door, appearing to be as well as usual In the twinkling of an eye a change came over her countenance ; with tottering steps she reached her eldest daughter, and sank upon the floor In a moment the spirit fled to the arms of her Saviour, and her place on earth knew her no more.

For her nothing more could have been asked than such a translation , for those whom she left, no better epitome of her life than that last day in which she finished her course, as the loving and faithful wife , the tender, affectionate mother ; the cultivated, intellectual companion; the active friend of the poor and lowly, and the mature, communing Christian

CHAPTER VIII

ENGLISH HOME AND ANCESTORS OF THE RHOADS FAMILY—JOSEPH RHOADS I. AND ABIGAIL RHOADS

Authorities —Dr George Smith's " History of Delaware County " Records of Friends' Meetings in Chesterfield, Derbyshire, England, and of the Southern Counties of Pennsylvania " Records of the Bonsall Family," by Spencer Bonsall Private family records in possession of Mary R Haines, and information from William J Ledward, vicar of Pentrich, in Derbyshire, England *

THE surname has in the course of centuries been variously spelled, as De Rodes, Rhodes, and Rhoads The family is pre-eminently English, being traceable in Derbyshire, the very heart of England, up to the twelfth century Something has been impressed upon it by the abode of numerous generations in that romantic county Its varied surface, high hills, rocky gorges, wooded valleys, caverns of spar, and numerous mines, the rivers Derwent, Dove, Rother, and Wye, with smaller sparkling streams, combine their attractions and foster in the denizens of highland and vale a love of home and of the beautiful, a free and thoughtful spirit

A few notes of my visits to the shire of my ancestors in 1875 may be transcribed here " Entering from the northeastern corner of Cheshire, with our friend Edward Godward as guide, a drive of nine miles into the Derbyshire hills brought us to ' The Wash,' which lies a little beyond Chapel-en-le-Frith In passing over a hill commanding a distant view, the parish of Marple was pointed out to us,—the only time I ever heard that

---

* The following extract from the parish register of the church of St Matthew, Pentrich, given by the rector, William J Ledward, to my brother, Charles Rhoads, is believed to relate to the same family,—a collateral branch

"'A D 1656, Dec 21 Elizabeth, daughter of George Rhodes, baptized , borne the 8th of December

"'A D. 1662 May 18th Jeremiah the sonne of George Rhodes jr baptized '

" These are the only entries in that parish from 1626 to 1700 "

When the Rhodes family became Friends they ceased to register in the Church of England and recorded in Friends' registers

name applied to any other place than my native township in Delaware County

"A Friend, William Bradburn, owns a cottage at The Wash, which stands on a steep slope. The second floor is fitted up for a meeting-room, and is entered from the hill-side behind the building It seemed as primitive as it may have been two hundred years ago when our forefathers withdrew from their parish church to worship in the way of George Fox and his friends I felt much sympathy with the people whom we met there and enjoyed our hour of worship, hoping the good seed sown would bear much fruit.

"With genuine hospitality, William Bradburn had brought tea and other refreshments from his home, a mile and a half distant, which were prepared for us by a woman who lives in the cottage

"Beautiful snow-wreaths lay along the road-sides At Woodside, where we spent the previous night, I asked the gardener where the mercury stood He answered, 'Fourteen degrees of frost.' That is the way they reckon there, and it means what we understand by saying 'eighteen degrees'"

On another occasion we came into Derbyshire from Mansfield, in the county of Nottingham, the 19th of Seventh month, 1875, taking the road for Heanor

It is said that Friends were first called Quakers in Derby, the term originating in the following circumstance

"In 1650 George Fox was imprisoned in Derby At his trial a cruel Justice struck him It was this Justice, Gervas Bennet, who first called Friends Quakers, because George Fox bid him to tremble at the word of the Lord"[*]

There is much manufacturing of iron in the eastern part of Derbyshire, particularly near Chesterfield The hills are bold, and fine streams of water run through the richly-green valleys, the air is pure and bracing, like the breezes that blow around Chestnut Bank Altogether, I felt singularly at home and as if breathing my native air

The family De Rodes has flourished for six hundred years in

[*] Memoir of George Fox in "Friends' Library"

the shires of Notts, York, and Derby, the name undergoing several orthographical changes

The following is extracted from a letter dated

"HEANOR   Seventh mo 20th 1875

"MY DEAR DAUGHTER,—Being near Ripley, in Derbyshire, the place from which our ancestors emigrated two centuries ago, I wish to write to thee while here

"As I sat in meeting last evening among a somewhat rustic people I looked back to the past, and thought how graciously the hand of our Lord has led us as a family all that time   And now after the lapse of two hundred years, I, the eldest of my generation, have been brought back to this spot to worship after the manner my forefathers had chosen, in spirit and in truth, as I trust, depending on Jesus Christ alone as Priest and Prophet.

"Our aged host is Francis Howitt, brother to the poet William Howitt,* and this home has sheltered the family for three successive generations. his grandchildren now come to play around the hearth-stone

"Heanor is a small town on a hill, we have seen it only in the rain, for the weather is wet and cool, and I still wear winter underclothing and sleep beneath blankets.

"*Bubwell Cottage. Afternoon*—Left Heanor this morning at 9 42 o'clock, with Mary, daughter of Francis Howitt, and came by train to Rowsley   We had to change trains near Ripley. the village and church are on a hill, and I could see them quite well from the railway   Ripley is a chapelry belonging to the parish of Pentrich   The road leads up the highly picturesque vale of the Derwent

"Near Cromford, which we pass, I was reminded of the scenery on Darby Creek below Leedom's Mills, although there is much less cultivation along the American stream than there is here I think it likely Crum Creek owes its name to Cromford, the neat market-town that was carried in memory by those early settlers in Delaware County from this locality, Crom being changed by phonetic spelling to Crum

---

* Francis and William Howitt died the same day, the one in his home at Heanor, the other in Italy

"This town is the birthplace of the great cotton-mills of the world, as it was here that Sir Richard Arkwright, in 1771, established the first cotton-mills, which eventually made him the founder of a wealthy family, whose handsome seat is in the neighborhood

"Having to change trains twice between Heanor and Rowsley, I made the most of my opportunities   Near Ripley I secured a smooth pebble as a memento   at another station (Fritchley?) I ran down the bank to pluck a flower or twig, and seeing two four-leaved clovers at my feet, transferred them to my velvet bag

"All through Matlock to Rowsley new charms were unfolding, and about half a mile from Rowsley the Derbyshire Wye, coming down from Bakewell, joins the Derwent   Taking a wagonette at Rowsley, we drove to Haddon Hall, two miles southeast from Bakewell in the river-dale   Haddon Hall, as you know, is the most perfect manor-house of the Middle Ages remaining, and belongs to the Duke of Rutland   It is uninhabited, but there are guides ; and one follows as in a dream the stream of mortal life that flowed through its arched gate-way and across the deserted court "

But I must not indulge in descriptions of this old Hall, nor of the Palace of the Peak and the beauty of its park, ten miles in circumference, nor refer to other spots of historic interest and to celebrated men and women who lived in the county   The foregoing gives a glimpse of the surroundings of our ancestors, and I will proceed with the story of lives less renowned, but redolent of truth, love, and peace

JOHN RODES, OR RHODES, OF WINFGREAVES

The name of Winegreaves has disappeared, but is believed to be the same as Waingrove, which lies beyond the parish of Pentrich   It was probably a farm or hamlet

John Rodes, or Rhodes, of Winegreaves, was one of the early Friends, and is supposed to have been a convert of George Fox   In Besse's "Sufferings of the Quakers" several

of the name of Rhodes are noticed as having endured fines and
imprisonment for their faith, hence it is probable that John
Roades and his family were impelled by suffering, and the liability to it, to seek a refuge in America. This John Roades
(whose name is spelled variously in different places, sometimes
in the same document) is believed to have been the fifth son of
Sir Francis Rodes, who married Elizabeth, daughter of Simon
Jessop, Esq *

John and Elizabeth Roades, having united with the Friends,
would cease to register in the parish church. Their children
were recorded in the books of Chesterfield Monthly Meeting of
Friends, in the county of Derby   There were five sons and
four daughters

    I Adam, born 30th of Sixth month, 1660, died, 13th
        First mo, 1744–45   He came to Pennsylvania in
        1684, in a vessel named "Sarah and John," and
        settled in Darby, Delaware County   He married
        Katharine, daughter of John Blunston, a Justice of
        the Court, Speaker of the Assembly, and a member
        of the Council of State by appointment of Governor
        William Penn

   II Mary, born 30th of Eleventh mo, 1662, married Wil-
        liam Maltby, 1689

  III John, born 13th of Sixth mo, 1664; married Hannah
        Willcox 10th of Ninth mo, 1692, died, 1733   He
        came to Darby, Pennsylvania, 1684, with his brother
        Adam. Subsequently settled in White Marsh, Mont-
        gomery County, Pennsylvania

  IV Elizabeth, born 7th of Eleventh mo, 1667, married
        Edward Daws, 1692–93

   V Jacob, born 16th of Twelfth mo, 1670

  VI. Abraham, born 11th of Tenth mo, 1672

 VII Sarah, born 5th of Third mo, 1675

VIII Hannah, born 15th of Twelfth mo, 1677

  IX JOSEPH, born 5th of Second mo, 1680, married Abigail
        Bonsall, 1702, died, 1732

Adam and John Rodes, or Rhodes, the eldest and second

* See Appendix

sons of John and Elizabeth Rodes, or Rhodes, of Winegreaves, England, were the first of the family to come to Pennsylvania They had certificates from the Monthly Meeting of Friends as to their membership, and another from their father and mother expressing their consent to their removal, and landed in 1684.

After the decease of his wife Elizabeth, John Rodes, or Rhodes, came to Pennsylvania, probably near 1690, certainly prior to 1699. He was accompanied by his sons Jacob and Joseph, and probably by his daughters Mary and Elizabeth. I have no further account of Abraham, Sarah, and Hannah than the time of their birth.

John Rodes, as stated in his will, was a yeoman and cordwainer He purchased lands in White Marsh, Montgomery County, and various tracts in Delaware County, amounting to five hundred and fifty acres. At the time of his death he resided in Upper Darby, Delaware County. In 1699 he bought one hundred acres of land in Marple, Delaware County, which, with other property, he bequeathed to his youngest son Joseph He deceased 27th of Eighth month, 1701, one week after the writing of his will

JOSEPH RHOADS I AND ABIGAIL RHOADS

Joseph Rodes, or Rhoads, of Marple, Delaware County, Pennsylvania, was born in Derbyshire, England, 5th of Second month, 1680. He had lately attained his majority when he came into possession of the place in Marple on which his lineal descendants have resided ever since, adding to it from time to time There he established a manufactory for leather, and enlarged his estate by purchasing two hundred and fifty acres lying between the property on which he had built a stone dwelling and Crum Creek

The 2d of Seventh month, 1702, he married Abigail Bonsall, daughter of Richard Bonsall She had a taste for gardening Two cedars planted by her, one on each side of the gate-way opening into the lane leading to the house, have been familiar objects all my life. One has recently fallen, the other is still standing (1893)   Other cedars and very old box-trees, nearer to the house, were probably planted by her also

Joseph and Abigail Rhoads had four sons and three daughters

    I   John, born in 1703, married Elizabeth Malin
    II. Mary
    III. Elizabeth
    IV Abigail
    V. Joseph, born 1715.
    VI Benjamin, born 1719, married Katharine Pugh
    VII. JAMES, born 15th of Fifth mo., 1722, married Elizabeth Owen

Joseph Rhoads deceased in 1732, aged fifty-two years.   His wife survived him eighteen years, departing this life the "eleventh day of the Ninth month, 1750, about six o'clock in the afternoon"

CHAPTER IX.

JAMES AND ELIZABETH RHOADS

JAMES RHOADS, the youngest son of Joseph and Abigail Rhoads, was born the 15th of Fifth month, 1722   It is believed that he was born and always resided on his father's estate at Marple   As his father deceased when he was about ten years old, his education from that time devolved upon his mother

At twenty-eight he appears to have come into possession of the whole property at Marple, to which he made considerable additions in land.

Traditions that have come to my knowledge represent him to have been of a refined and gentle nature, loving and generous in his domestic relations, and successful in business transactions and in the care of his property   He kept the faith of his parents as a Friend, and sustained the family characteristics of uprightness and scrupulous honesty   An aged Friend named Forsythe, of Chester County, told my father that she was ac-

quainted with his grandfather, James Rhoads , that he was remarkably honest in his dealings, and whoever bought of him
was sure of a fair bargain

When twenty-three years of age he brought a lovely bride to
share the home at Marple. His mother was still living, and five
years longer she continued a blessing in their house before she
was called away to her heavenly inheritance. Ample room was
provided for the two families by additions to the original dwelling, and all lived harmoniously in the pleasant residence amidst
undulating fields and meadows, bowery woodlands, and sparkling streams of purest water   The young wife was Elizabeth
Owen, whose personal charms and graceful manners indicated
her amiable qualities and solid worth   She came of honorable
Welsh ancestry, as may be seen by ancient marriage certificates
now in my possession.* Her birth is recorded in a Welsh
Bible belonging to our family, but the records are all in the
English language   From it I take the following

"Elizabeth ye Daughter of John and Hannah Owen was born
the 20th day of ye 11th mo 172 2/3 and the 5th day of the week,
at sunrise, in Springfield "

And so this beautiful gift came " in the sweet hour of prime,"
and was " a joy forever," scattering gladness and love all along
her pathway through life

We have no account of her childhood, but it appears that
she resided for a time in Philadelphia, probably for better edu-
cational advantages than such as the country districts afforded.
On returning to her home in Springfield, her young friends in
the city gave her a testimonial of their appreciation of her
character, which I copy below

"To Friends at Springfield or Elsewhere.

"Dear Friends,—Our respected ffriend Elizth Owen the Bearer hereof Upon her
Removal from Amongst us requested our certificate of her behaviour whilst here,
these therefore may Inform that During her Residence with us, she hath Conducted
herSelf Soberly and is Justly Esteemed and beloved of her acquaintance being
Chearfull yet Easy and Inofencive in her Conversation, without affectation, a
frequenter of religious meetings and is as far as we know Clear from any contracts
of Marriage So Commending her to Divine Protection and to be assissted by your

* See Appendix

Religious Care under which we hope and Desire her Growth in Piety, and sincerely wish her Welfare and Happiness here and hereafter So Conclude ourSelves Your Real Friends —

"Signed at a Meeting of Junior Friends held at Philadelphia the 18th Day of 10mo 1742 by—

SAM'LL MORRIS	REBECCA OWEN
JUDAH FOULKE	MARGARET LAWRENCE
ROBT OWEN	TACY OWEN
JOHN BIDDLE	REBECCA EVANS
SARAH BIDDLE	SIDNEY EVANS
CAD EVANS	SARAH EVANS
DAN'LL MORRIS	MARY REEVE
ISAAC GRIFFITTS	MARY BRINGHURST
JOHN BRINGHURST JR "	

Attractive in appearance and with such qualities of mind and heart, it is not surprising that the youthful yeoman of Marple was drawn into the charmed circle of her acquaintance. He sought a more intimate friendship and prospered in his suit "Having consent of Parents and Relations concerned," the "Twenty-second day of the Sixth month in the year of our Lord One Thousand seven hundred and forty-five," James Rhoads and Elizabeth Owen appeared in a public meeting of the Friends at "Springfield in the County of Chester and Province of Pennsylvania," and taking each other by the hand solemnly promised to be loving and faithful to each other as husband and wife "with the Lord's assistance" till death should separate them

Sixty-three friends signed the certificate of marriage as witnesses, many of whose names are still represented in highly-respectable families *

Contentedly occupying the ancestral home, with firmly-established Christian principles and hearts loving and loyal, truest foundation for happiness in this life, time flowed on for more than thirty years unmarked by any great events in the experience of the wedded pair, yet full of occurrences and colored by circumstances that give the deepest interest and liveliest charms to existence

* This event occurred just one century, wanting seventeen days, before the eldest of their great-great-grandchildren—in the line of their son Joseph—was born at Springfield, she for whose sake I am writing these memoirs chiefly, Hannah Rhoads Garrett, *nee* Haines

Three sons and five daughters were given to them Two sons and three daughters grew to maturity and married into respectable families Three children died in childhood, and it is touching to read the minutiæ in the day and hour when the child was received as a priceless treasure, and again when the parents yielded it up to the Author of all their blessings

Some objects at this moment before me give a slight peep into their domestic economy. One of them is a rather handsome arm-chair of walnut that was presented by my great-grand-father to his son Joseph ; a similar one was also given to his son Owen. Another is a high-backed rocking-chair that looks as if it might last centuries longer It came to me rather curiously, having been sent by Elizabeth Rhoads, daughter of Owen Rhoads, to my dear husband when he was seriously ill some years before our marriage, that he might have a comfortable support when able to sit up On the brocade-covered seat of the walnut chair are lying two books that came into our family through Elizabeth Owen One is a Welsh Bible bound in leather, with clasps, printed " yn Popes-Head Alley yn Cornhil. 1678." On the first blank leaf is written,—

> " Evan Owen his book, 1708
> " Witness to the same
>> " Robert Jones
>>> " June the 5th 1709
>> " James Rhoads his Book
>>> " Oct 19 1765 "

On the next page is a Welsh metrical verse on " Robert," signed " John Owen His hand " This stanza was translated for us by Joseph Harrison, a Welsh miner from one of our Penn-sylvania counties, who attended our meeting in Eleventh month, 1886, and came home with us to dine He said the verse was in a rhythm peculiar to the Welsh language

> " Robert, faithful son of Owen,
> Full of life passed his journey.
> What was mortal went to earth,
> The soul has reached the realm of heavenly cheerfulness " *

> * Robert Owen, grandfather of Elizabeth Owen

The other book alluded to is "The English and Welsh Dictionary Salop Printed and sold there by the author, John Roderick, 1725" It was given by Grace Lloyd to "John Owen, His book," 1737.

Our English forefathers brought to the Province of Penn their habits of thrift and thoroughness Their buildings for dwelling-houses, carriages, horses, and dairy were constructed of stone so well cemented that even in our climate they remained firm for centuries They had a love for gardening, and were successful in the cultivation of shrubbery and many beautiful flowering-plants. A fancy for china, cut-glass, and silver was conspicuous in corner cupboards and old-fashioned buffets

The children of James and Elizabeth Rhoads were

    I Hannah, born 6th of Sixth mo., 1746; married Nathan Garrett, of Upper Darby

 * II Joseph, born 3d of Twelfth mo, 1748, married Mary Ashbridge

  III Susanna, born 28th of Fourth mo., 1751, "Departed this life the 23rd day of ye 6 month 1752, and was buried the 25th of the same."

  IV Rebecca, born 1754? married Hugh Lownes, of Springfield.

   V Owen, born 1756, married Mary Hall; deceased 10th of Eighth mo., 1838

  VI Tacy, born 25th of Third mo, 1759; married Joseph Davis

 VII "James Rhoads son of James and Elizabeth Rhoads was born the 26th day of the Second month 1763 and the 7th day of the week Near 9 A'clock in the morning He Departed this life the 4th day of the 9th month 1770 and 3rd day of the week at 1 Aclock in the Morning and was buried the 5th of the same aged 7 years and six months"

VIII Elizabeth Rhoads, "Daughter of James and Elizabeth Rhoads was born the 17th day of the 4th month 1768 and First day of the week between 8 and 9 Aclock in the morning She Departed this Life the 9th day

        * Date taken from his own journal

of the 8th mo 1778, it being the First day of the
week near 9 Aclock in the morning, and was buried
the 10th of the same in the afternoon Aged 10 years
3 months & 23 days, it being the 13th day of her
sickness "

And so the child that gladdened the meridian of their days
passed into "the realms of heavenly cheerfulness" with the dew
of her youth fresh upon her But already the tender father
had preceded her Six days before, his illness of eighteen days'
duration was ended On the "3rd day of the 8th month 1778,
it being the second day of the week, between 5 and 6 a'clock in
the afternoon," his "soul to Him who gave it rose," and in the
presence of the Saviour whose footsteps he had endeavored to
follow, he doubtless heard the welcome "Enter thou into the
joy of thy Lord" He was fifty-six years, two months, and
nineteen days old, the funeral was on the fifth of the same
month "in the forenoon "

The stricken wife and mother, gentle and affectionate as she
was, bore her sorrows with meekness, and for seventeen years
longer her children enjoyed the blessing of her love and care
and the benefit of her example

Her son Owen and the three daughters, Hannah, Rebecca,
and Tacy, appear to have married early and settled in homes of
their own in the same county

Joseph, the eldest son, always resided on the paternal estate
To his mother he was a man after her own heart, and when he
chose a companion for life her refined and noble nature must
have completely satisfied the maternal taste and judgment
Mother and daughter-in-law were well suited to occupy the
same abode

Elizabeth Rhoads chose for her apartments the western end
of the long building, which was less connected with the business
operations of the place. In my day it was called "The Far-
house;" and its well-lighted rooms and large closets, almost
deserted by our elders, furnished my generation with free and
ample space for the amusements of many happy hours Good
work had been put into the walls by English trained masons,
and when they were removed in after-years, to be replaced by a

modern but less æsthetic structure, it was difficult to separate the stone and mortar that had grown rock-like together

There the honored mother saw her grandchildren come around her, from year to year new faces added to the groups of young life   My father remembered her well, and she left a very agreeable impression on his mind   He has told me that she was a handsome woman, and that the forehead of my brother James resembled hers

One by one the generations must pass away, and our great-grandmother Rhoads closed her earthly career on the 5th day of the Fifth month, 1795, and rejoined the loved of her early days where life is ever new and joyous

CHAPTER X

JOSEPH RHOADS II AND MARY RHOADS—THE ASHBRIDGE FAMILY.

JOSEPH RHOADS, the eldest son of James and Elizabeth Rhoads, was born at Marple the 3d day of Twelfth month, 1748. In him the characteristics of both parents were happily blended. Thoughtful, tenderly conscientious, with a high sense of honor, warm and steadfast in his domestic affections, a lover of good society, earnest, diligent, and persevering in the employment of his time and talents, he was greatly beloved by his family and friends, and a trusted and very serviceable member of the civil and religious communities in which he lived

He was later in winning his bride than some of his predecessors had been, not marrying till he was thirty   Ten years her senior, he had to wait till she grew up to womanhood, but the waiting was well rewarded, for none other—by birth and position, kindred faith, and the endowment of a nature at once gentle and strong—could so well have fitted into his sphere.

As typical of the best class among the rural population of Pennsylvania in provincial days, a glance at the genealogy and circumstances of his wife, Mary Ashbridge, may be allowed to interrupt the narrative of my grandfather's life.

GEORGE ASHBRIDGE I

George Ashbridge came from Yorkshire, England, and arrived in Philadelphia the 5th of Fifth month, 1698. He purchased a tract of land extending from Sugartown to Milltown, in Chester County, Pennsylvania At that time Chester County included what is now known as Delaware County, and the residence of George Ashbridge was on this estate On the 23d of Eighth month, 1701, he married, at Providence Meeting of Friends, Mary Malin, whose family also came from England among the early settlers of Pennsylvania

It is said that on landing at Philadelphia George Ashbridge had with him a Bible, an axe, and an English coin of some value The coin he gave to one who needed it more than himself, the axe was no doubt kept for use, and the Bible is probably still in possession of one of his descendants

George and Mary Ashbridge had five sons and five daughters, —viz., John, GEORGE, Jonathan, Elizabeth, Mary, Aaron, Hannah, Phebe, Lydia, and Joseph

Mary (Malin) Ashbridge deceased the 15th of Second month, 1728 George Ashbridge married again, his second wife being Margaret Paschall, and soon after removed to Chester, where he continued to reside till his decease, in 1748

GEORGE ASHBRIDGE II ,

the second son of George and Mary Ashbridge, was born the 19th of Twelfth month, 1703–04, and named for his father. As he grew to manhood he developed great physical strength and indomitable courage, but with it all a kind and generous spirit It is related of him that he said he would rather be six feet under ground than fear the face of any man.

He owned the first carriage used in that part of the county As he could not enjoy his hour of public worship unless his horses were made comfortable, he erected a stone building to shelter them and his carriage on the premises of the Friends' meeting-house at Goshen, with a door-way at each end, because he "never liked to back out."

He married Jane Hoopes on the 21st of Eighth month, 1730.

9

Their home was the paternal mansion in Goshen, his father having chosen to reside in Chester a few months previous to the son's wedding   Near it he had a flour-mill doing a good business, and he never took toll out of a grist that a laboring-man brought to it on his back *

In 1743 he was elected member of the Provincial Assembly, which held its sessions in Philadelphia, and was returned by his constituents of Chester County to the end of his life   However late the Assembly adjourned, he mounted his horse and rode twenty miles to his home, in Goshen, that night

George II and Jane Ashbridge had four sons and five daughters,—Mary, GEORGE, William, Susanna, Phebe, Jane, Daniel, Joshua, and Lydia

His daughter, Jane Maris, has left this short testimony of love and veneration for her father.

"On the 6ᵗʰ of Third month 1773 departed this life at Goshen in Chester County George Ashbridge (the II) after a short but severe illness, which he bore with great patience, being in the seventieth year of his age

"He seemed not to have much apprehension of his dissolution being so near till the day before he departed, at which he did not discover any surprise, nor the least discomposure   Two of his children coming in the evening before he departed, who had not seen him in his sickness till then, he seemed well pleased, but had little inclination for discourse   And so remained till early next morning when he quietly departed, to the great grief of his wife and children, as also a great number of his friends and neighbors, which was manifested by the vast concourse that attended his funeral, whose countenances were generally expressing sorrow, for indeed it was a general loss

"He was a true friend to the poor and afflicted who shared largely of his bounty   He had a great faculty for composing differences in which he often assisted with great success

"He was a useful member of (religious) society, and was for thirty years a member of Assembly, which station he filled with

---

* It was formerly customary to pay laborers on farms partly in produce, and they would take home or to mill a sack of grain on their shoulders

dignity and always acquitted himself well in his country's cause He was not fond of fine-spun discourses, but his arguments were sound, pathetic and pertinent to the matter.

" His appearance at home and abroad was manly and bold few men of the age were endowed with a more constant and even temper for transacting business He acquired a laige estate by honest frugality, with which he was very liberal in his contributions both public and private He was a very kind husband and as tender a father, his bounty to his children was almost unbounded

" His steady decorum in his family was beautiful, he was solid in his deportment, not very talkative though pleasant and cheerful in the company of his friends, which he was fond of It may be truly said that he was good without noise, without ostentation great

" JANE MARIS "

GEORGE ASHBRIDGE III ,

the eldest son of George and Jane Ashbridge, was born the 1st of First month, 1732/3.

The halcyon days inaugurated by William Penn were gliding peacefully on as he grew from youth to manhood In Philadelphia his father was promoting the cause of truth and freedom, and Franklin was pursuing his philosophical experiments and strengthening the political growth of his country Between the Potomac and Rappahannock another son of 1732 was rapidly evolving those mental and moral qualities that made him worthy of the first place in a new and independent nation

Amid such favoring circumstances George the younger attained his majority But a change was approaching, and soon the first notes of war rang through the forests of Pennsylvania as Colonel Washington led his forces, under British command, through Indian ambuscades to the spot where Pittsburg spires now rise amidst the smoke of countless chimneys Dauntless and true to liberty as were George Ashbridge and his son, they were no less true to their principles of peace and of good-will to all men, and were ever ready to obey the order of their Heavenly King, not only to love their neighbor as themselves, but to love their enemies also, and to return good for evil

With such a pacific career in view, the younger George sought the hand of Rebekah Garrett, daughter of one of the original settlers of Philadelphia, and they were married on the 5th day of the Twelfth month, 1754 To receive her he had already provided a substantial stone dwelling at Milltown, on the picturesque banks of Chester Creek, soon to be surrounded with trees and all that was then deemed essential to comfort and beauty in a rural residence. About lay an ample farm, and a short distance below the house a busy mill took in the products of fertile fields in its vicinity My grandmother used to speak of Goshen, her native township, as a land flowing with milk and honey, and when the wants of the immediate neighborhood were supplied the surplus was sent to Philadelphia or Chester. To carry the merchandise from his mill, as well as for the accommodation of his large family, her father kept a fine supply of horses that had their full share in the kind care extended to all under his charge

By nature a nobleman, independent in spirit, and strong in religious integrity, George Ashbridge's hardier virtues were tempered by an affectionate disposition and regard to the amenities of polite life Observing the limits of Christian moderation, he felt a liberty in his mode of living to adopt such refinements as were becoming his means and station His personal appearance was made none the less agreeable by his suit of fine broadcloth and silver buckles in his well-polished shoes.

Such a man would not have failed to choose for the companion of his life a woman whose worth and attractions were genuine and abiding, and her character, as reflected in her children, was one of true virtue and loveliness A pleasant glimpse of her ways was given to my brother James, her great-grandson, by Jane Vernon, who, in her ninetieth year, showed much of her original vigor in relating it She said that to our great-grandmother she was indebted for all the schooling that she ever received One cold, snowy day she was taken by her father to the Ashbridge mill, where he had some business to transact While attending to his affairs the little Jane was sent to the house Business despatched, her father walked up with the proprietor for his daughter As they entered the house

Rebekah Ashbridge said to her husband, "My dear, this little girl tells me that she has never been to school Had she not better stay with us and attend school with our children?" The child was left there accordingly and remained through the winter

I recently met with a cousin, who is also a great-granddaughter of the above-mentioned lady, and asked her what she could tell me of our common ancestress Not being given to folk-lore, she could only say that in her home they had a tea-set of richly-painted china that came to them through her, and besides this a curious chair of still older date, with "I H , 1704" inlaid on the back

As years passed, prosperity smiled upon the family at Milltown . their country was advancing in wealth and influence , in their own house sons and daughters were growing up around them,—two boys, energetic and enterprising, five lovely girls, a good deal varied in appearance and character

These were Lydia, stately and beautiful, regarded by the younger sisters with especial love and respect, MARY, gentle and affectionate, her clear intellect and calm judgment veiled by a slightly timid and shrinking modesty, Susanna, petite and sprightly, Jane, lively, ambitious, prompt in thought and act, Phebe, the youngest, graceful, refined, and almost luxurious in her tastes The sons, George and William, were younger than their sisters, but equally marked in character and venerated in the memory of their descendants

The girls were taught by Mistress Hollis, who conducted a small school in her own residence, about a mile from their home She enforced habits of strict obedience and attention, regulated their manners, and required an erect posture in their exercises Punctuality was exacted while under her care, although their path homeward led through their father's orchard, where tempting fruits often lay on the ground, they were expected to walk straight to their own door, enter, and hang up their bonnets before they were at liberty to touch apple, plum, or pear

Probably their literary advantages were few compared with those now enjoyed by young ladies, but the result was a facility for action in every department of woman's life and the art of

producing an extraordinary amount of fine needle-work   I remember many specimens of my grandmother's skill and dex-
terity, and so clear was her eyesight that she could embroider
by moonlight

The simple Christian creed professed by George Ashbridge
and his wife led them into few religious forms, but its spirit
pervaded their lives   They regularly attended Divine worship
at the Friends' meeting-house in Goshen, where I have seen the
stone stable that was built by his father to accommodate his
horses and carriage.   George Ashbridge took an active part in
the Monthly Meetings, and for twenty years served as clerk

In the peaceful valleys between the Blue Mountains and the
Atlantic, where the fellow-believers of Fox and Penn had come
to breathe the air of freedom and live in accordance with an
enlightened conscience, they might have thought themselves
secure from war and political commotion.   But unjust assump-
tion on one side and impatience of control on the other led to
provocations and aggression   The apparently safe abode of
our ancestor was encircled by armies ; the battle of Brandywine
was fought on one hand and the massacre at Paoli darkened a
night of horror on the other   Lying in the route from Chadd's
Ford to Valley Forge, martial troops passed to and fro over the
place   One day the teams for carrying flour to Chester would
be seized, on another a company of light-horse would call
uninvited to dine   On such occasions my grandmother would
retire from sight, but not so her lively sister Jane, who could
almost forgive the unceremonious visit for the sake of a casual
conversation with English officers and the excitement of a
repartee   Among family traditions an anecdote of these times
is related of this aunt of ours.   It was customary for the
younger members of this household to ride to their place of
worship, and one meeting-day, when a considerable number of
horses were standing on the premises during the hour of worship, a company of British soldiers arrived   Just as they were
securing their prizes the Friends came out of their meeting-
house ; Jane's quick eye saw that her favorite was being led off
by an officer, and having no mind to lose him, she walked
directly up and claimed her steed   The officer was so thrown

off his guard by the demand of this girl of thirteen that he immediately helped her to mount, and she rode away in triumph, retaining one horse at least for home service

With years comes change, not only in the larger national life, but as inevitably in each household   The parents, in the full maturity of their powers, with daughters and sons growing into womanhood and manly strength, had reached the climax of domestic happiness, and in the natural course of events would come a lessening of the circle around the cheerful fireside.

While her country was struggling for independence the beloved wife and mother was called to the peaceful home

> " Where no storms ever beat on the glittering strand,
> While the years of eternity roll "

This event is commemorated by a time-stained paper now lying before me, on which is written in a clear, strong hand the following ·

> " By way of Memorial
> concerning my near and dearly beloved wife
> REBEKAH ASHBRIDGE

" DEAR CHILDREN,—I do herein effectionately salute you and desire your growth and perseverance in the Truth , which if you abide under the teachings thereof, manifest in your own hearts, will keep you from evil and enable you to dwell in Love one towards another and seek the good and welfare of all mankind

" I believe it my duty to leave you some account concerning my dearly beloved and effectionate wife Rebekah Ashbridge, your loving and tender mother (deceased), whose care over you both for your spiritual and temporal welfare hath been great   Therefore not knowing how soon, or in what manner it may please the Divine Being to dispose of me, whether in life or death, absent or present I know not, but having had frequent opportunities of observing how soon a short sickness brings these bodies of ours down to the·grave to be seen of men no more, I do embrace this opportunity, hoping it may through Divine assistance put you upon pressing after such a life and conduct

"I think I may justly say in remembrance of her that she was a woman of a meek and tender spirit, living in the fear of the Lord, was quick in discerning evil in herself and others, from which by the tender mercies of the Lord she was in a great degree preserved through life and in that meekness which becomes the followers of Christ

"We were married about the twenty-second year of our age, in which weighty undertaking and discoursings thereon I believe there was a true desire in each of us to know the will of the Lord concerning us, and I believe our proceedings therein were with Divine approbation   Thus dwelling in a good degree of humility she became a loving wife, a tender mother, a careful, tender, and diligent mistress over our family: but words are wanting to express her loving, constant and tender care for me, your poor weakly Father, often in many pains and weaknesses through life

"It was evident to me that her care and concern for our meetings grew much, that Friends might more and more be preserved from vain imaginations and wrong things, and that she might act consistent with the Truth in the station of over-seer in which she was placed, being often mindful to assist and sympathise with the poor of all sorts so long as it pleased the Lord to give her ability in this transitory and fading world

"But above all, O how hath she been enabled in the many sore conflicts and temptations, which the Enemy of our souls is suffered to pour in on us like a mighty flood for our tryals through life, such as the many hurries of business and outward distresses in this perishing world, as it were meekly to lay her hand on this or the other thing and say this is not best to be so, or to do so, which has often appeared to me as pure oil poured on around by a skillful physician

"With such a truly beloved and helpful companion the Lord in His great mercy hath been pleased to assist me for almost twenty-three years, to whom alone for this and all His other mercies be all attribute and praises, for to Him it is due   Greatly desiring I and you may so walk through life as that it may please Him still to continue His mercies and blessings to us, that we may have to give up our accounts with joy when time here is no more, as she, to our great loss and her everlasting comfort amidst all the great outward commotions of war and bloodshed, all which tumults she appeared to bear with great fortitude of mind.

"She was taken unwell in the morning of the 16th day of Ninth month 1777, which did mightily increase On the 17th she said she did not know where she could have catch'd the distemper,* and with great composure of mind said she believed it was come to take her from this troublesome world

"On the 18th she said to me she hoped I could forgive her everything she had done amiss to me: soon after added, 'I believe we have lived as well together as most,' but she thought our time of parting would soon be On the 19th she said to one of her children, 'Look on me and see what a short time of sickness will do and be not too much concerned about thy cloaths' On the 20th she said to me 'I am very weak, I believe much weaker than thee may think, and if I should now be taken from thee thou will not be left in so hard a case as many are, for none of our children are very young'

"On the 21st being very weak desired me to raise her up and sit behind her, which I did. soon after she said, 'I have often had to remember the saying of an ancient friend, "What an awful thing it is to die," which I believe I shall soon experience' Then exhorted her children thus, 'Children, live together in the fear of the Lord, and do all the good you can one for another:' then said to one, 'Thee must be as a mother to the rest,' and gave particular directions concerning others, and as to the plainness of her coffin and cloaths, and lay down again

"Soon after observing me said 'Fret not thyself for me, I believe I go and do not know that I need desire to live longer in this troublesome world,' then was a considerable time silent, then said 'O Lord have mercy on me!' A little time after she said, 'O Lord receive my soul up into Thy mansions of everlasting glory where there is joy and peace forever,' then lay still a considerable time like one departing But on perceiving her move a little I asked her if she wanted anything,—she said 'I am waiting—I am waiting—O how hard it is to wait' Then

* Believed to have been dysentery

she putting her hand to my head we took a solemn farewell as for the last   She lay a considerable part of the night in which we did not expect her to speak again but by degrees she recovered a little by the 22nd so that we had some small hopes of her recovery, and on the 23^d also, she being relieved some little from the sharp pain got some small time of sleep, and being told she slept some she said ' Ah what a mercy it is, and how thankful I ought to be for it '   At night she seemed to sleep for the most part, but I asked her at several times how she felt, to which she replied ' I feel very little pain,' and though towards morning her departure seemed to appear yet she remained sensible and quietly departed this life about 10 o'clock in the morning of the 24th day of the Ninth month 1777

" Now, dear children, believing through the mercy of the Lord she is fully at rest in the mansions of peace where she so earnestly prayed to be it remains our duty daily to endeavor to follow her footsteps in such a virtuous and exemplary life, having our eyes towards the Lord for daily help   Let us submit, as much as may be, without murmurings to His providence in every dispensation whether in prosperity, or adversity in this life, for the Lord alone is the preserver and disposer of mankind, to whom all praises and fear are due now, henceforth, and forever.

" I could say much of my solitaryness and loss in her [here some words are worn away from the manuscript] and forbear and remain your effectionate father

                                    " GEORGE ASHBRIDGE.

" GOSHEN, the 10th mo   the 10th day, 1777 "

The expression " troublesome world" will be understood if we realize that these events were occurring during the Revolutionary War and while the noise of battles was booming through the air   Losses, imprisonment, and much suffering of mind and body had to be endured by those whose Christian principles forbade their taking an active part in the struggle.   The future was shrouded   No one could yet see the end and the result.

How heavily the times pressed on the minds of Friends may be inferred from verses written by George Ashbridge, which indicate more love and faith than poetic talent   A few of the closing stanzas may be given from " Some lines written in the forepart of the year 1780 as an encouragement to Christians to put their trust in the immovable Rock which faileth not " The text chosen for the title is Deuteronomy xxxii 31

" Their Rock is Zion's holy King,
    Whose doctrine's peace, and all good-will to men ,
Thus at His birth did angels sing,
    Let Zion s children join in chorus then

" Though laws may threat with cruel rage,
    Though blinded men increasing havock make,
Our Rock is strong from age to age,
    He never did His righteous ones forsake

" Pure waters issue from its spring,
    Sustaining Bread is here forever sure ,
Here peaceful ones in covert sing,
    Here strength's received all trials to endure

" Though foolish men may scoff and mock,
    Our life is peace, our practice breathes good-will,
Our trust is in the Eternal Rock,
    We neither strengthen bloody hands, nor kill.

" Though troubles rage these are secure ;
    By storms unhurt, unmoved by fear, can sing,
Our Rock is strong, our Refuge sure ,
    Good-will to men, all praise to Zion's King "'

In another effusion he portrays a " scheme" that would nullify the projects of communists and socialists.

" A DISTANT PROSPECT OF THE MILLENNIUM, OR PROMISED HAPPY DAY OF PEACE
IN THE SIMILITUDE OF A DREAM

" Tired with the world s tumultuous jars,
Religious broils and bloody wars,
    I laid me down to sleep,
And chargéd my domesticks round
To keep off all obstructing sound,
    And solemn silence keep

" My troubled mind no rest could find,
    But still I felt distressed,
Until a scene did intervene
    Which put my soul to rest

" For in my dream the Quaker scheme
    Prevailed throughout the earth :
The swords and spears made hooks and shears,
    The promised day took birth.

" The thundering bombs and killing guns
    Throughout the world did cease,
And murderers steeled forsook the field,
    And left the world in peace.

" None tries to cheat, or to defeat,
    Or over-reach his neighbour,
The strong do seek to support the weak
    In the produce of his labour.

" The lame and blind relief do find
    And bounteous supply,
Where all men strive in love to live
    And boundless charity.

" No lawyers' pleas, nor double fees ;
    No Judges set to hear them,
Their destiny is work or die,
    No client e'er comes near them.

" No mammon priest mankind opprest
    Or sent to jail his neighbour,
But each possest as God hath blest
    The produce of his labour.

" All that can preach do freely teach
    The knowledge God hath lent them,
And mean to stay and take their pay
    From Him who freely sent them,

" More pleased to give than to receive
    The words of our Redeemer :
A hireling is a man of sin,
    An antichristian schemer.

" When the wolf comes away he runs,
    But if the wolf he faces
He freely gives their carcasses
    So he can have their fleeces.

" Now, God of love, look from above,
    And bottle all our tears.
When Christ descends on earth to reign,
    At least, a thousand years,

" Men live in love, like saints above,
　　In peace and unity;
　The fear of God spreads o'er the globe
　　As waters do the sea

" Under their vines each head reclines,
　　The fig-tree yields her store,
　The arts of war men are not for
　　Nor learn them any more.

" No baneful strife 'twixt man and wife,
　　Faith feeds their mutual love,
　And virtue chains the happy swains
　　As turtle to the dove

" The balmy youth, nursed up in Truth
　　And grateful harmony,
　Anthems do sing to God our King
　　Who reigns above the sky

" The children young begin their song
　　As they begin their days,
　And from their undissembling tongue
　　The Lord perfects His praise

" Both old and young join in the song
　　As they have utterance given,
　Sweet harmony mounts to the sky
　　And joins the courts of heaven

" Oh! Glorious Day! then did I say,
　　Oh! blessed be that scheme!
　I, overjoyed, my sleep destroyed,
　　And quite dissolved my dream "

Such was the occupation of some of George Ashbridge's solitary hours after the departure of his lovely wife, but he had much else claiming his attention in the training of his young sons, and the marriage of his daughters, as one by one they went to form the centres of new homes   For eight years his children were favored with his paternal aid and counsel, and then, having seen his country restored to tranquillity and taking her place among the nations, he, too, passed over to the inheritance incorruptible on the 25th day of the Tenth month, 1785

CHAPTER XI

JOSEPH RHOADS II AND MARY RHOADS—(*Continued*)

RETURNING from this genealogical digression respecting the Ashbridge family, I will take again the story of Joseph Rhoads the second where it was dropped, just previous to his marriage with the gentle and judicious Mary His thoughtful gray eye won her confidence, although his brilliant complexion and dark-brown hair—falling, cavalier-fashion, in ringlets to his shoulders —may have lessened the gravity of his appearance.

The bride's outfit was liberal, judging from a memorandum turned out of an old chest in her garret three-quarters of a century afterwards. Clothing, house-linen, silver, china and other furniture, horses, cows, and sheep were included One of the most valued of the relics of that assemblage is a tall clock now in the possession of my brother, Jonathan E Rhoads, at Wilmington, Delaware

From their marriage certificate, now in my hand, I take the date of their wedding, which was solemnized at Friends' meeting-house in Goshen the "twenty-seventh day of the Fifth month in the year of our Lord one thousand seven hundred and seventy-nine"

Below their own names are the signatures of eighty of their relations and friends as witnesses of the vows then made and ever faithfully kept

A home was in readiness for the bride, one at which her father had been hospitably entertained a few years previously, probably when, as companion to some minister, he had visited the meetings of Friends in that vicinity. Ambitious only to answer her vocation perfectly, unwavering and affectionate, my grandmother left her father's house trustfully and contentedly, taking her place in the family mansion at Marple with the desire and expectation of abiding there all her days

A part of this old homestead was still occupied by the
widowed mother and her three daughters, but there was room
enough for all, and the three young sisters, shortly to be married themselves, enlivened the secluded place and adorned it
with plants they delighted to cultivate For five years the
sweet mother was permitted to bless her household with her
presence before her happy reunion with the husband of her
early days where there are no more partings

In the seventeen years immediately following the marriage of
Joseph and Mary Rhoads, four sons and three daughters
brought new life and love into their home

An accident that occurred in the infancy of their eldest boy
grieved the tender hearts of the parents Somehow he fell
from the arms of his nurse, and the spine was injured so that
he never became robust like his younger brothers He grew
to manhood and at thirty-three passed from earth His character made a deep impression on his family by its strength,
its purity, and its gentleness, and the tone of voice whenever
after "Brother James" was spoken of was full of love and
tender memory

George was the second son, and of him there is a little sketch
to be appended to these memoirs

JOSEPH, the third son, my father, is Joseph Rhoads III in
our family history

Next were Rebecca and Elizabeth, twins,—pure, transparent
characters, in which there appeared no moral flaw, but sweet
domestic virtues and humble, Christian spirits From my aunt
Rebecca I have the liveliest impressions of my grandfather's
personal appearance and of his relations with his children
Her health was delicate in early life, and her father frequently
took her out for a drive, on one such occasion he asked her
which she would prefer as an inheritance, land or money, she
artlessly answered that she liked both "And so" (she added,
in telling me) "he left me both in his will"

After the twins, my aunt Phebe was next in order, and she
seems to have been heiress not only to the name and handsome
silver spoons of her aunt Phebe Valentine, but also to some of
her delicate and slightly luxurious tastes To her province

were relegated the most æsthetic employments of the household, and her image is indelibly stamped in my memory, as she
sat in her prolonged maidenhood by the winter fireside, between
its glowing brands and the low windows filled with blooming
plants, her fingers deftly turning textile fabrics into articles of
ornament or use   In the nearest window drawer were her
books, a treasure of delight to me as I pored over them beside
her, amused now and then with the crackling logs and their
flying sparks riddling the nearest breadths of my aunt's dress.

Her wedding was the first I ever attended,—a bright, happy
day, and full of happy auguries for me

The youngest of the band was William, distinct from all the
others in some qualities, yet in all sterling attributes substantially the same.   He had more of the spirit of fun in his composition, and added much to the merriment of our childhood in
our frequent seasons of intercourse   All were bound together
by the most intimate and the strongest ties of affection, and
were ever ready to serve and succor one another

There was always a transparency in thought and action
throughout the family, agreeing well with some simple lines
now lying before me, written by my grandmother on paper
grown yellow with age   I copy the paper below.

> " Flee youthful lusts, the omniscient God revere,
>   Whether with others, or alone you are,
>   Suffer no idle word, nor secret act to be,
>   Which ought to cause a blush if all mankind could see

" 1783   6 mo 11th

" This being a copy of a small piece of verse which our
ancient and worthy friend, Thomas Goodwin, gave as a present
to several of the children of Goshen Meeting, after his return
from England the last time, of which I was one

                                  " MARY RHOADS "

She certainly instilled this reverential and watchful spirit with
much success in the training of her children   Notwithstanding
the regularity of his habits and strict temperance after passing
his fiftieth year, my grandfather's health became somewhat pre-
carious and for several years he suffered from dyspepsia, and at

times had to combat the tendency of that disease to disturb
the cheerful serenity of mind that he believed it right to
maintain

At this period he occasionally wrote down his reflections, or
the occurrences of the day   I will transcribe some passages
from the journal.   It begins with expressing his affectionate
solicitude for his children, and his admonitions for their conduct
in life

EXTRACTS FROM THE JOURNAL.

" I, Joseph Rhoads, having been for some time past in a weak
state of health, and for two days past much declining and much
concerned for the sober, orderly and regular conducting of my
children, do this evening, being the 11th of Seventh month 1801,
feel concerned to put something in writing

" In the first place I exhort you all to be sober and dress
yourselves in plain clothing and attend religious meetings   and
when you go there, if about the time, go into the house as soon
as conveniently may be, and endeavor to take seats as much
from amongst such as are light and vain as you well can, then
endeavor to turn your minds inward and compose your thoughts
with earnest desire that your Creator may instruct you and incline your hearts to serve Him, which as you attend to the first
pointings of Truth you may be instructed what you ought to do

" I also exhort and admonish you to shun taverns and places
of public resort except where your business really calls you.
As to company keeping I advise you to only accompany with
such as are really virtuous and good   but when your lot is
thrown amongst vain people get clear of them as soon as possible.

" Observe punctuality and justice in all your dealings, and in
selling your goods or property be careful to not overrate, or use
many words praising the same, and in buying carefully avoid
running down or undervaluing what you are about to buy

" By honestly attending to these things and using no deception you may preserve your consciences in a good measure
clear, and probably get along in the world in a way that you
will not be so much afraid to leave it as if you conducted
otherwise

10

" *Third-day,* 14*th* (*Seventh month* 1801)—I think I was weaker this morning than I have been before, though better after riding a little

" This is not the first time I have felt myself surrounded by doubtful apprehensions of being very soon removed out of this state of being   If any of my friends shall wish to know my thoughts at this time I may inform them that I consider that I shall at some awful period die, that I am turned of fifty-two years of age, of weakly constitution for some time back, and cannot expect to live long, but have not yet seen my way in that manner as I could wish and have always desired into another state, yet I think I feel that support in my mind that it cannot, or will not be consistent with Divine goodness to punish one whose intentions have been like mine

" *First-day morning,* 19*th*—My anxiety still is great that I may have all things in readiness and be so redeemed from things, thoughts and desires contrary to the will of the Supreme Being that I may be in a fit disposition to receive the agreeable witness in myself that I shall at the close here be received into everlasting happiness

" Then, O Lord! my desire is that I may be willing at this, or any other time, to give up my stewardship with joy   But if it shall so happen that I continue here and am restored to a state of middling health be it remembered by me that I have entered into solemn engagement to dedicate my time and talent to such things and in such manner as appears most consistent with the will of the great Creator

" Lord God Almighty, I humbly beseech Thee to enable me to call on Thy name and to pray acceptably unto Thee   I feel something within at this present time which I wish may be increased   I think I have a degree of faith to believe that my wife and children, if I am removed, may live very comfortably together if the Lord is sought unto for direction   Live in love, do good to and for one another   Oh, my children, be not proud, do not be going about unnecessarily, but stay much of your time together   Learn to live frugal, then less labour will support you   be cautious in great undertakings.

" *Second-day,* 20*th* (*Seventh month*)—My weakness is so

great that it has become a matter of serious consideration how
it shall go with me at this time My desire is that I may be
instructed by the Supreme Being how to ask aright, and above
all things that my faith and confidence may be fixed and placed
on Him and have full assurance that I shall enter into life
eternal with joy

" I believe it will be unsafe for such as are in the practice of
using spirituous liquors to excess to expect any benefit from
them as medicine, except they have so long abstained therefrom
as for nature to require it It has been productive of much
evil my desire is that my children may be very careful in
habituating themselves to the tasting of them I believe it
hurts the digestion, inflames the blood and weakens the bowels,
where they are used in the manner they often are The very
smell of one that is in the constant habit of drinking spirituous
liquors is intolerable to a sober temperate person But what
good is to be derived from spirits is to such as have been careful
of the use of them in health. . .

" *Fourth-day, 26th (Eighth month)* —My desire for the welfare
of you my children, still continuing, and not knowing how long
I may be permitted to continue with you, am free to caution
you against reading pernicious books, or such things as may
lessen your thoughts of religion ; but give much diligence to
make your peace with the Almighty, live lives of strict piety,
justice, virtue, and pursue every good work

" It was a remark of the great William Penn, I think, that he
that is taught to live on a little owes more to his father's wisdom
than he that has a great deal left to him does to his father's care
This I want you all to observe so far as to guard against im-
moderate extravagance, and confine your wants within moderate
bounds · less labour may support you, you may have more to
spare one unto another, also to help the needy you may have
more time to visit the afflicted and needy and comfort them in
such things as their situations may require

" Be willing to help the widow and the orphan, attend to
acts of religious duty; and to visit, help and counsel one another

" My meaning is to live plentifully and enjoy the necessaries of life where they have them, but to be very careful not to imitate such as live out of the bounds of true moderation and wisdom   There is a danger of such as live in the gratification of self getting out of the limits of Truth, living above their circumstances, and in order to make an appearance and support themselves therein oppressing their hirelings and exacting more in the course of their business for their property than what may be really just.

"*Second-day the* 31*st*, 8 *mo*—Justice and uprightness in dealings are in a good measure observed by most men, and in general mankind speak nearly the truth, although sometimes there are certain evasions that are not right   May we all be careful not to deceive one another, that thing called pride is of such a nature that is very likely to lay hold in some way unless we are very guarded   O Lord, that I may be kept in humility before Thee, and be guided by Thee

"*Fourth-day the second of Ninth mo* 1801.—I think I may truly say ' as the hart in the wilderness panteth after the water-brooks, so doth my heart pant after thy presence, O Lord '   I have no desire to call any more time mine, but all to serve the Lord and do good to His people, and in everything promote His cause

"Dear John Parrish came to see me, had something comfortable to communicate wherewith I hope to be refreshed

"*Fifth-day the third of Ninth mo* 1801.—Some people may suppose there is some cause for my affliction ; I know of none but what I have mentioned   I do acknowledge that I have mist it in many things, but I have a tolerable conscience, and rather think I shall not meet with condemnation

"The situation of my outward affairs is very little uneasiness to me, such as business &c   My wife and children are dearly Beloved by me, and show me love and respect, I have enough to pay all and as much as I seem to need or want

"Roger Dicks and Eli Yarnall have been to see me this afternoon, whose company was agreeable and I hope of real advantage. . .

"*Third-day the eighth,* 9 *mo* 1801 —I think this has been nearly as warm a day as we have had , I have continued toler-

able through it so far   My desire is that I may acknowledge
it with thankfulness to Him whom I wish to love and serve in
preference to every other joy

"*Fourth-day the ninth*, 9 *mo* 1801 —O Lord, I pray thee still
the perturbations of my mind and preserve me in quietude   be
pleased to enlighten my understanding and let me know what .
Thy will is concerning me, and I do humbly beseech Thee to
enable me to do and perform the same

"I have made some observations in the course of business of
late, and am fully convinced in my own mind that it will not be
to advantage to keep many hired people when there is no proper
person who seems to have authority, or to give directions in such
a way that they may think they ought to comply

" My son James has been engaged in business in such a manner
that he is much fatigued, which is contrary to my mind, as his
situation is such that it cannot be expected that he can do near
so much as some others   And my mind is that my children be
not kept constant to hard labour, though I wish them to be
attentive to care and business, and by no means to spend their
time idle, and to live frugal, and to be careful and not go unnecessarily rambling about   If they go on a visit let them
choose well whom they go to see, let them be of the more
virtuous sort   I have been the more careful, or thoughtful on
account of these things as I have had opportunity of seeing and
judging and find a right application to these things may be of
great advantage to their future happiness

" Happiness doth not so much consist in great possessions as
it doth in a good conscience, a quiet serene mind, and, I may
add, a good constitution is also a blessing

"*Fifth-day the tenth*, 9 *mo*. 1801 —I have had a desire to
write to some of my connections, but being so very low in health
and strength I seem unwilling, as I could not consistent with my
present feelings write anything but what would convey an idea
of my weak state and such an account would be unpleasant to
my friends   But if the Lord would be pleased to restore me
to a middling state of health and a sound mind I should esteem
it a favor and a blessing never to be forgot by me and should
then look upon it as a duty to write to my friends in humility

and fear, but with pleasure and satisfaction, also to visit the afflicted and endeavour to comfort and help them

".   I think it right to endeavour on every occasion to do what to us appears just, consistent and so agreeable to what we think right as to conclude then that we shall never after be uneasy about the same, yea conduct ourselves towards all others in such a way that if we were used by them in the same manner we should be satisfied and call it right   And after having on all occasions conducted agreeable to the best of our knowledge, and making restoration where we have mist it, it may then be best to not think too much on matters beyond our comprehension, but trust in the Lord to enlighten our understandings as far as it is consistent with His goodness to reveal unto us   Oh, that I may be preserved in stability and my whole confidence be fixed in the Lord alone, and enjoy a quiet calm

"*First-day the thirteenth* (9 *mo* 1801).—I think I can truly say it is my earnest desire to conduct myself so as to be in favor with the Almighty and above all things serve Him and enjoy His favor and presence   I have also wished earnestly to conduct myself in such a manner as to have the countenance, Love, respect and real good will of my own particular family and all mankind

" . . I may acknowledge my weakness and manifold transgressions and, as far as they have presented to my view, I hope I have sincerely repented of them all   However I do earnestly beseech the Almighty to bring all things to my remembrance and set my sins in order before me, and to put an opportunity into my power to fully accomplish all that I ought to do, to fully do justice to every one, and that I may in the depth of humility beseech forgiveness of Him is the prayer and ardent desire of my heart and mind

"*Second-day the fourteenth* (9 *mo* 1801)—   William Jackson with his companion Joshua Pusey, in the course of his visit to meetings hereaway, was at our meeting at Springfield to-day   I have thought myself in too weak a state to attend meetings two or three weeks past, I may confess it something of a cross to my desire   I feel more concerned on that account than I ever thought of, and if I am restored to a state suitable to at-

tend religious meetings again my desire is that I may prize the
favour and endeavor to apply the time and service therein
agreeable to the intent and institution wherein they were set up

"Now I am prepared to leave a caution for myself and others
that may read these lines to prize their time whilst in their
power, and to use all diligence to make their calling and election sure In the first place to seek for an inheritance in the
kingdom of heaven by pursuing the means which look most
likely to consist therewith and persevere therein, and then I
have no doubt but all things needful will be added

"*Fourth-day the sixteenth* (9 *mo.* 1801) —This afternoon
near three o'clock George Fairlamb came down and informed
me that William Jackson and Joshua Pusey were at Joseph
Hood's and wished me to go up there as they should like to
see me I being better than common concluded I would try to
go I went there in the chair and found them and several other
friends we spent the afternoon in agreeable and I hope edifying conversation, and after parting I think I may say I felt real
affection and esteem for them. I have sometimes of late experienced the fulfilling of that saying ' As iron sharpeneth iron
so doth the countenance of a man his friend.' May I be thankful
to the Author of every good for this day's favour, is the desire
of my heart , and I humbly pray for more such times as this
afternoon

"*Seventh-day the* 19*th* (9 *mo.* 1801)— . Of ourselves we
can do little , not even command our own thoughts I think
I have seen the littleness of man or human nature in the course
of these few weeks past more clearly than ever before The
most bright and shining parts in such as could think and judge
with great accuracy, how small an obstruction in the human
frame may impair and reduce those faculties and clearly show
unto us how poor, weak and little we are of ourselves.

"*First-day the* 20*th* (9 *mo* 1801) —I may appear to some in
a low state, as indeed I am, but let such as judge of me judge
in the Light I feel disposed to do justly, love mercy, and
walk humbly I cannot delight myself at this time with transitory things, my desire is to be possessed of something permanent It is not any outward concern that affects my mind I

consider myself as one possessed of all the outward comforts, such as a beloved wife and children in whom I have much delighted, and the necessaries and conveniences of this life plentifully, and my business in a prosperous way In all these things I desire to be a just steward, that when called upon I may give up with joy, being ready

"I have been on the stage of action for many years past, have given up much of my time to serve other people, and hope I have always done to the best of my judgment When I have been called upon to decide in matters of controversy, or to assist in any business, I have thought my mind often very serene and quiet, possessed of much calmness and capable of thinking with some degree of steadiness

"The serenity of the mind much depends on the health of the body, though the mind may be disturbed and affect the body and both thereby be disordered . . .

"*Second-day the* 21*st* (9 *mo*. 1801) —Towards twelve o'clock Abraham Pennell and Jacob Hibberd came to see me and stayed till after three. Spent the time I hope to profit as well as agreeably They are friends in whose company I should wish to spend more time than, perhaps, may soon be convenient

"*Third-day the* 22*nd* (9 *mo* 1801) —My dear wife is also very poorly, she hath been a great comfort to me in this my weak state Indeed I have thought her my principal support on this earth as an individual My prayer is that the Lord may be her support and preserve her in safety.

"In the course of my late and present exercises and afflictions both of body and mind I think I have gathered some experience. In a weak state of bodily health where the nerves are affected it is most proper to guard against everything that would discompose the mind; and even when disagreeable objects do present use all endeavours to guard against showing any discomposure, put on the best face we can and try to carry it off with pleasantry . .

"*Sixth-day the* 25*th* (9 *mo* 1801) —My dear wife and self went to Hugh Lownes' about ten o'clock and continued till about five. I was a good deal unwell much of the time, but got better towards evening   Caleb Lownes came there towards evening, we had conversation on various subjects, I hope to some degree of edification, and I desire to profit thereby

" Perhaps it may be best for me to use as much exercise as my strength will bear as I do not know of any method more likely to succeed   Although of ourselves, in a spiritual sense, we can do very little, it may be right to use every endeavour to promote both spiritual and temporal health by a right exertion of the means put in our power

" *Seventh-day the 26th* (9 mo. 1801) —   . . I have had some very cordial visits which were so reviving that perhaps it may be easier to conceive than to express   As I am rather better than common this evening I feel gratefulness, and considering the many obligations and engagements I feel myself under do earnestly desire to be possest of a heart full of gratitude, likewise of strength and resolution to do what service I can to mankind universally. . . .

" I feel free to make some remarks wherein I think I have mist it   I have often looked at the situation of some young people wherein I have had a thoughtfulness of having some friendly conversation and giving some cautions where I have thought they were in danger, and by letting the opportunity pass, it may be that I have not been that faithful watchman to give warning when I should have done so   .

" *First-day the 27th* (9 mo 1801) — . . . About 11 o'clock brother George Ashbridge and Jane Ashbridge came to see me, and from meeting Abraham Hibberd and Jeffry Smedley Good and agreeable company seems to cheer the mind, and cheerfulness in innocence may help the body   .

" *Second-day the 12th* (10 mo 1801) —Rested well and am in good health   Spent last evening and this morning agreeably with my cousins Joseph and Jane Walker   A cloudy morning and damp, but it is warm towards noon.   Oh, how thankful I wish to be for the health, strength, and serenity of mind which I enjoy, blessings far exceeding great riches.

" *Second-day the 19th* (10 mo 1801) —I have had the company of Sarah Levis Sen[r] and Sarah Levis, Joseph's wife, very agreeably this afternoon   also Joseph Levis and Nathan Garrett

came towards evening, and Mary Lawrence, whose company
was pleasant   I rode a little after dinner but was very unwell
Sarah Levis Sen' had something very encouraging to communicate, and as she had passed through a scene of affliction
similar to mine her affectionate sympathy and concern for my
support and preservation was truly consoling.   I desire to
return the visit, and hope to be thankful for the favor

"*Fourth-day the 21st* (10 *mo* 1801)—If I do recover may it
be a part of my covenant or resolution to visit the afflicted and
seek or strive to help and comfort the orphan   Now let me
make one remark, I believe it doth happen sometimes that children whose parents are deceased are under the care of such as
very much oppress them and require more from them than their
constitutions can well bear, whereby they are often so borne
down that their spirits get sunk or their health destroyed that
they are wretched while they live, and at the same time many
quiet people will behold them in silence   What I wish at present is to awaken the attention of such as may have an opportunity of beholding oppression to step forward in a mild and
entreating manner and use such endeavours as may be in their
power to prevent the oppression or hard usage that sometimes
happens

"I myself wish to examine whether I stand clear of requiring or exacting more from such as I may have as hirelings
or children or anything to do with than what is right   Let
people first look to themselves and endeavour so to conduct as
that they may be clean-handed so that they may step forward
and help others.   A gentle hint to the oppressor might sometimes be of great use to the distressed   Let us all seek for a
right qualification to help the needy

"*Fourth-day the 28th* (10 *mo* 1801).—My desire is that while
I am recommending the virtue of temperance to others I may
know the benefit of it myself   I hope to be truly cautious how
I live, and govern my own passions and appetite   Oh, that the
Supreme Being may enable me to be firm in my intentions con-
cerning temperance and every other virtue

"*Seventh-day the 31st* (10 *mo* 1801)—   Now I desire,
pray and beseech the Almighty to fix the things of this world

in their proper light, that the things of this world are only things of time, transitory and fleeting, and that my mind may be fixed to lean upon something permanent and durable with a confidential dependence that the Lord will be my support. Oh, that I may enjoy calmness and serenity, let things of this world be as they may.

"*First-day the 1st of* 11 *mo.* (1801).—I went to meeting to-day which I have not done for some weeks past; it was what I much desired and truly it was grateful to me to see the faces of many friends in that place. I think I enjoyed as much calmness and serenity of mind during the solemnity thereof as I had any reason to expect, though there was considerable interruption by the untimely coming of some of our members and some others. . . .

"O Lord, I pray Thee open my understanding and show me the way wherein I ought to go. I desire to be subject to Thy will and requirings; I pray Thee to stain the things of this world in my view so that I may not be improperly concerned at losses or disappointments here, but be wholly given up and willing to give up all I have so that it may be as my meat and drink to do Thy will. . . .

"*First-day the 8th* (11 *mo.* 1801).—We went to see sister Rebecca Lownes who, we had word, was very low. We got there a little after ten o'clock and found her very weak, she seemed to take little notice and did scarcely speak while I was there. I returned home near the middle of the day and left my dear wife there. . . .

"Oh, that I may be inspired with a heart and willing mind to do justice in its fullest extent, to love mercy and be merciful and walk humbly, living in a state of true humility. O Lord, I pray Thee instruct me in that which I ought to do.

"*Past six o'clock.*—I went down to Hugh Lownes' this afternoon after three o'clock. I found sister Rebecca very low, to appearance near her end: I returned home with my dear wife near evening.

"*Second-day the 9th* (11 *mo.* 1801).—I was informed of the death of sister Rebecca about twelve o'clock to-day just as I was getting ready to go there. I went to the house and found a number of people there, but I felt so low, depressed and unfit for being of much use among them that I returned home as soon as I could without being noticed   After I returned I stirred a good deal about but felt thoughtful

" I feel much concerned that all things which are my proper business may be conducted in a right manner while I have time and opportunity, that I may regulate my affairs and set my house in right order, that I may impress something on the minds of my children that may promote their peace and felicity here, and especially that they may be encouraged to use the right means to strive to be admitted hereafter into a state of joy and peace by having faithfully done the will of their Creator

" As my sister Rebecca is deceased I feel concerned for her children, and if I live I hope to be in some degree useful to them

" But I leave it as a charge to my children to be good examples to them and endeavour to cultivate their plainness, sobriety and real good in a religious sense.   Caution and counsel in meekness and wisdom probably may have a good effect "

This charge was faithfully kept   Rebecca Lownes left two sons and two daughters, — Joseph, Benanual, Elizabeth, and Sidney. Joseph married and had a large family of children, residing always on his father's place   His brother Benanual was a bachelor and lived with him   Elizabeth and Sidney, after their father's decease, lived together on a farm of their own, conducted their affairs with ability, and had a pleasant, attractive home   They were agreeable in person, gentle and refined in manners, amiable and affectionate, and examples of true Christian living

The descendants of Joseph Rhoads and Rebecca Lownes keep up their friendly relations with one another, and a grandson of each now sit side by side at the head of Springfield Meeting.

" *Seventh-day the* 14*th* (11 *mo.* 1801) —I rode into the woods towards evening in order to examine and search out such chestnut timber as would not do well for rails and have it cut for coal wood so that it might leave the room for more, and perhaps better, to grow   My judgment is that it is rather best to cut away the old scrubby and twisty chestnuts and sell the wood, as I observe it in common sprouts plentifully from the stumps, though I wish to be careful to commit as little waste as may be. If proper attention is paid to those things and some of the young stuff trimmed I apprehend a considerable advantage would arise to them that may be the owners in some years to come. As our forefathers have done for us also let us endeavour to do something to the advantage of succeeding generations. But in all our actions and conduct strive to do that which is just and right, so that no one can say we have used oppression or fraud in gaining or procuring an inheritance for our children. Mark the perfect man and observe the upright, for we read the end of such is peace.

"I have thought that a man of strict justice and integrity would have no inclination to defraud, but would do what appeared to him to be right with a willing mind from a true principle, having no inclination to do otherways, not for the reward's sake only, but would have no desire to do otherwise.

"*First-day the 15th* (11 *mo.* 1801).—Oh, that the Lord would be pleased to grant me the favor of His living presence and fix my confidence secure in Him, so that neither heights nor depths, nor anything else might be able to hinder me.

"*Second-day the 16th* (11 *mo.* 1801).—I do earnestly wish that I may not be disturbed with overanxiousness about worldly concerns either profit or loss. I believe it is very proper and right for mankind while in health and strength suitable to be moderately industrious and careful to provide a living or things to live on for themselves and family : and whatsoever they may be blest or entrusted with more to use it in a way most likely to do good to them that may succeed them, or apply it for the good of the needy as far as to them may appear right. But if they wish it to be of use to their offspring it will be prudent in them to instruct them in the paths of piety, equity, justice, prudence, frugality, charity, and every virtue, and then there may be hopes of a moderate portion of riches being a blessing to them. But riches given to children who are void of virtue is not likely to be of much use to them.

"*Third-day the 17th* (11 *mo.* 1801).—I feel very desirous to get into my usual way of going among my friends and doing such services for the good of such as stand in need as may be in my power.

"*Fourth-day the 18th* (11 *mo* 1801) —   . I desire to stand ready for any service that may be appointed in Divine wisdom for me   I hope no worldly concern may ever hinder me from doing the will of Him that hath thus far preserved and supported me   All that I have I have received. my worldly affairs seem to have been blest almost beyond what I would have looked Oh, that I may be a just steward and do the will of Him, who hath been thus bountiful unto me, do what is right with a willing mind and for righteousness' sake, not only for the reward, but also for the good of my fellow-creatures

"*Sixth-day the 20th* (11 *mo* 1801) —In the course of many years in which I have been an observer of men and times I have discovered something like a disposition too common for people to try to gain points, or have things settled to their advantage or liking too much without being fully convinced of that principle of doing as they would be done by.   But for some time I have been fearful of standing for what I thought was my right in some cases lest I should gain more than what was my due and thereby commit an evil   My desire is rather to suffer wrong than wrong any individual   When we judge for ourselves we see all in our favour, and perhaps interest may swerve us from doing or judging right, it is therefore safest to say as little in our own defence as the nature of the case will admit, and carefully guard against using a deception or wrong means to gain a cause, and rather be contented with less than our due than use improper means even to gain a right

"*First-day the 22nd* (11 *mo* 1801) —I went to meeting to-day and sat very comfortably "

Here it may be admissible to refer to the meetings of Friends at Springfield. The meeting for worship held there was among the earliest established in Pennsylvania, and belonged to the district of Chester Monthly Meeting; it was frequently visited by ministers of the Society travelling on religious service

The house was built of stone partly dressed, and had a curb roof, stone arching over the doors and windows, a flight of stone steps to the door in the gable-end opening between the ministers' galleries, a flag pavement along the front of the house, on to which opened two doors, with corresponding doors at the opposite side of the building.

The interior was originally finished with a ceiling arching up to the roof, a ministers' gallery running the length of the north gable-end, and a youths' gallery over the farther end, supported by wooden pillars and reached by a staircase inside. The whole was capable of seating several-hundred persons, and altogether a very respectable edifice and more picturesque than most of the modern meeting-houses of Friends near Philadelphia. The grounds around were large, grassy, and well planted with oaks and other trees. The burial-ground for the members and their connections was inclosed by a low stone wall. As an indication of the distinction that color made in those earlier days, and also of the thoughtful care of the Friends in providing for those who could not provide for themselves, it is interesting to recall a small " graveyard," fenced in by itself and shaded by a great oak-tree, where those of African descent were laid to rest.

I regret that the old meeting-house was taken down somewhere about the fifties of our century, and a new one erected to promote the comfort of the congregation. With the increased knowledge of architecture now at command it might have been so renovated as to serve its purpose well and retain past associations.

" *Fifth-day the 3rd of* 12 *mo.* (1801).—Joshua Lawrence came here and mentioned the following recipe for a cough: viz. Elecampane root, indian turnip, hoarhound, ground ivy, fennel seed, liquorice stick, in equal proportions mixed together. Take a table-spoonful of the mixture made into tea, take a tea-cup full of the tea in a morning fasting, and noon and evening; as he grew better he omitted taking at noon. This he had from Doctor Benual and supposed he had received much benefit from the use of it.

" *Sixth-day the 4th* (12 *mo.* 1801).—I suppose according to the account that is entered of my birth I was yesterday evening fifty three years of age. I lived with my parents chiefly till I was nearly thirty years of age in a single state and much of my

time in my father's service I have been married upwards of
twenty-two years, my principal business has been tanning and
currying in which I have much delighted

"*Seventh-day the 5th* (12 *mo* 1801)—   I think I have
long and earnestly endeavoured to do that which is lawful and
right, and in some doubtful cases refused to take that which I
believed to be my due lest I should fall under condemnation,
and if there is anything in which I have erred and not made
restitution I pray the Lord to ·put it into my power to do
justice where I have missed

"I cannot say that I wish for the reward of the righteous
without doing the works thereof .   .

"O Lord, I pray Thee let me die the death of the righteous,
and let my last end be like theirs I desire not to deceive myself, but that all things may be put in order before me and
opportunity put into my hands, as I have expressed to do that
which I ought to do

"I have looked for better days and hope continually to keep
striving never, never do I intend to cease until I obtain, or
finish my course here

"*Third-day the 8th* (12 *mo* 1801)—I had a middling good
night of sleep and rest, not much cough, though the soreness
in my breast is very alarming   O Lord! I pray thee
prepare the way wherein I have to go and guide my steps in
safety Furnish me with a willing heart and obedient mind to
comply with all Thy requirings Oh, fix my delight in doing
Thy will above every other joy

"*Fourth-day the 9th* (12 *mo* 1801)— .   . Moderate exercise
I believe to be good for health My advice to my connections
is to follow some business, though not more than they can
manage well. to follow such business as that their labour may
be of use both to themselves and mankind in general, and fix
not their affection too much on any earthly treasure

"*Fifth-day the 10th* (12 *mo* 1801).—I sometimes walk much
after supper till very near bedtime, and go to bed with my mind
as calm as possible, with desires that the Lord may compose
every roving thought and grant me rest and sleep   I feel
thankful for the favours which I have of late received of sweet

sleep, and, if I am worthy to use the expression, of Divine protection.

"O Lord, I pray Thee to enable me to return thanks for the many favors received; and to bless the rod which hath chastised me. I hope to be instructed by the afflictions which I have undergone. O Lord, I desire to bear all the chastising which Thou seest meet to bring upon me, only let Thy presence go with me and support me therein.

"*Third-day the 22nd* (12 *mo.* 1801).—I desire to do the best I can both for myself and all others, to promote peace, quietness, harmony, good-will, justice, temperance, health, love and every other virtue and such things as may lead thereto. . . .

"*Fifth-day the 31st* (12 *mo.* 1801).—This is the last day of the year. Oh, that I may be preserved in humility and confidence, and trust all my cares with the Author of my being with full assurance of His care and preservation of me now and forever.

"*Second-day the 4th of the First mo.* 1802.— . . . If I should be removed off this stage of being without expressing much more on the subject of a future state I am free to state that according to my present apprehension I feel not anything like condemnation. But what I wish for is justification, sanctification, and to know redemption, which is what I seek after, and never intend to cease striving until I find it, or pursue it during my time here. . . . They that seek shall find.

"*First-day the 10th* (1 *mo.* 1802).—I am convinced of the importance of moderate exercise to strengthen the nerves, if there is bodily strength to use it. Observe temperance in eating and drinking as well as in action with strict care to endeavour to keep a quiet and serene mind. In order thereto it is sometimes needful to pass some things which may not be exactly agreeable without much notice, except we think it is a duty to warn or caution the offender: and then let it be done in such manner as to endeavour to convince the understanding with calmness and composure. But shun and avoid useless controversies where no good is likely to follow.

"*Fifth-day the 4th of the 2nd mo.* (1802).—I sat meeting agreeably, had the company of several friends from meeting, viz. Roger Dicks, Daniel Sharpless, Abraham Pennell and John Powell being of the school committee; and Edward Fell came after dinner. Their company was very agreeable. Samuel Pancoast and myself also (went with them) to our school in the afternoon and spent some time in noticing the order and conduct of the school: towards the close we had a time of silence and I hope it may be called a religious opportunity: our friend Roger Dicks had some things to communicate tending to encourage both the teacher and the scholars to a perseverance and attention to a life of piety and virtue. On the whole we thought the school in a good degree orderly conducted. . . . I may call this a day of favor; have been as well in health or better than some time of late; also had such agreeable company that it was I thought reviving every way.

"*First-day the 7th* (2 *mo.* 1802).—Was at and sat meeting with considerable satisfaction. . . . My dear wife set off for Concord Quarterly Meeting this afternoon about half after two o'clock, since which I was at Joshua Lawrence's and spent some time there agreeably: Clement Lawrence and Elizabeth Maris were there.

"This day has been moderate and some cloudy. I have been thoughtful of my lonely situation as I do not expect my dear wife to return till Third-day night or Fourth-day, but I hope the Lord will strengthen and support me.

"*Third day the 9th* (2 *mo.* 1802).—A man called in and sat a little. I had been informed that he was one who set light by the Scriptures; he proffered to lend me some of T. Paine's writings but I excused my accepting, believing them to be hurtful. I may remark that it is unsafe to enter into familiar conversation with such as hold principles contrary to the Scriptures of Truth. In short I believe it best not to search too curiously into or after such things as we do not understand or hath not been made known unto us, but endeavour faithfully to perform and do according to the knowledge we have received, and as much as may be shun the company of such as would weaken this faith, and when we discourse on religious subjects do it in an orderly and becoming manner.

"*Fourth-day the 10th* (2 *mo.* 1802).—I slept very well last night; the weather is fine; temperately cool. My dear wife returned from Quarterly Meeting last evening between seven and eight o'clock.

"*Second-day the* 15*th* (2 *mo.* 1802).—I desire to be thankful for the health and quietude of mind and body which I have enjoyed this day.

"*First-day the* 28*th* (2 *mo.* 1802).— . . . I may just remark that for such as are, or have been, reduced in body and mind and wish to get along in calmness, I believe it is most safe to be very careful in all their words, thoughts, desires and actions not to require things that appear unreasonable; to endeavour to cultivate love, harmony and goodwill with all mankind, but in an especial manner with such as our situation in life hath placed us amongst; and endeavour to be contented with the conduct or management of our business when it is done by people that use some endeavours to give satisfaction and appear obliging although it may not be exactly as we once could have done ourselves.

"But remember we are not always to continue here and our possessions of course will fall into other hands and belong to others, therefore let us possess these things as not coveting them. . . .

"*Seventh-day the* 13*th* (3 *mo.* 1802).—John Parrish was at our house: we went to Henry Lawrence's in the afternoon and staid, perhaps, an hour and a half: I have had much satisfaction in his company though I have not been so well as at some other times."

John Parrish was at meeting with him the next day. Subsequently he had some weeks of trying illness, and records his concern about some business that he had entered into for the benefit of other persons, such as building a house for John and Leah Farr, his executorship in the estate of Henry Effinger, and his care as guardian of Elizabeth, Sarah, and Rebecca Gibbons. Should he not live to see all those affairs settled, he requested that his friends Abraham Pennell and David Pratt would assist on his behalf. After recovery, he writes,—

"*Third-day the* 30*th* (3 *mo.* 1802).—I wish to be thankful for the health and composure I (now) enjoy. The cool weather we have had of late I apprehend has conduced to my recovery, though I wish to attribute all to the great Physician, whose Divine presence, protection and support is, above all, what I crave and secretly desire. . . .

" *Sixth-day the 9th* (4 *mo.* 1802).—I enjoyed a blessed night of sweet sleep for which favor I desire to return thanks. . . .

" *Fifth-day the 22nd* (4 *mo.* 1802).—I lay awake considerably, though I may call it a tolerable night's rest, and have been brave through the day : was at meeting which was our preparative, and had great satisfaction. Truly I wish to bless and adore the Author of such favors and humbly pray for a continuance thereof. . . .

" *First-day* 5 *mo.* 2*nd* (1802).—I feel very desirous of getting into that resigned, quiet and humble state of contentment as to be perfectly satisfied with everything that is permitted to befall me. The mind being of a very active nature appears to be, when awake, almost continually pursuing some object, or searching into something out of reach. But when the body is weak it often fixes on the most disagreeable subjects that either have happened, or probably may happen. My earnest desire is to be so redeemed from all worldly things as to look beyond them, and after doing what may appear right humbly submit to what may happen with a mind unshaken.

" O Lord! I pray Thee to stain all the treasures of this world so far in my view as to fix my thoughts and delights and pleasant contemplations on Thy royal law, therein to meditate with composure and full assurance of Thy notice and heavenly regard. . . .

" *First-day the 9th* (5 *mo.* 1802).— . . . I wish such as consider me a friend of theirs and see it right to counsel and advise my remaining family would use such freedom in the same manner they would wish their friends to do towards their children &c. after their decease. As ye would other men should do unto you or your offspring do ye also. If I had spent more time in religiously cautioning and advising the younger people than I have done it would have added to my present prospect of having done more service than I have, although I have spent much time in the outward affairs of many people. . . .

"*Fourth-day the* 12*th* (5 *mo.* 1802).— . . . My desire is to do, suffer, and perform all things here that are consistent with the will of the Almighty, so that I may know His will concerning me and may know myself fitted and prepared for His kingdom of felicity and joy.

"*Fourth-day, Sixth mo.* 2*nd* (1802).— . . . Though I know I have deviated and fallen short of steady attention or perseverance in the paths of true virtue, yet I have the consolation that I do not know that I have ever drawn an individual into any iniquity or sin: where I have erred I have stood alone or at least as far as I know have not been the occasion of leading another into any wrong. Neither can I charge myself with willfully or designedly ever having wronged mankind out of one shilling, neither do I remember ever having been tempted to want or covet the property of another contrary to their wish or willingness. But I believe I may say I have given up many pounds where I have really thought it due to me, but from a fear of falling short of doing right and to enjoy sweetness of mind and justification of conscience I have given up in many doubtful cases rather judged against my interest. I cannot say that if I had these twenty five years past to live over again that in the general I should mend it by a second trial. . . .

"*Fifth-day the* 3*rd* (6 *mo.* 1802).—I was at meeting; it rained as we went and much of the time till we returned. I went in much weakness though I enjoyed as much satisfaction as I could expect. I have repeatedly been thoughtful when I have got to meeting whether it would not be the last time. However, if the Lord will be pleased to enlighten my understanding to see the way with that clearness that I have long and ardently desired, oh, then I trust all would be light and joy. I feel a submission to the greatest humility or lowest office of any of the Lord's servants, or any performance that He may require of me, only that His presence may go with and support me, and manifest His requirings. . . .

"*Third-day the* 15*th* (6 *mo.* 1802).—I have thought that person whose justice, virtue and good works were only performed for fear of future punishment could not feel that justification, or have that well-founded hope of the full and happy reward equal with him who from the real principle of justice, love and integrity acted not from fear of suffering so much as from a real grounded principle of truth and equity, having no inclination to do a wrong act even if they had no prospect of being accountable therefor.

" The right education of youth appears to me at this time to be one of the greatest affairs, and one of the most probable means of promoting their happiness even in this life, and of preparing them to seek with meekness, love and humility for that which is to come.

" What I mean by right education is to endeavour to preserve them in innocency and strive to inspire their tender minds with the love of every virtue, truth, humility, temperance, frugality, reasonable industry, and all such things as would fit them to go along in a smooth, easy, quiet way. I believe it to be a delicate thing to preserve the youth from the two extremes of fixing ideas in them which may occasion them to think higher of themselves than they ought to think and copying after such as pursue vanity, high-mindedness, and such things as do not make for peace and quietude, which I wish to promote ; and on the other hand there is a danger of keeping those under our care so much under the level as to beget mean and low ideas in them to accompany with low characters. As it is a natural consequence for young people to have companions therefore it may be best to fit them in outward garb, or appearance, so as to be in some degree an invitation to accompany with such as would be most agreeable to us. It has been remarked that some things nearly alike in nature are attracting, and in company-keeping I think it commonly happens that we imitate such as we love to be with : and I believe it may happen that people may be almost necessitated to keep company in the course of things that at first may be disagreeable, but by degrees at length become familiar, and at last they may become a party both in form and substance. Then how needful it is that we fix aright, and use all diligence to promote forming right connections.

" *First-day the 20th* (6 *mo.* 1802).—I went to meeting ; Nathan Smith was there and had very considerable to communicate which I hope may have its use. He and his daughter called and took dinner with us on their way to Westtown.

"*Sixth-day 25th* (6 *mo.* 1802).—I may remark in this place that if I am removed from this state of being it is my earnest request and charge that no person may be imposed upon by my family, in a way that is known I should be uneasy with if I were living, but rather (let them) exceed in paying all people who have done work for me, or over-pay rather than under in doubtful cases.

"When people that are engaged in doing work for us get cross, pettish and are a disturbance to the family give them fair words, reason with them in truth and good-nature, pay them the utmost farthing, and part with them in friendship. It may be better to part with such as we cannot confide in, or if they cannot place confidence in us we had best not have them. There is a possibility of all of us missing in some things without design, even in our good intentions, wherefore I think it right to make considerable allowances where there is reason to believe others have intended well and there has been some miss.

"Let us measure that charity and forgiveness to others which we think in justice ought to be extended to us. But observe that it is no degree of goodness to have fellowship and unity with wicked or ungodly people: shun or be cautious in being much conversant with liars, drunkards, or profane swearers, slanderers or such as delight in telling or spreading evil reports of others, or sowing discord.

"He or she that can unjustly ridicule or falsify another to us probably will use us in like manner when opportunity serves. And when we hear these reports be very careful that we stand clear by not spreading them lest we become a party and fall also into condemnation. I believe many a truth had better die in oblivion than be told again, wherefore rather cover and conceal than expose, hoping to receive such measure hereafter as we give unto others.

"*Seventh-day the 26th* (6 *mo.* 1802).— . . . If I am necessitated to be unable to earn my living I hope it may be remembered that for many years great part of my time I was one of the labouring department and spent as little time in idleness as the

greatest part of mankind. I think I was as much of a labourer
as an overseer and wrought with a willing mind and delighted in
measure in it, therefore if I cannot do much hereafter perhaps
I have done a good share of the useful part of business.

"*Fourth-day the* 30*th* (6 *mo.* 1802).—As I have been in better
health and feelings for a few days past than in some other times
I do wish to walk worthy of the favor and return thanks to the
Author of my being therefor.

"*Third-day the 6th* (7 *mo.* 1802).—Was at the burial of old
Mary Levis turned of eighty years. There was a meeting held
after in which Sarah Talbert and William Canby both appeared
in the ministerial line I thought to edification, and I hope to the
satisfaction of all present. I left home in much weakness yet
sat meeting with great satisfaction and bodily ease and serenity
of mind. My earnest desire is to live here in such manner as
to impress some feeling thoughtfulness on my friends and connections that may beget a serious time at my funeral, at least
that I may die in their esteem and good liking.

"*Fifth-day the* 15*th* (7 *mo.* 1802).—I think it is the general
opinion of physicians that barks are strengthening and at times
I find a use in it. But my advice is to such as are blessed with
middling good health to just observe temperance in eating and
drinking and moderation in labour, strict attention to going
timely to bed in order to sleep and rest, and avoid meddling
with medical drugs until real necessity obliges them.

"*Seventh-day the* 17*th* (7 *mo.* 1802).—Went to the burial of
Ann Levis an ancient widow of Haverford. It was showery
and wetting much of the way both from the house and after
till we returned when we found Ellis Yarnall and his wife at our
house. They staid till near five o'clock which time we spent I
thought agreeably pleasant. They were on their way to his
brother Eli Yarnall's.

"*First-day the* 18*th* (7 *mo.* 1802).—I was at meeting with considerable satisfaction. With thankfulness and I hope humility
I may remark that I am much relieved from a numbness and
cramp in my thighs, legs, and soles of my feet for some weeks
past. Now if I can conduct myself so as not to administer new
cause for a return of that disagreeable feeling, and the Almighty

will preserve and strengthen me so as to get along in a middling way, my desire is to do and perform such things as may consist with my duty to myself and all mankind. . . .

"O Lord, instruct and support me! is the prayer of my heart. . . .

"*First-day the 25th* (7 *mo.* 1802).—I went to meeting : had as much satisfaction as I had reason to expect.

"This has been a very growing, fine time as to the outward and great crops of hay and grain have been gathered. The prospect looks something like what we read of where on certain conditions the Lord would pour out a blessing that there should not be room enough to receive it, if it meant an outward blessing. I am thoughtful whether we are in a condition fit to receive it as such, because crops are so great and the provision so plentiful that there appears a danger of people murmuring at the low prices of the markets and ready to fear they cannot dispose of the abundance. I wish us to be thankful receivers and endeavour to apply rightly what we have to spare, remembering that the earth is the Lord's and the fullness thereof, and that we are but stewards and must give an account. Oh, that we may rightly apply for instruction so as to dispose of these things according to the will of the great Giver. But if we squander and waste these things on our lusts and vain desires they may be far from anything like a blessing to us. These things may be considered.

"*First-day the 1st of* 8 *mo.* (1802).—I was at meeting with tolerable satisfaction. Eli Yarnall, Thomas Leacock and wife came home with us, and returned to an afternoon meeting appointed on account of Roger Dicks and Eli Yarnall. It was wet about the time appointed, though people continued coming a long while as it cleared off.

"*Second-day the 9th* (8 *mo.* 1802).— . . . If it is the will of the Almighty to call me hence at this time my prayer is that He may enlighten my understanding so far as to leave some comfortable expression with my near and dear connections whereby they may be informed of that clearness and foresight of eternal life and happiness which I have long and earnestly sought after. . . .

"*Seventh-day the 4th of* 9 *mo.* (1802).—I rode to Thomas Holland's this afternoon and spent some time with General Erwin agreeably. This has been one of my better days. . . .

"*Sixth-day the* 17*th* (9 *mo.* 1802).—Thomas and William Garrett called here on their way home from the burial of Nathan Garrett Sen'. I rode with them to Newtown towards evening as my dear wife had gone to see her sister Susanna Fairlamb who was unwell. We got home just before a shower of rain in the evening.

"*Third-day the* 21*st* (9 *mo.* 1802).—Elizabeth Morris was buried to-day ; she was an old woman, and had long been a neighbour.

"*First-day the* 26*th* (9 *mo.* 1802).—Was at meeting with tolerable satisfaction. Mary Worrall aged about eighty-eight years, widow of Peter Worrall, was buried at Springfield in forenoon. . . .

"*Seventh-day the* 2*nd of* 10 *mo.* (1802).—Was at Hugh Lownes' this forenoon to acquaint him of the burial of uncle Josiah Hibberd.

"*Fourth-day the* 6*th* (10 *mo.* 1802).—I got up rather sooner than common being informed that a man who had wrought for us had gone off, as I supposed, to his hurt. I immediately rode to where I found him beginning to indulge his intoxicating appetite : however I prevailed on him to return and go to work.

"Oh! the stupidity, that some men should be so base and foolish as to sacrifice their credit, interest, peace, happiness, and even life itself to gratify their carnal appetite in intoxicating liquor : and then they are unfit to have the care or command of a brute.

"While I am on the subject my desire is that every one may be warned to flee from the wrath to come by living sober, godly, self-denying lives.

"It appears to be the judgment of many eminent physicians that distilled spirits used in the common way are injurious to health, we generally allow it is a disgrace to be found in the intoxicating use of them, as also the almost ruin of many a man of great parts, also of their estates, and, perhaps, of their present and future happiness. . . .

"*Sixth-day the* 29*th* (10 *mo.* 1802).—James Wilson came here yesterday evening and staid till this. A man of considerable information and instructive discourse: he taught school at our school house a few years ago, and from his account hath taught in Maryland since in one place. Being queried with concerning the different dispositions of children he remarked that he found that the children he had last taught being the offspring of slave-holders had acquired a superiority of mind and overbearing strong wills which seemed to be at enmity with all good and were hard to be brought under restraint. . . .

"*First-day the seventh of* 11 *mo.* (1802).—I was at meeting. James Wilson, John Simpson and John Shoemaker were there and came with us from meeting, also John Hunt and wife, and went in the afternoon towards Concord. My dear wife and self went also towards Concord Quarterly Meeting. . . .

"*Third-day the* 30*th* (11 *mo.* 1802).—The friends who came with us from Monthly Meeting had a meeting at Springfield and returned with us after meeting, also Nathan Sharpless, Joseph Churchman and Caleb Lownes. These three days past I had comfortable satisfaction with being at meetings. . . .

"*Fifth-day the* 16*th* (12 *mo.* 1802).—I had a tolerable night though considerable time awake as it was very blustering, windy, froze exceedingly and continued remarkably cold through the day. I suppose it will be remembered as the cold Fifth-day. I was at meeting as well as common, or rather better. . . .

"*Fourth-day the* 29*th* (12 *mo.* 1802).—I spent some of the day in framing a petition or remonstrance in order to endeavour to put a stop to a tavern in Springfield as many of us believe it to be productive of evil consequences. . . .

"*Third-day the* 22*nd* (2 *mo.* 1803).—We had an account of the death of Hugh Ogden, an industrious man of a good character who will be much mist by his family. . . .

"*Fifth-day the* 24*th* (3 *mo.* 1803).—Several friends were at our meeting and came with us to dinner, viz. Samuel Smith, Martha Routh, Edward Garrigues and wife, Jonathan Evans and Rebecca Archer. . . .

"*Fifth-day the* 28*th* (4 *mo.* 1803).—I was at meeting: it was the marriage of Yeamens Gillingham and Sarah Lewis, daughter of John Lewis.

"*Fifth-day the 5th* (5 *mo.* 1803).—I was at the marriage of Samuel Davis and Eliza Maris; also spent much of the latter part of the day at Elizabeth Maris' with considerable satisfaction. John Parrish and Thomas Scattergood were there.

"*First-day the 8th* (5 *mo.* 1803).—This morning there was a good deal of snow on the ground and it continued snowing for some time. I was at meeting with satisfaction.

"*Fifth-day the 19th* (5 *mo.* 1803).—I was at meeting : sundry friends were there and came here after, viz. Mary Dickinson, Hannah Gibbons, John Truman, Benjamin White : and sister-in-law Phebe Valentine was here some days past and went to Newtown this afternoon. . . .

"*Second-day the 30th* (5 *mo.* 1803).—I went to Monthly Meeting and returned better. Joseph Malin and Rachel came with us from meeting. . . .

"*Second-day the 4th* (7 *mo.* 1803).—I was at the burial of Sarah, the wife of Thomas Levis, this afternoon. I believe her to have been a woman who had been concerned to be ready to leave this world, and she lately desired my wife to inform me that she was willing and waiting her change. I was acquainted with her when young and for many years she was of a cast-down disposition seeking solitude. Perhaps it may be safe to conclude that she was a woman who hath left a good report deserving of double honour, having sought the Lord early, and persevered therein.

"I have spent much of this cool day and pleasant weather in a solitary manner very desirous of more refreshing times though I wish to be thankful for the easy conscience which I hope I feel. My prayer and desire is that the Lord may be pleased to enlighten my understanding and enable me to get along the residue of my time in calmness, serenity, and confidential dependence and trust on acquaintance with Him.

"*Fifth-day the 14th* (7 *mo.* 1803).— . . . If I discover anything of impatience or imprudent expressions I desire such to be buried in oblivion and not repeated or remembered any more ; if any good can be gathered from what I have written it is well and all the other be obliterated.

"*Sixth-day the 15th* (7 *mo.* 1803).—Oh, that I may be preserved in humility and patience, trust and waiting, confiding in Divine support and aid, perceiving that no man can redeem another or give a ransome for his own soul. . . .

"*First-day the 24th* (7 *mo.* 1803).— . . . When I think of right and wrong I may give it as my opinion that with regard to dealings amongst men I should have no desire of wronging any one if I had no idea of future rewards or punishment, so that I have very little to war with in that respect, yet nevertheless in some respects I have met with many difficulties.

" I have desired to refrain from all things which in my own conscience I believed to be wrong; I have also wished not to transgress in such things as were forbid in Scripture. From anything that I have yet been able to discover a reasonable and moderate interest for the use of money looks just, and where I have acted as executor or guardian, or caretaker for others I have thought it a duty and almost a command to take it if there was no circumstance that forbid it. But in my own money where I could have had it I have long found my way hedged in. Perhaps a literal observation of the Scripture and a weak mind were all that appeared to forbid in some cases, though I believe if I had been a usurer I should have been a very liberal one : I have no desire that any should copy after me in that part but be governed by what they think just and right. I have thought it my duty to pay usury in full."

The words " usury" and " usurer" were used here in their old-time sense of interest, and one who accepts interest, now become obsolete.

There is little doubt that my grandfather was sensitive in some respects, but his close adherence to what he believed to be right in a moderate pursuit of business, in choosing to overpay in some instances instead of pressing his own just claims, his refusal to take interest for the use of his money, and his liberality to the poor, were honored by the Giver of every good and perfect gift. His outward affairs prospered, he had sufficient for all the requirements of his family and a generous hospitality, and left his wife and children in easy circumstances.

With all his scrupulosity he did not weakly give up his rights. A man who bought leather of him, when offering the money in payment, remarked, " I made all that by fiddling," supposing it would be refused because of my grandfather's well-known conscientiousness, but he calmly replied, " I made it by honest labor." His example in not taking interest bore good fruit many years after. Among others to whom he lent money in that way was George Bolton Lownes, a young man in the neighborhood, whose capacity for business enabled him to acquire a large estate. Remembering how he had been helped in his early life, he left by his will a considerable sum to be loaned in portions of five hundred dollars for a term of five years free of interest to such young men in the county as the trustees believed to be suitable recipients of such aid.

" *Sixth-day the 29th* (7 *mo.* 1803).— . . . Sister Tacy Davis and her two daughters came here this afternoon. I have enjoyed more satisfaction in the company of my friends than I could have expected; this has been one of my better days.

" *First-day the* 31*st* (7 *mo.* 1803).—Jesse Garrett and his wife came here from meeting, whose company was I hope of use to me.

" *Sixth-day the* 5*th* (8 *mo.* 1803).— . . . I want it to be noted that anything bitter, especially if there is spirits in it, ought to be cautiously used, or not used at all by people with nervous affections. A very little sound wine may on some occasions be of use, but probably oftener doth hurt. . . . Temperance in its full extent is a fine thing: attend to the calls of nature and don't fast too long, but observe timely and regular meals: do not force more than the stomach can digest, rather eat sparingly and if hunger should ensue before the next meal attend to it in moderation; long fasting is hurtful to enervated constitutions. . . .

" *Third-day the 9th* (8 *mo.* 1803).—I have thought sometimes the cravings of the appetite might dictate such things as are suitable to be used for health. Smoking tobacco was very agreeable some time back, but at this time I almost feel opposed to it and all kinds of liquor, so that my inclination seems within narrow bounds, wherefore according to my present feelings I may have but little temptation to deviate. I note this apprehending, if I live to observe the consequence, I may gather some experience. It has often been recommended to me by physicians and others, but my apprehension is that it hath not been of much use if any.

"*Sixth-day the* 19*th* (8 *mo.* 1803).—I desire humbly to be thankful for the easy, peaceful, and serene nights that I have had for some time past. Although the days have been almost a continued scene of weakness and low sensations yet truly when I consider that I am not in much pain and have a tolerable good conscience, and some other comforts I wish to not murmur, but rouse up and endeavour all in my power to make things pleasant and agreeable both to myself and friends, and earnestly engage in doing all things that I ought to do with a willing and obedient heart and mind. I do not count upon having much time, therefore desire to stand ready to enter into such service as may be pointed out as my proper business be it ever so mean or low. . . .

"*Fourth-day the* 24*th* (8 *mo.* 1803).—Abraham Hibberd called here this morning on his way to the burial of Isaac Lobb of Darby.

"*Fifth-day the* 25*th* (8 *mo.* 1803).—Jesse Garrett and Mary Garrett came here near meeting time on their way from the burial of I. Lobb. Mary went with our people to meeting and I had Jesse's company a good deal of the day and am well satisfied with their having been here.

"*Third-day the* 30*th* (8 *mo.* 1803).— . . . My attention is turned to the young: perhaps it may be as easy to contract good habits as bad, and the surest time to imbibe good sentiments is before bad ones have taken place. And I am convinced that a life of piety, virtue and good works is much more comfortable than its contrary, and in order to promote such a life my advice is for parents and caretakers to engage early in the instruction of such as come under their notice. Good habits early fixt are the surest: by early attention to what is right it will become as your meat and drink to do the will of your heavenly Father.

"Now I am not for fixing a perpetual gloom, believing the way to be sufficiently wide for to enjoy the most substantial delight and real, pleasant happiness this world can afford, there being liberty and society in the Truth which is pleasant and

agreeable, yea desirable   As happiness is our main object my
judgment is that by attending to these things, and observing
moderate industry, frugality and temperance as necessary means
to preserve health, the enjoyment of which added to a sound
mind and peaceful conscience are the greatest blessings this
world can give, I have not any doubt but such as attend thereto
will possess all things necessary.

"I remember in my youth one direction of my father to me
was when I went from home to do a certain piece of business,
in the first attend to do what I went about, and after having finished my real business my time, if any to spare, would be the
more at my command   There is something of a similitude to
this in that he or she, who in the first place observes every act
of virtue, temperance and good works, which may be compared
to seeking first the kingdom of heaven and the righteousness
thereof, and all other things being added thereto   .

"*Fourth-day the* 31st (8 mo 1803)—I spent part of the day
reading some in a book containing memoirs of Catharine Philips
It appears that she was exercised with many fears, insomuch
that she was weary in the conflict and ready to hope for death
rather than life and tried in her passage almost from youth to
old age, yet she was supported almost against hope in extreme
infirmity and weakness, which she called a nervous disorder

"There are bodily disorders which are closely connected with
the mind wherein life itself appears to be invaded   There are
also different dispositions and inclinations in mankind, it seems
that some have little to war with in getting along in the paths
of virtue, their inclinations and habits seem disposed to doing
justly and equitably in their transactions and perhaps they have
very little temptation to do otherways.

"On the other hand it looks as if there were some dispositions inclined to deceive, defraud and take advantage of their
fellow creatures   As I have looked at these things I have sometimes thought that when the individual acted uprightly only for
fear either of present or future punishment virtue was still
wanting   These may look like strange remarks to some, but in
order to remedy this last danger let us train up our children in
the way they should go that it may be fixt in their natures

and when they are old they will not be likely to depart there-from.

"*Seventh-day the 3rd of the 9th mo.* (1803).—I feel humbly thankful for the sweet and easy nights I often enjoy. I have a very great desire of being so far supported as to show forth more pleasantness to my family and friends, having lately been in such a dull, weak and low-spirited way. . . .

"We read that light is sown for the righteous and joy and gladness for the upright in heart. My prayer is that the Almighty may enable me to do everything agreeable to His requirings and instruct me in His will concerning me. I think I have no reserve to make, but feel disposed to surrender all. My desire is to stand as a humble servant waiting the command of the most beloved Master with full determination to comply therewith according to the ability I may receive. But if my day's work is over my prayer is that this light and joy may be experienced.

"*Third-day the 6th* (9 *mo.* 1803).—All our family except myself and son Joseph are gone to the burial of Abigail the wife of John Grim Jr. She was the daughter of my cousin Joseph Rhoads who has been deceased many years.

"*First-day the 11th* (9 *mo.* 1803).—Eli Yarnall and Abraham Pennell came with our people from meeting and continued till near evening. I had great satisfaction with their company.

"*First-day the 25th* (9 *mo.* 1803).—George and Joseph were at the burial of Sarah Bonsall at Darby: she was upwards of eighty years of age. She was my father's first cousin.

"*First-day the 2nd of* 10 *mo.* (1803).—I was at meeting with a degree of satisfaction. Roger Dicks had appointed to be there which undoubtedly occasioned a great number more than common to attend; he appeared largely in the ministry. . . .

"*Third-day the 11th* (10 *mo.* 1803).—I spent the morning in company with Peter Andrews and Jacob Maule very agreeably. They went to Newtown meeting, son James went with them.

"*First-day the 16th* (10 *mo.* 1803).— . . . I rode a good deal about the fields and woods in the afternoon as I often have done both for bodily health and observation or contemplation and meditation. Even the uncultivated parts of the earth seem

12

to show forth the kindness of the Author of nature: the lofty oaks, beautiful chestnut, hickory and a variety of other timber producing provender in abundance at this season for the little inhabitants of the woods, with the murmuring streams gliding through the same, all delightful and beautiful to behold, as also greatly useful to man with the fields producing in a bountiful manner.

"I have thought that if we had confined our wants more within the reach of what we might gather from our own farms we might probably have been a happier and hardier race of inhabitants in this highly favored country. But alas, how is it all the luxuries of the East that many can procure will scarcely satisfy. If we will continue to gratify and indulge ourselves in their delicacies, luxuries and poisonous liquors we must, or may peradventure, expect to partake of their plagues.

"*First-day the 23rd* (10 *mo*. 1803).—I was at meeting with much satisfaction, though our meeting at Springfield was small in number as there were several burials. My dear wife and son George were at the burial of William Malin at Providence: he was ninety five years of age; also Eleanor Jones was buried at Radnor aged nearly seventy four, and Ann Pennell, wife of Robert Pennel J^{un} at Concord: she was daughter of Joseph Gibbons.

"*Sixth-day the 25th* (11 *mo*. 1803).—I went to Philadelphia in the forenoon where I had not been for two years and five months past and settled some business agreeably and returned early in the evening. The day was fine and mild. . . .

"*Third-day the 29th* (11 *mo*. 1803).—I was at Chester and met Edward Hunter and David Pratt in order to settle our accounts as executors to the estate of Henry Effinger at the Orphans' Court, which we accomplished to satisfaction. . . .

"*Third-day the 17th of the 1st mo*. 1804.— . . . We had word that sister Tacy Davis was very low;* my dear wife and myself went there almost immediately and found her extremely weak and somewhat flighty in her mind and in great anguish. I believe her to be in a state wherein she hath no need of terror or fear of appearing before the just Judge, believing her sins

* A son was born on the 14th.

are forgiven from her having sought after the ways of justice and peace. A woman of a meek and humble spirit, my prayer is that the Almighty may be with her at this trying period.

" When I went into her sight she seemed to know me and in distress said ' What will become of us.' I was in some degree supported to say that I saw nothing to hinder our happiness, believing that the means most likely to attain thereto have been long and ardently pursued: my desire is to stand ready by having all my day's work done in the day time.

" *Fourth-day the 18th* (1 *mo.* 1804).—Soon after I returned on Third-day evening sister Tacy departed this life about six in the evening. My dear wife returned this forenoon, I was there in the afternoon. . . .

" *Sixth-day the 20th* (1 *mo.* 1804).—I was at the burial of my beloved sister Tacy Davis.* Eli Yarnall appeared in the ministry, I trust to the edification and great satisfaction of a crowded assembly: he came with us from meeting and spent the afternoon. Owen and Josiah Hibberd and John Pharis were here also.

" *Third-day the 24th* (1 *mo.* 1804).—We have more snow on the ground than has been a long time, perhaps fifteen inches on a level.

" *First-day the 29th* (1 *mo.* 1804).—I was at meeting: there was a large gathering as it was the burial of our ancient friend Lewis Davis, who deceased in his eighty eighth year. Eli Yarnall, Randall and Joseph Malin, Joseph Malin jr. and Rebecca Fairlamb were here from meeting.

" *Fourth-day the 1st of 2nd mo.* (1804).—Isaac Jacobs, William Milhouse and Caleb Maris came here yesterday and had a meeting at Springfield to-day.

" *First-day the 26th* (2 *mo.* 1804).—I was at meeting: Ann Mifflin and Jane Cresson were there and appeared in the ministry: they and John Folwell came with us from meeting.

" *First-day the 11th* (3 *mo.* 1804).—I was at meeting with real satisfaction therein and quietly about home the remainder of the day.

" Notwithstanding many low and deep probations which I

---

* Her husband was Joseph Davis; they lived in Marple, or near it.

have frequently experienced, I still have hope that better days are before me, days of joy and rejoicing, and am humbly trusting in that Being who hath I hope been my Preserver.

"Although I dare not say much of my experiences or establishment in Divine things I feel a degree of confidential trust that I shall not be numbered with the transgressors, knowing that I have long and ardently sought to do that which is lawful and right, not only for the reward, but for righteousness' sake, or from an inclination in my nature Divinely implanted to do justly, love mercy and be merciful: humble I think I have long been.

"*Sixth-day the* 23rd (3 *mo.* 1804).—John Simpson and John Parrish had a meeting at Springfield and went toward Chester.

"*Second-day the* 26th (3 *mo.* 1804).—I was at monthly meeting though not very well, but enjoyed considerable satisfaction. John Simpson and John Parrish were there, who both appeared in the ministry, also had sundry things to remark in the meeting for business which I wish may have its use.

"*Fifth-day the* 10th *of the* 5th *mo.* (1804).—I was at meeting at which was the marriage of Jacob Jackson and Elizabeth Ogden.

"*First-day the* 13th (5 *mo.* 1804).—Roger Dicks, Jeffrey Smedley and wife came with us from meeting, and went on to Willistown, as Roger Dicks had appointed an afternoon meeting there.

"*First-day the* 3rd (6 *mo.* 1804).—I was at meeting with much satisfaction. Abraham Hibberd and wife, Jeffrey Smedley and Deborah Passmore came with us from meeting. . . .

"*Second-day the* 11th (6 *mo.* 1804).—Davis Richards and Cyrus Lewis shingling the shed room. . . .

"*First-day the* 8th *of* 7th *mo.* (1804).—Some evil disposed person took off in the night thirty one yards of flax lining which had been left on the green. . . .

"*Second-day the* 20th *of* 8th *mo.* (1804).—I have been in better health for some days than common and hope to be thankful therefor. . . .

"*Second-day the* 3rd *of* 9th *mo.* (1804).—I was at W. Moore's *

* William Moore was husband of Mary Moore, whom I knew for many years. She took care of the meeting-house at Springfield, as I suppose her husband had done before.

in the morning, also at the grave-yard fixing on a suitable place for John Grim, who fell out of an apple tree on Sixth-day evening last and deceased yesterday: a short and sudden stroke to be removed out of time to eternity. . . .

"*Second-day the 24th* (9 *mo.* 1804).—I was at monthly meeting with satisfaction. Eli Yarnall appeared largely in the ministry (I trust) much to the edification and consoling of many friends. I thought it a good meeting. . . .

"*Fifth-day the 4th of* 10th *mo.* (1804).—I was at meeting whereat were married Asa Wilson and Mary Paist.

"*Second-day the 29th* (10 *mo.* 1804).—I was at monthly meeting. Arthur Howell was there and came with us and lodged.

"*Third-day the 30th* (10 *mo.* 1804).—I took Arthur Howell in the chair and we were at Haverford meeting, after which stopped at Amos Lukens' and dined: went from thence to Joseph Hood's, where I left Arthur and returned home.

"*Fourth-day the 31st* (10 *mo.* 1804).—I went to Joseph Hood's; from thence with Arthur Howell to Newtown meeting; called at John Lewis's and dined; Jeffrey Smedley and Caleb Maris were also there; then went with Caleb Maris and lodged, where we were entertained and treated with much kindness and respect.

"*Fifth-day the* 1st *of* 11th *mo.* (1804).—Went to Willistown meeting, called at Mordecai Thomas's and dined. From thence I went with Arthur Howell to Samuel Briggs' in Haverford on his way to Merion meeting, whence I returned home in the evening with satisfaction. . . .

"*Third-day the 5th of* 2 *mo.* (1805).—George was at the burial of Hannah Garretson. I was about home in tolerable health, as I have been some considerable time and hope to be thankful for the same.

"*First-day the* 17th (2 *mo.* 1805).—I was at meeting: received a letter from Leah Farr giving an account of the death of her husband and only son last fall of a violent fever which prevailed much in that country, Virginia.

"*Second-day the 25th* (2 *mo.* 1805).—I was at monthly meeting after which I went with Eli Yarnall to visit Roger Dicks, who was much indisposed."

Here the journal appears to have ended; the entries had become fewer and more brief within the last year. As his health had been improving, a more active life was resumed, so that, probably, time and attention were chiefly given to the performance of those religious, social, and domestic duties that impressed his mind during the long period of physical debility.

His desires, so often expressed, to do everything that might be required of him do not indicate a dependence on works, as the many prayers for instruction, assistance, and support clearly show. Looking to the Lord alone for help, his petitions were for preservation in humility, patience, lowly waiting on Him, and a firm trust in His love and mercy, well assured that no man can redeem his brother or give a ransom for his own soul.

Far from looking upon the Christian religion as being gloomy, he was constantly reaching forward to joy and happiness, and his loving spirit wished to leave with his family and friends only the impression of peace and pleasantness.

About four years after the last date in his journal some memorandums of his illness and decease were written by my dear father, Joseph Rhoads III., from which the following are transcribed:

" 1809. Fourth mo. 28th and Sixth of the week: cold. My dear Father was this day at Providence select preparative meeting, and sitting pretty long and having other business there to attend to came home unwell in the evening, having taken some cold before, I believe. He was very unwell on Seventh-day, having a high fever and being in pain, but slept on Seventh-day night.

" First-day Father was still very poorly and restless.

" Charity Cook and some others were at our meeting and came to our house and staid over night. Father rested but poorly this night.

" Second-day Father continued very unwell.

" Third-day I believe we thought Father some easier.

" Fourth-day Father seemed, I thought, rather better: he moved into the middle-room.

" Fifth-day he was very poorly, suffering much. I was several times in the room with him, having been in the room most of last night. I believe he got some sleep having taken some anodyne.

"On Fifth-day night I believe a considerable change took place in my Father. He had the few preceding days of this sickness been at times in considerable pain of body and his nerves much affected so that the fever which he had rendered him mostly restless and uneasy though sensible almost all the time.

"Towards Sixth-day morning it appeared as though he was drawing near the close: he became composed and more still, being quite sensible and, I hope, resigned to his heavenly Father's will. Expecting the time of his departure was nigh he was frequently exercised in prayer to the Lord, and appeared to have a comfortable hope, and faith to believe it would be well with him, and so quietly departed, near two o'clock on Sixth-day afternoon, the 5th of Fifth month 1809, aged sixty years and five months. He was buried on First-day forenoon following, his funeral being largely attended.

"He was a man useful in his day amongst many of those with whom he was acquainted in several respects, and generally esteemed by those who knew him. He was a man of great honesty and integrity, and conscientiously careful in his dealings amongst men. A very tender Father he was to us his children, governing in gentleness and mildness, and more by gaining the assent or judgment in a kind and friendly way than by positive command. Deeply and tenderly concerned he was for our present and future welfare."

He was remarkably social and affectionate, enjoying the company of his friends and relations and desirous to have his children near him. Could he have watched the course of his sons and daughters through life his heart would have been fully satisfied: from youth to age they walked in the ways he so ardently wished them to choose, and are now without doubt united to their loving parents, "a family in heaven."

Hospitable in welcoming and entertaining his guests, he was careful to return the kindness of those who came to see him by visiting them in their homes as far as he was able to do so, and frequently called upon his neighbors in a friendly and familiar manner, as he once said, " It does good if only to ride up to the house and inquire after their welfare."

At the time of her husband's departure my dear grandmother was in her fifty-first year. For the nearly twenty-one years that followed she honored his memory by the simplicity, dignity, and Christian loveliness of her daily walk and conversation, revered and beloved by her children, and esteemed by all who knew her.

During the last four or five years she was obliged to relinquish her wonted activity : rheumatism deprived her of the full use of her limbs, but her mind was unclouded, her judgment sound, and she still governed her household by the law of love, and drew around her relations and friends.

On the 9th of Second month, 1830, she peacefully passed from her home on earth to "a house not made with hands, eternal in the heavens," aged seventy-one years, four months, and nine days.

Some recollections of her and the residence to which she came in her youth, and which was contentedly occupied by her for more than a half-century, were written several years ago in a sketch hereafter inserted under the title " The Old Homestead."

My grandmother's brother and sister who survived her kept up their affectionate intercourse with her children as before. It was an event of some importance when Uncle George and Aunt Rachel Ashbridge drove down from the valley in their roomy carriage, with colored coachman, to make a circuit among their relations at the old place, Chestnut Bank, and at Ashley Farm. On some fine summer morning our aunt Thomazine Ashbridge would drive out in handsome style from her house,—in Arch Street, near Ninth, Philadelphia,—with her son William or Richard and her daughters Mary and Jane, to spend a day or more among their country cousins.

I seem still to have before me my aunt Susan Fairlamb's lively eye and slight figure enveloped in brown fur cape and muff of ample size. And Aunt Jane Downing always brought with her an atmosphere of spirited sociability; her Friend's costume of silk gown, clear cap and kerchief relieved of all stiffness by the touch of her own individuality.

CHAPTER XII.

THE EVANS AND BACON FAMILIES.

THE earlier part of the genealogy of my mother—Hannah Rhoads, *née* Evans—is taken from a work by Howard M. Jenkins, "Historical Collections," relating to the township of Gwynedd, in the county of Montgomery, Pennsylvania. It was settled in 1698 by immigrants from Wales (page 143 and farther):

"The origin of the Evans family in Wales is indicated by notes given on a following page by the late Mrs. William Parker Foulke, the ancestress of her husband having been the daughter of Robert Evans. Her facts are drawn from a very elaborate family document, prepared by the late Rowland E. Evans, son of Cadwalader Evans, of Philadelphia.

"It traces the descent of the four brothers of Gwynedd back to Mervyn Vrych, King of the Isle of Man,* who was killed in battle with the King of Mercia, A.D. 843.

"Mervyn married Essylt, the daughter and sole heiress of Conan Tyndacthivy, King of Wales, who died in 818 or 820. Both Mervyn and Essylt traced their descent from Lludd, King of Britain, brother of Cassivelaunas or Caswallon, the chief who resisted the invasion of Cæsar before the Christian era.

"Passing over a number of intermediate generations from Mervyn Vrych, the following may be noted.

I. David Goch, of Penllech, lessee of crown lands in Caernarvonshire, in the eighteenth year of Edward II.; living November 9th 1314; married Maud, daughter of David Lloyd, descended from Prince Gwynedd; had three sons, one being

---

* So stated in the manuscript from which this account was taken. It is probably a mistake, and should be Anglesey. Anciently Anglesey was called Mona and the Isle of Man Monapia or Monarina; both named Mona by Cæsar, I think. The early kings of the Isle of Man were of the same line as the Scottish kings for a time, and then a second came from a king of Norway.

II Ievan Goch, of Gramnor and Penllech, one of a jury
1352, owner of lands, as shown in titles of that age
Married Eva, daughter of Einion Cynvelyn, descended from Bleddyn, Prince of Wales, had two
sons, eldest being

III. Madoc, who appears in the Cwm Amwlch pedigree
as ancestor of the gentleman Ysbitty Evan in Denbighshire. His son was

IV. Deikws ddu, who married Gwen, daughter of Ievan
ddu (who traced his descent to Maelor Crwm, head
of the 7th of the noble tribes of Wales), had a son

V Einion, who married Morvydd, daughter of Matw ap
Llowarch, and had a son

VI Howel, who married Mali, daughter of Llewellyn ap
Ievan, and had a son

VII. Griffith, who married Gwenllian, daughter of Einion ap
Ievan Lloyd, and had four children, the third being

VIII Lewis, who married Ethli, daughter of Edward ap
Ievan, and had six children, the fourth being

IX. Robert, who married Gwrvyl, daughter of Llewllyn
ap David, of Llan Rwst, Denbighshire, and had by
her six sons and six daughters, the fourth son
being

X. Ievan, known as Evan Robert Lewis He was living
in 1601 He removed from Rhiwlas, or its neighborhood, in Merionethshire to Vron Coch, probably
in Denbighshire, and there passed the remainder of
his life In the genealogy of the Owen family, descended from his son Owen, it is said he was 'an
honest, sober man,' and was 'born near the end of
the reign of Queen Elizabeth.' He had five sons,
all taking for themselves, in the Welsh manner, the
surname ap Evan They were,—

I. John ap Evan,

II Cadwalader ap Evan,

III Griffith ap Evan,

IV Owen ap Evan,

V Evan ap Evan."

fifth son of Ievan, known as Evan Robeit Lewis, had four sons
born in Wales He and his wife and their sons appear to have
lived in Merionethshire and Denbighshire previous to the emi-
gration of the sons. They came to Gwynedd, Pennsylvania, in
1698 I have been told that each son brought ten thousand
dollars with him, which would enable them to settle handsomely in the new country Of these four brothers Thomas
was the eldest

THOMAS EVANS

He came to Pennsylvania in 1698 with his wife and older
children. They settled in Gwynedd, and must have had some
hardships to endure in those early days of the colony. History
relates that their first houses were built of logs, and that the
house of Thomas Evans was made of logs with the bark taken
off, indicating more care than usual in its erection

His first wife's name was Ann, and she was the mother of all
his children She departed this life at Gwynedd on the 26th of
First month, 1716

Thomas Evans married again, the 14th of Tenth month, 1722,
at Friends' meeting-house in Goshen, Chester County His
second wife was Ann Davies, and after this marriage he removed from Gwynedd to Goshen The record quaintly remarks that it would probably have been as well for him to have
remained in his own home at Gwynedd He was born in 1650,
and departed this life on the 12th of Tenth month, 1738, aged
eighty-seven years

The children of Thomas and Ann Evans were four sons and
three daughters, all of whom were probably born in Wales

The Welsh are profoundly attached to their country and their
language , they are proud of ancient ancestry and careful to
preserve family records The Welsh language has still "a
genuine literary as well as oral existence;" is "essentially the
same tongue that Cæsar and Agricola heard," a living link that
unites those distant ages with our own It belongs to the
Cymric branch of the Celtic language, of Indo-German origin
Many of the Welsh immigrants who established themselves in

parts of Delaware and Montgomery Counties belonged to old
and honorable families, and had good estates in their own romantic land, but for the sake of religious freedom sought new
homes in the genial colony of Pennsylvania, with its many
advantages of soil, scenery, and climate

True to their national character, they transferred to the land
of their adoption names familiar in their earliest years and endeared by long associations   It was well for them to do so as belonging to a people of whom it can be truly said, "Their name,
their language, and their honor they have preserved to this day "

Haverford (Aber fford, the ford of the confluence), Merion,
from Meyren, or Meirion, a prince who ruled over a part of
Britain in the eighth century, Radnor, so named since 1196,
Bryn-Mawr, the great hill, and many others distinctly mark
the localities whence came the early settlers of tracts lying on
either side of the Schuylkill River, northwest of Philadelphia

The sons and daughters of Thomas and Ann Evans, according to the records to which I have access, are as follow .

Robert, who was twice married   His first wife's name was
    Jane, the second, Sarah   His decease was in 1754
Hugh, who also married twice   His first wife was Catharine
    Morgan, the second, Alice Lewis   He deceased in 1772.
Lowry Lloyd   married Evan Jones, son of John Jones of Rad-
    nor, at Gwynedd Meeting-house, 8th of Fourth month, 1711
Owen was married twice   His first wife was Ruth Miles, the
    second, Mary Nichols   He deceased 1757
Evan married Elizabeth Musgrave, 13th of Seventh month,
    1713
Ellen married Rowland Hugh, yeoman, of Gwynedd, at
    Gwynedd Meeting-house, 31st of Fifth month, 1712
Sarah married Edward Jones, son of John Jones of Radnor,
    at Gwynedd Meeting-house, 25th of Sixth month, 1715

EVAN EVANS,

son of Thomas and Ann Evans, was born in Wales in 1684,
and came to Gwynedd, Pennsylvania, with his parents in 1698
He was married to Elizabeth Musgrave, at Haverford Meeting-

house, 13th of Seventh month, 1713. His wife was the daughter of Thomas Musgrave, a yeoman of Halifax, England. His home was by the mill on the Wissahickon, owned in 1884 by Henry Mumbower. The children of Evan and Elizabeth Evans were,—

JONATHAN, born 1714, married to Hannah Walton 1740, deceased 1795;

Abraham, born ——, married to Lydia Thomas;

Daniel, born ——, married to Eleanor Rittenhouse, sister of David;

Barbara, born ——, married to Isaiah Bell;

Musgrave, born ——, married to Lydia Harry 1753, deceased 1769;

David, born 1733, married to Letitia Thomas 1755, deceased 1817.

Three other children are mentioned in the Gwynedd records: a daughter Hannah, who deceased in 1720; another of the same name, who deceased in 1745; and a son William, who deceased the same year.

Evan Evans departed this life the 24th of Fifth month, 1747. His will was dated 3d of Fifth month, 1747, and proved 3d of Eighth month following.

He bequeathed property to his sons—Jonathan, Abraham, Daniel, Musgrave, and David—and to his daughter Barbara. He mentioned his wife's uncle, Jonathan Cocleshaw, and appointed his wife Elizabeth and son Jonathan executors, with authority to sell the farm they lived on,—about two hundred acres. He appointed his brother Owen Evans, his cousin Thomas Evans, son of Owen, and William Foulke trustees for his children.

He was a minister of the gospel in the religious Society of Friends, and Gwynedd Monthly Meeting placed on record a memorial of him, which is printed in the fourth volume of "Piety Promoted," edited by William Evans and Thomas Evans in 1854, a copy of which follows:

"MEMORIAL OF GWYNEDD MONTHLY MEETING.

"Evan Evans, of Gwynedd in Pennsylvania, was born in Merionethshire, in the principality of Wales, in the year 1684, and came to Pennsylvania with his parents in 1698, under whom he received a sober, religious education. But being early in life convinced that a form of godliness without the real enjoyment of the quickening principle of grace and truth would not afford solid and lasting peace to his soul, he sought earnestly after it, and resigned his heart to the baptizing power of God, which fitted him for eminent services in the church.

" In his constant attendance at our religious meetings, he was a remarkable example of unaffected piety; for whilst he sat in silence, the earnestness wherewith his soul wrestled for a blessing was obvious in the steady, engaged appearance of his countenance. He was favored with an excellent gift in the ministry, which he exercised in solemn dread and reverence; and, as he always retained an awful sense of appearing in public testimony, he was particularly cautious and watchful not to presume to speak without assurance of a necessity being laid upon him, and equally careful to attend to the continuance of it; and therefore his ' preaching was not with enticing words of man's wisdom, but in the demonstration of the Spirit and of power.' His service was rendered more effectual by the distinguishing marks which he bore of 'an Israelite indeed, in whom was no guile,' adorned by a plainness and simplicity of manner in word and deed, with a zeal seasoned by divine love; and as he had large experience in the work of regeneration and the mysteries of the heavenly kingdom, as well as the snares of the world, he was thereby well qualified to administer to the states of the people.

" He travelled through many of the colonies of North America in the service of the ministry, in company with his relation and dear friend, John Evans. Their friendship was pure, fervent, and lasting as their lives, and their separation a wound to the latter, the remembrance of which he never wholly survived. He also frequently visited the several counties in Pennsylvania, and, more particularly, many of the adjacent meetings in their infancy, wherein his unwearied labors of love tended much to their comfort, growth, and establishment in the truth.

" He was religiously concerned for the support of the Christian discipline of the Society, and as he was always diffident of himself, he labored faithfully for the discovery of truth, and a disposition of mind to embrace it, whereby he was often enabled to lay 'judgment to the line, and righteousness to the plummet,' whether in reproof to the obdurate, or instruction and comfort to the penitent In visiting Friends' families, his service was great; for being endued with a spirit of discerning and the authority of truth, his advice was adapted, with great propriety and advantage, to the particular states and conditions of persons and families His conduct and conversation in common life adorned the doctrine he preached, being a good example of plainness, moderation, and uprightness of heart

"He was abroad in the service of truth when attacked with his last illness, and as the disorder was slow and tedious, he attended several meetings in the forepart thereof, in some of which his lively, powerful testimonies clearly manifested that the God of his youth, who had raised him up an instrument in His hand, and on whom he had relied all his life, continued to be his shield and support in the evening of his days and close of life, which was on the 24th of the Fifth month, 1747. He was buried at Gwynedd"

JONATHAN EVANS I. AND HANNAH (WALTON) EVANS.

Jonathan Evans was the eldest son of Evan and Elizabeth Evans, of Gwynedd, Montgomery County, Pennsylvania, and was born in the year 1714

His early life gained the confidence of his father, who appointed him, in connection with his mother, executor of his will

He established himself in Philadelphia as a wine-merchant, and on the 19th of Fourth month, 1740, married Hannah, daughter of Michael Walton, of the same city

Their residence was on Dock Street, at that time one of the finest localities in the town Tradition relates that they lived in a free and generous style, and I well remember many articles of handsome plate and elegant china inherited by my grandfather Evans, that would now be considered valuable family treasures, but were then scarcely appreciated.

As the gradual abolition of slavery did not begin in Pennsylvania till 1780, their household service was performed by negro slaves Two of them continued in their employment and under the care of the family till after the decease of my great-grandfather, and I have often heard my mother and her sister speak of Cæsar and Sela They were husband and wife, and Sela had the reputation of being the best cook in Philadelphia No doubt her skill contributed largely to the family festivities My great-grandfather and a number of other gentlemen were in the habit of meeting socially at each other's homes, where they had a handsome supper provided, and naturally preferring the best entertainment, their choice led them most frequently to the house of Jonathan Evans on Dock Street.

In a large family Bible, published in London " By John Baskett, Printer to the King's Most Excellent Majesty, and by the Assigns of Thomas Newcombe, and Henry Hills, deceased, in 1722 and 1723," there are recorded, in a clear, strong hand, the day and hour of the birth of Jonathan and Hannah Evans's children,—two daughters and six sons,—viz

Elizabeth, born 1741 , deceased 1746

Samuel, born 1742 , deceased 1744

Joel, born 1743 , deceased in West Indies

Mary, born 1746 , deceased 1794

William, born 1749 ; supposed to have been lost at sea

Benjamin, born 1751 , deceased 1793

John, born 1753 , deceased 1798

JONATHAN, born 1759 , deceased 1839

Of these, Elizabeth deceased "August 26, 1746," and Samuel "August 22, 1744 "

Joel, William, and John are probably those mentioned in vol ii of Sabine's " Loyalists " There it states that " Joel (a merchant) and William and John, all of Philadelphia, and William of Philadelphia County, were attainted of treason, and their estates confiscated "

I feel assured that they never did anything that they could consider as dishonorable, but being determined Tories, they no doubt actively favored the English government after the Declaration of American Independence

Joel was a merchant, and went to the island of Jamaica to

reside. There he was married and had two children,—a son and daughter.

He was a remarkably handsome man, and appears to have had a very affectionate disposition. His wife deceased in rather early life, then his little daughter Grace quickly followed. Thus bereaved, his heart turned towards his native land, and preparatory to coming here himself he sent his fine boy of about twelve years to America, as the child's health seemed to require a more bracing climate. Providing every possible comfort for the voyage, including a goat that he might have fresh milk while at sea, he gave his son into the care of a captain in whom he had confidence. The captain proved unworthy of his trust: the child was neglected, the voyage was tedious, and the weather grew colder. The clothing furnished by the father was misapplied, and the poor boy landed in a thin suit adapted to the warm climate of Jamaica, ill and sad. His short career speedily ended, and the father, soon after hearing of his son's fate, died of a broken heart, away from his old home and his kindred.

I have often heard my mother and aunt Mary Evans speak of this uncle and the pathetic story of his life. Whether his estate was confiscated, or whether a similar treachery absorbed it to the one that robbed the son, I do not know, but there seems to have been nothing returned to the family in Philadelphia but some boxes of books that were placed in my grandfather's garret, and where my mother and aunt used to read them by the hour. From their account there were classical volumes among them, but not altogether such as their father kept on his own shelves, which were devoted to books of the most substantial character.

William, the third son, was a man of great physical powers. With his single hand he could do what two or three other men tried in vain to accomplish. His will was as strong as his arm, and he was such a determined royalist that when the Revolutionary War broke out he went into the British navy. It is supposed that he perished in some engagement, or was lost at sea, no account coming back to his father's family, and his estate was confiscated.

13

We have no record of the time of these events, nor of the year of Joel Evans's decease, but it is probable from other circumstances that all occurred before 1780.

Benjamin, the fourth son, lived in Philadelphia, and I believe that he continued the business in which their father had been engaged, both he and his son, Joseph R. Evans, being wine-merchants. He deceased the 1st of Third month, 1793.

Joseph R. Evans and his wife Margaret resided next door to my grandfather, and I remember the family well, as I knew them in my childhood. There were three sons—William, Edward, and Joseph—and one daughter, Elizabeth, who was much admired for her beauty and other amiable traits. She married her first cousin, Samuel Welsh, and was residing in Germantown, the beloved mistress of a charming home on School Lane, when my mother removed to Germantown in 1862.

Mary Evans, the only daughter who reached maturity, married Adam Hubley. She deceased 14th of Sixth month, 1794, in her forty-eighth year. I think her husband must have survived her some years, as I used to hear "Uncle Adam Hubley" frequently spoken of in our family. I believe they had no children.

John, the fifth son, went to New York to reside, and departed this life there in 1798, aged about forty-five.

In the record from which these names and most of the dates have been transcribed are two entries in the firm handwriting of my grandfather, Jonathan Evans. The first one is this:

"My father, Jonathan Evans, deceased the 3rd of 2nd month 1795, at his dwelling house on Dock Street."

Of his more than fourscore years, fifty-five of married life had been passed with the wife of his youth. Left alone in the old home, and feeling that age had touched her physical vigor, she was induced to accept the filial care of her son Jonathan, and removed to his house on Union Street near Fourth. Her servant Sela went with her, and was contented to remain with her mistress and enjoy the frequent visits of her husband Cæsar, who could not be accommodated with a home under the same roof. Our great-grandmother had her favorites among the children of her son's household, and was particularly attached

to Joel, the namesake of her own handsome son, and who
grew up with a similar dower of manly beauty.

Five years passed on; and then, as the leaves of another
spring were unfolding, the second entry in the record previously referred to tells us its brief story:

"My mother, Hannah Evans, deceased at my house the 23rd
of 4th month 1801."

And so her earthly day was over, and of her eight children
the youngest only survived the mother.

JONATHAN EVANS II. AND HANNAH (BACON) EVANS.

In the family record his history begins thus:

"Jonathan Evans, son of Jonathan Evans and Hannah his
wife, was born the twenty fifth January 1759, between three and
four o'clock in the morning, Fifth day of the week," in Philadelphia.

"His parents gave him a liberal education at the schools
under the care of Friends in this city; and possessing strong
mental powers and quick perceptions, he made considerable
proficiency in most of the branches of useful learning." *
Through life he cultivated an acquaintance with literature, and
was very exact in speaking and writing the English language,
keeping to the most approved pronunciation, giving the long
sound of i in either and neither, and being particular as to the
definite meaning of terms. This was done so naturally that it
has only been on reflection that I have become aware of it.

He learned the art of carpentry, an occupation that has had
a higher honor put upon it than any other, not excepting that
of "the grand old gardener and his wife." When of age he
engaged for a time in building, but subsequently merged the
business into the purchase and sale of timber for a few years,
and finally retired in comparatively early life. Whatever he
put his hand to was done in the most thorough manner; order,
punctuality, and accuracy seeming to be inherent.

Tall, handsome, athletic, with a good voice and exuberant
spirits, he was a favorite in the gay circle of his young com-

* Memorial of the Monthly Meeting.

panions, and in those early years indulged in mirth and con-
viviality   In his twenty-first year he accidentally met with a
copy of William Penn's "No Cross, No Crown"   The title induced him to look into it, and his eye caught the words "The
Light of Christ," but, seeing the subject was not to his taste, he
laid the book away   However, the phrase, The Light of Christ,
came again and again to his mind, and he took up the volume
a second time and examined its contents   This made such an
impression that it was followed by conversion and a new life.

Accepting the exhortation, "Whether therefore ye eat, or
drink, or whatsoever ye do, do all to the glory of God," he
withdrew from jovial circles and refrained from indulgence in
the luxuries of his father's table, confining himself to a plain,
wholesome diet   Convinced of the injustice of holding men
and women as slaves, he avoided, as far as possible, sharing in
the products of their unpaid labor

Unwilling to lose his lively companionship, his former gay
associates solicited his return   One of them, Daniel Offley, was
especially anxious to win him back again, representing the
change in his conduct as the result of melancholy, and that it
would wear off in a cheerful atmosphere   But Jonathan Evans
explained to him so clearly the reasons for his altered course
that he was convinced of their reality, accepted the glad tidings
of salvation through the Lord Jesus, became a witness for
Christ, and a minister of His gospel   The early friendship
thus sanctified and strengthened, the two young men were
united in a warm Christian fellowship for life

My grandfather had a birthright in the religious Society of
Friends, which was now confirmed by convincement and choice ;
whatever he did was done with his might, and ever after he
conformed to their doctrines and practices   His membership
was vested in the Monthly Meeting of Friends of Philadelphia
for the Southern District, and in his twenty-fourth year he was
placed in the office of overseer

These circumstances occurred during the commotions of the
Revolutionary War, and my grandfather was drafted as a soldier
for the American army   Having enlisted under the Prince of
Peace, he could not take up arms against any of his fellow-men,

and for his refusal to do so was put in prison and confined there for sixteen weeks.

On the 13th of Fourth month, 1786, he was married to Hannah Bacon, daughter of David and Mary Bacon, of Philadelphia. The marriage was solemnized in a public meeting of Friends in their native city, and the names of relations and many other well-known citizens are placed as witnesses on the certificate. The bride had just reached her majority. She was endowed with strong common sense and a sound judgment; was attractive in person and pleasing in manners, cheerful and affable in disposition. Both had warm and strong affections, and were fully united in religious belief and in their views of domestic life and economy.

Their house was furnished simply but substantially for neatness and comfort. My grandmother was a model housekeeper and looked faithfully after her children's health and training. With her desire to observe moderation in all things, she kept to what was reasonable. A visitor one day reproved her for being so luxurious as to carpet the floors. She informed her mentor that she could not have her little children falling on bare boards, to the injury of their tender faces and arms. She was a skilful nurse, and her warm sympathies led her often to minister to the sick and afflicted. Her naturally kind and amiable disposition was an inheritance from her parents, and a sketch of her ancestry will follow this narrative.

My grandfather was conscientiously restrained from putting much ornamental work on the buildings he erected, and for a time his income was lessened in consequence. He and his young wife carefully confined their expenses within its limits, and were finally blessed with sufficiency for all their needs.

Five energetic boys and two daughters must have given them much to think of and to do, but it did not prevent them from tenderly caring for and waiting upon the aged mother whose last years were passed under their roof. Both were accurate in all business transactions, and this gave them leisure of mind to attend to other and higher duties, if one duty can be called higher than another where all form one chain in right living.

In the latter part of the eighteenth century Philadelphia was occasionally visited by yellow fever, and this circumstance probably led to the practice of taking a house in the country for a summer residence A place in Upper Darby, near what is now Lansdowne, was their usual resort before the older sons were grown up

One day after the family had left town for the summer, the house on Union Street was entered by a company of thieves. They made themselves quite at home there for some time, removed some articles of value, and were preparing to carry off a quantity of plate that had been left in the closets, when a fright caused a hasty retreat, and a number of silver vessels were thrown into a well in the yard No trace of the culprits was discovered that could identify them. Long after this, a poor fellow was arrested, convicted, and executed for a capital crime In his confession he stated, among other misdeeds, a robbery in which he had been concerned. He said that in a certain year a gentleman was observed leaving his house on Union Street and driving away in a chaise No one was left in the house, which was taken possession of by the criminal and his accomplices, and a part of what they intended to appropriate was carried away, the alarm alluded to inducing them to conceal the rest.

My grandfather was a diligent and devout student of the Holy Scriptures, in a knowledge of which all his children were carefully trained He was also well read in many of the religious writings of the last few centuries A firm believer in the spiritual nature of Christianity and in the immediate power and presence of the Holy Spirit operating in every human heart, he was equally clear and settled in his belief in the divinity and offices of the Lord Jesus as the atonement and propitiatory sacrifice for a fallen race, and as our ever-living mediator and High-Priest, He by whom all things were created, and in whom all things consist To the service of his Lord he willingly gave time and strength, and in addition to the office of overseer was recorded by his Monthly Meeting as an elder, a station that he filled with fidelity to the close of his earthly career At one time he was sent, in company with one or more other Friends, on a religious mission to Canada They were from home three months in wintry weather, and on their return drove in a sleigh on the ice down the Hudson River.

He was one of the founders of Westtown Boarding-School, and warmly interested in its success. His intense earnestness and the old-time ideas of obedience to authority gave something of sternness to his character, but underneath there was a solid foundation of true love and tenderness.

In his family this was conspicuous. He watched over his children with a deep paternal interest for their best welfare, and as they grew in years provision was made for their education and settlement in life ungrudgingly and wisely.

The mother's softer sway and innocently mirthful temper gave a sunny aspect to their home and warmed the domestic atmosphere. My grandfather was devotedly attached to his wife, and when she was removed to her home in the celestial city, it was touching to see the depth of his sorrow. Already " the days of his years were threescore years and ten," and I remember how, declining to take the arm of a son, he walked alone at the head of the funeral procession from his house to the burial-ground on Arch Street, the personification of silent, solitary grief. Long after, in conversation with one of his children about their mother, he said, " I am married to her grave."

But he did not refuse the sympathy of his friends and the filial attentions of his children, always living in the midst of his family, visiting his married sons and daughter, interested in his grandchildren, and keeping open house for them all.

My recollection of him becomes more distinct after the decease of my grandmother. Our aunt Mary was his faithful companion and mistress of the household, cordial in the reception of their varied guests, and affectionate in her attention to the brothers and sisters, doubled in number by marriage. Her father's chair, of ample dimensions, was always ready by the blazing hickory fire in winter, and his Bible within reach of his hand on the end of the mantel-piece. When the hall clock struck nine in the evening, a tidy Irish maiden who waited on him was at the foot of the staircase to hand him a silver can of water and a lighted candle as he left the parlor and went up for the night's repose.

In summer, Samuel-like, he made a circuit among his children in Springfield and Marple. He had purchased a fine tract of land and divided it into two farms for his sons Joseph and Joel. Each had a pleasant dwelling-house and suitable farm-buildings on its premises. In my uncle Joel's house he retained certain rooms for his own use in the summer season, as he should have occasion for it, but all his children felt it the greatest honor to have him visit them. The grandchildren were always addressed as "My child," and he seemed to have at hand a perennial supply of spice-nuts and raisins for the little ones.

His remarkable figure is not easily forgotten, and was aptly described by Henry Cope as reminding of a Roman senator. Dressed in a long broadcloth coat and knee-breeches to match, ribbed stockings, shining shoes and silver buckles, overshadowed by a broad-brimmed beaver hat, with a cane in his gloved hand, he was ready for whatever might come in his daily round.

Slowly as he had transferred his fealty from the English government to the new republic in early life, when the independence of the United States became an accomplished fact he did not shrink from his responsibilities as an American citizen. He was regularly at the polls with his vote, and after the snows of age had whitened his locks, his grandson and namesake used to tell us how the men would open a passage for him as he appeared on the day of election, that he might cast in his decision without the fatigue of waiting.

His aspect in the deliberative bodies of his own religious Society is described in the following extract from an article on "The Close of the Yearly Meeting of 1836," by William J. Allinson.

"Next sat the man whose first name is sufficient designation in all the Society of Friends. As he leaned upon his cane he reminded you of Rome, and everything that is rendered venerable by antiquity and stern endurance. His very appearance was a grand moral spectacle, the more so to those who knew him.

"Versed in all the doctrines, opinions, and usages of the Society, he detected at a glance the first appearance of whatever is unseemly. The Discipline is an open book before him, and he is an oracle to expound its meaning. When Jonathan Evans speaks, and he is not lavish of his speeches, the clerk may safely make a minute, for the question is settled; Jonathan is not mistaken. Not that he assumes dictation, not that he wishes to carry his point, but, as I said, the Discipline is an open book before him, and he knows all about it without thinking twice.

" Be it that he is fallible like the rest, he has overcome more within himself than almost any ten men had to contend with. When he is gathered to his fathers the Society will miss him, and then, and not till then, will they appreciate his worth."

To this extract may be added another from verses by a rhyming chronicler of a half-century ago, referring to my grandfather :·

> " A pillar of the church, erect and strong,
> Swayed by no friendship to the church's wrong;
> Unwarped, unmoved, sound to the very core,
> And rendered firmer by the weight he bore.
> An honest watchman the alarm to sound,
> When foes were sowing tares within our ground.
> *　　*　　*　　*　　*　　*　　*
> Their malice moved not, and their threats were vain,
> Fixed at his post, determined to remain.
> And when at last the final goal was won,
> Death's message found him with his armor on ;
> No oilless lamp to trim, no loins to gird,
> Ready to enter at the Bridegroom's word."

He had so long cultivated a habit of meditation on subjects divine and eternal in their nature that time never seemed wearisome to him, even after he was obliged by age to lay aside some occupations requiring physical vigor. With faculties clear and strong, he passed the closing years of his life with us in Christian serenity and hopefulness.

On the 30th of First month, 1839, he had a severe chill, and from that hour gradually declined in strength, but suffered very little pain. His children gathered round him, and many friends called to express their affectionate interest and inquire as to his health. When asked by his son, Dr. Charles Evans, how he felt, he replied, " Very quiet, very quiet, but very weak." Nine days after his seizure, in the morning of 8th of Second month, in holy composure he passed over the river, his countenance glowing with heavenly light

> " His soul to Him who gave it rose,
> God led him to his long repose
> And glorious rest
> And though the good man's sun is set,
> His light shall linger round us yet,
> Bright, radiant, blest "

My own dear mother, who watched by the bedside of both her parents in their last illness, gave me the particulars of each scene   Ten years before the departure of her husband my grandmother had left the circle of her beloved ones on earth With her latest words she testified her unfaltering love and trust in the Lord Jesus, and her affection for them   So gently and peacefully did she leave us that, as my mother said, it seemed as if she were only gone into an adjoining room.

After the central bond was removed, the families of the sons and daughters did not fall apart   I think no band of brothers and sisters could have been more closely united, although my father's was equally so   A community of interests was always drawing them together   Their early training had fostered their domestic affections, given them one faith and very similar views of the responsibilities of life.

Special characteristics and varied abilities gave to each one a distinctive individuality, making it possible for them to find their greatest social pleasures in the society of one another, the children of each household were adopted by all the rest, and the weal or woe of any member of the clan vibrated from end to end

As they heeded the warning against putting their light under a bushel, this family trait was well known among their contemporaries, of which I once had a curious proof   Dining at the house of a friend in Aberdeen, in 1874, with a large party, the conversation turned to Philadelphia Yearly Meeting and its isolation from Friends in general, a circumstance few can regret more than I   The discussion was carried on at a distance from me, and I heard nothing of it till in explanation of some point William Ball remarked that he had been told that Jonathan Evans, on his death-bed, had solemnly bound his children to stand by and support one another. Unwilling for such an idea to be entertained, I made use of a pause in the conversation to say that Jonathan Evans was my grandfather, and that there must have been some mistake in regard to the supposed fact. There had never been any such promise exacted of his family by my grandfather, but his children had all been so taught and trained from infancy that they were bound together in love and naturally supported and aided one another. The surprise at finding so near a relation of Jonathan Evans at the table gave a brilliant color to the countenance of the courtly divine.

It is time to give something of my grandmother Hannah Evans's lineage, which might have belonged to an earlier place, but could not be inserted without too much interruption to the narrative.

I cannot begin it more appropriately than by transcribing a letter from my cousin Richard Morris Smith.

"Stanley, 3715 Chestnut Street, Philadelphia,
"Fourth month 24th, 1891.

"My dear Cousin Mary R. Haines,—I am now fulfilling a neglected duty. Thy sister Elizabeth wrote me nearly two years ago inquiring about our common Bacon ancestry. The letter did not arrive till after we had sailed for Europe; it was forwarded and reached us (I think) at Antwerp. I felt puzzled how to reply, being fearful of making mistakes in the absence of my documents, and not knowing exactly what to say, postponed reply till in the hurries of travel it passed from my mind. I had a pleasant call from her on the way to meeting this morning, and she recalled the subject to my memory, asking me to write anything I felt inclined to, to *thee*.

"Working up the family history of the ' Burlington Smith' family led me to much information about the Bacons, with whom the Smiths several times intermarried. Nathaniel Bacon was mayor or recorder (I think both) of Barnstable, Massachusetts, on the first arrival there of the ' Pilgrim Fathers' who first landed at Plymouth by the Mayflower. His brothers Samuel and John and a sister* arrived some years later on another 'Pilgrim' vessel. These vessels sailed from a port in Holland, I think Dordrecht, near which many Puritans, expelled from England, were temporarily settled. The most powerful and typical Puritan sect was the 'Independents,' but the Bacons (except Nathaniel) were 'Free-will Baptists,' and not very comfortable, I imagine, among the Independents. Samuel and John, after living in Barnstable till about 1672, 'turn up' near the present Greenwich, N.J., where they bought land from the Indian sachems. Here they were among Friendly or 'Quaker' settlers. The now rare and curious 'Annals of Barnstable' has the following notes of Samuel,—

"'Mr Samuel Bacon takes the oath of fidelity 1657'—'Mr Bacon had a grant of land in this town in 1662, and has been thought a brother of Mr Nathaniel and Elizabeth, who were early here. Mr Samuel Bacon married Martha Foxwell, May 9th, 1669, and had Samuel, March 9th, 1670, and Martha, 1671 ; but at what time he came, or when or how the family *disappeared* from town, is a question yet to be settled.'

" The question of the disappearance of the family from Barnstable is settled by their reappearance in Salem County N.J., accompanied by Samuel's much younger brother John, quite a youth and barely mentioned in the 'Annals.' John must have been a boy when they came from England, but was now grown up. My 'Burlington Smiths' says,—

"'In 1685 another collateral ancestor of our family, Samuel Bacon, appears in the history of the province, having been appointed in that year a justice of the peace for Salem tenth. He was also a member of Assembly in this year. Some years before, he had purchased lands on the Cohansey River, near where Greenwich now stands, from the Indian sachems there ; these lands, forming a peninsula between the Cohansey and Delaware Rivers, have ever since been known as "Bacon's Neck." '

" Probably both brothers, certainly John, left the Free-will Baptists and joined the Friends. John Bacon married, in 1688,

* The sister's name was Elizabeth.

Elizabeth Smith, daughter of the well-known early settler the Honorable John Smith of 'Smithfield,' a fine place near Salem. John Bacon was appointed justice of the peace in 1696 and continued to serve in that capacity till 1701 inclusive. He was also a justice of the quorum for Salem County, and properly styled Judge. 'Judge Bacon also owned property at Chesterfield, Burlington County, where he some time resided.' I possess the certificate of his second marriage, to Elizabeth Leppington, of the city of York, England, which took place in York Meeting, and bears the names of many eminent early Friends. We are, however, descended from his first wife, Elizabeth Smith.

"John and Elizabeth (Smith) Bacon's *eldest son* was John Bacon 2d, of 'Bacon's Neck' (who married in Salem meeting Elizabeth, daughter of John Test, of Salem, a well-known Friend). Their (J. B. No. 1's) *daughter Elizabeth* (Elizabeth Smith's daughter) married my great-great-grandfather Robert Smith, of Burlington (grandfather of the editor of *The Friend*). John Bacon 2d and Elizabeth Test had sons and daughters, of whom were David Bacon *your* ancestor and Job Bacon my great-grandfather, whose daughter Mary married my grandfather Robert Smith (Junior), many years editor of *The Friend*.

"In our family the descent from the 'Barnstable Bacons' was a matter perfectly known to the older members.

"Going back to the 'Pilgrims,' the name of Nathaniel Bacon, the member of Parliament and Puritan author, appears in several biographical dictionaries, accompanied by the statement that he was a member of the celebrated 'Long Parliament' in the Restoration period, when the 'Church of England' was firmly established. Nathaniel Bacon, considering such establishment an outrage on the rights of non-conformists or 'Dissenters,' wrote a book against it, for which he was banished in the first year of Charles II. He is stated to have died in Holland in the same year (A.D. 1660), being then certainly an aged man. His would not agree with the career of Nathaniel, Recorder of Barnstable, who lived many years later. In the absence of positive evidence, I can only conclude it as extremely probable that this second Nathaniel, together with Samuel, Elizabeth, and the boy John (our ancestor), were children of this first Nathaniel. The identity of name, sect, and location all favors this high probability, which is further confirmed by the family tradition of descent from 'Lord Bacon,' and by the fact that the 'Herald's College' (of London) granted to my great-uncle Job Bacon the arms of the 'Lord' Bacon family.

"Supposing, then, that we are descended from the Puritan Parliamentarian Nathaniel Bacon, I trace his (our?) earlier descent.

"Nathaniel Bacon, Esquire, M.P., was son to Sir Nathaniel Bacon, a country gentleman of fortune, who had an eminent talent as a landscape-painter, and flourished under James I. and Charles I. before Puritanism existed. This Sir Nathaniel Bacon was younger brother of the very eminent Sir Francis Bacon, Viscount St. Alban's and Baron Verulam, Lord Chancellor of England, the prince of philosophers. They were sons of Sir Nicholas Bacon, Queen Elizabeth's Lord Keeper of the Great Seal. Sir Nicholas was son to Sir Edmund Bacon of Redgrave, Suffolk, who was son to George Bacon of Redgrave, Esquire, a wealthy country gentleman.

"This is as far as I have traced the family. The name is unquestionably Norman, being derived from Bucon (the beech-trees) in Normandy. On the grant of the original arms the heralds of the period, according to the custom of selecting some wild and warlike animal as typical of knightly bravery, gave the Bacons the crest of the wild boar, doubtless because of the name. Their name, however, as above-said, does not derive from the common word bacon, but from Bucon (beech-tree or the beeches), a local name. The word bacon is supposed to be similarly derived, because of wild swine feeding much on the mast or fruit of the beech (bucon).

"Now, my dear cousin, thee has 'all I know about the Bacons,' *excepting, however,* that I know some of them, with whom I have had the happiness to spend part of my lifetime, to have been among the loveliest of our Father's children.

"Affectionately thy cousin,

"R. MORRIS SMITH."

From this letter and other accessible sources we trace the descent of my mother from

John Bacon I., married to Elizabeth Smith; their son
John Bacon II., married to Elizabeth Test; their son
David Bacon, married to Mary Trotter; their daughter
Hannah, married to Jonathan Evans.

David Bacon, son of John II. and Elizabeth (Test) Bacon, was born the 14th day of the First month, old style, in the year 1729.

Mary Bacon, wife of David Bacon and daughter of Joseph and Dinah Trotter, was born the 23d of Eleventh month, old style, 1727. She departed this life 15th of Tenth month, 1793, aged nearly sixty-six years.

They had five sons and five daughters, whose birth is carefully recorded to the day and hour in a page lying before me as I write. Two of them, at least, must have died in early childhood,—John and David,—as their names were given a second time to younger sons.

Elizabeth, born 1752; married Thomas Scattergood; left one son, Joseph.

Rebecca, born 1754; unmarried.

Joseph, born 1756.

John, born 1757.

Mary, born 1759; married John Olden; second, married Timothy Mount.

John, born 1761; married.

David, born 1763.

HANNAH, born 1765; married Jonathan Evans.

David, born 1766.

Rachel, born 1767.

Of these there are numerous descendants, many of whom I know and esteem.

David Bacon lived in Philadelphia, on Second Street, I think, at the corner of Trotter's Alley.

He was a genial man, "given to hospitality, and a highly esteemed member of the religious Society of Friends." He accompanied one of our ministers on a religious visit to England, and his sea-chest is now in the possession of my brother, Dr. James E. Rhoads. He was a liberal householder, and among other provisions for winter had some means of storing large supplies of oysters in the cellar, so as to have them fresh for use when the Delaware River was frozen over.

When Friends collected in the city to attend their Quarterly and Yearly Meetings, he kept an open house for their entertainment, and used to encourage them to come without regard to numbers, by telling them that while horned cattle required a great deal of room, many sheep would be happy together in a comparatively small fold.

He and his wife, my great-grandmother, passed away from earth long before my day, but they left a pleasant memory behind them, and perhaps in the hereafter I shall know and love them. I remember my great-uncle Joseph Bacon's house on Front Street, and my great-aunt Mary Mount, who was unlike my grandmother in many respects, but seemed to me a woman of a good deal of spirit.

My recollections of my grandmother are distinct on three occasions, all of them in our house at Marple. I had a slight illness, and she prescribed and weighed the medicine for me in a delicate pair of apothecary scales. At another time she sat in the front door and I on a step at her feet, as she gave me a sewing-lesson in gathering a shirt-sleeve, two threads up, four down. The last was of an evening in the parlor, and some one relating a ludicrous occurrence, at which her laugh rang out as merry as a girl's.

The dear grandmother! May her sterling virtues and pleasant temper mould the inheritance of her descendants!

My great-grandfather, David Bacon, had a sister who was known to her nieces and nephews of later generations as "Aunt Hough." I never knew her first name, and think she passed away before my day; but Aunt Hough made an impression on her contemporaries. I believe she was a lovely woman, although she seems to have led an independent career, living unmarried till she was forty years old, and then changing her name three times. Her first husband was a gentleman of the name of Gilbert. Some time after his death she married Richard Wistar. Wishing to have a very quiet wedding, they went to Greenwich to perform the ceremony. Their union could not have been a long one, for her name was finally changed to Hough; but of Mr. Hough, or the circumstances that brought about their connection, I have heard nothing more than that some of her nieces would have been better pleased had she remained Mrs. Wistar. Even this third alliance she survived. The only person now living who can remember her, I suppose, my cousin Hannah W. Scull, told me a few days ago that she recollected being taken by her mother to visit Aunt Hough in Philadelphia. She was then solaced by the companionship of a niece, my mother's aunt, Rebecca Bacon. But a fatality seemed to follow her in the choice of her heart and home, for one morning, on coming down to breakfast, she observed that her niece had not yet taken her place at the table. Sending to her room to see what was detaining her, she was presently informed that Rebecca Bacon was lying in bed, as if asleep, with her cheek on her hand, but life had fled, and once more Aunt Hough was alone.

CHAPTER XIII.

JOSEPH RHOADS III. AND HANNAH RHOADS.

JOSEPH RHOADS III., the third son of Joseph and Mary Rhoads, was born the second day of the First month, 1787, in the house that had been occupied by the family for three successive generations, at Marple, Delaware County, Pennsylvania. He grew up, healthy and vigorous, in the fine atmosphere of that favored locality, under the gentle, loving, yet steadfast training of his parents, in which just so much of indulgence was mingled as was needed to soften and adjust the rule of principles that governed their own lives.

His home education was supplemented by attendance at a day-school in the neighborhood under the care of Friends, and afterwards at Westtown, then a recently-established boarding-school. Industry was natural to him, and the most was made of the opportunities he had for acquiring knowledge. He once

14

gave me an account of what he accomplished in study the year
that he was at Westtown   I cannot recall it with accuracy, but
it seemed almost incredible that so much could have been done
in so short a time

From letters written to him by his father, and treasured
through life, it is clear that he had his ambitions, and would
have gladly continued his course as student to prepare for an
active career in some city   But the strong desire of his father
to keep his children near him prevailed, and the school-days
were shortened, not, as he was assured, because of expense;
that gave his parents no concern   Their opinion was, that
"as much peace of mind and comfort of life might be enjoyed"
if their son should follow some country business for which he
was already qualified, as could be attained were he to choose a
more ambitious path, and probably they were right.

When about twenty-two years of age the decease of his
father threw much responsibility upon him as being the strongest
and most energetic of the older sons   Very faithfully did he
fulfil his part in guiding affairs, sustaining and comforting his
mother, and in loving care for his sisters and younger brother
My aunt Rebecca used to say of him, " He has been both father
and brother to me," and my aunts have told me of his ability
in small details, and how well, when weather or other circumstances prevented their going to the city, he would do their
shopping, and bring home the fine muslin for the mother's cap,
her velvet shoes, and materials for their dresses, choosing what
he thought appropriate, whatever the cost, as being the most
truly economical

In anticipation of a separate establishment for himself, he
early planted a large orchard of the best selected apple trees,
set out pear, plum, peach, and cherry trees, and began preparations for building   With his strong love of social life, it is
not likely that he intended to be a solitary occupant of the new
home, but his plans matured gradually

Near this time a gentleman in Philadelphia purchased a tract
of land in Springfield, about as far south of the old meeting-
house as my father's place is to the northwest, and divided
it into farms for two of his sons   As soon as the older one

became of age he was installed as resident proprietor in a picturesque old mansion on one of the divisions, with his sisters
Mary and Hannah, both younger than himself, as alternate
mistresses of the house. It was with joy that my father found
a congenial companion in Joseph Evans, the young farmer, and
the friendship then formed flowed on without chill or ruffle, and
with increasing sweetness to the close of time to him.

One day, while the mother and her daughter Hannah were
settling in for the new housekeeping, they drove in a chair* to
the meeting at Springfield. As they passed through the gate
and towards the ancient building, a young man stepped up,
helped them to alight, and took care of their horse. A glance
left on Hannah's mind the impression of a remarkably fair
forehead beneath the dark, waving hair ; how he was impressed
I never heard, but he was drawn towards her .by a cord that
never slackened, and finally he won the hand of the maiden.

They were united in marriage on the fourth day of the
Eleventh month, 1818, in the Friends' meeting-house on Pine
Street, in Philadelphia, a large number of their relations and
friends being present, who were afterwards liberally entertained
at the house of my grandfather, Jonathan Evans, on Union
Street near Fourth.

As the result of preparations begun years before, there were
an ample, cheerful, gray-stone dwelling, wherein were " all
things in order stored," a barn, other out-buildings, and surrounding premises, ready for occupation. Here, a few weeks
after the wedding, a family dinner-party assembled and inaugurated the heads of a new household.

In looking over the more than forty years of married life
that our parents shared together in that home, it seems to me
that seldom, if ever, has there been a family that has enjoyed
more of substantial comfort, physical health, cheerfulness, mental pleasure, and domestic love, with hearts open to the world
around them, than was their portion.

Of course they had cares, perplexities, trials, but these were as
foils to the brightness ; and their experience was a beautiful illustration of the truth that " godliness is profitable unto all things,

* A vehicle with seats for two only.

having promise of the life that now is, and of that which is to come "

Four daughters and four sons came in the first twelve years to gladden that country home   The third daughter, named for the mother and the mother's mother, a child of remarkable sweetness and beauty, but ominously precocious, lived two years and eight months to entwine around her the affections of all who knew her, and then went to grow and unfold in the congenial air of Paradise   All the others are yet here,* although even the youngest has measured threescore years

With a large family dependent upon them, it was still plain to us that our parents, in some silent, indefinable way, kept the heavens above the earth.   All their worldly affairs, within doors and without, were punctually and strictly cared for, their children's interests were never overlooked or neglected, but duty to God came first, and all religious meetings of which they were members were habitually attended in all weathers without comment, and as naturally as they came to the breakfast-table each morning

Our father filled the offices of elder and overseer, I think from his thirty-first year, besides having many other appointments in the religious Society of Friends   At twenty-four our mother was one of the committee on Westtown Boarding-School, and although that was relinquished for a short time, even while her children were in their infancy she was clerk of the Monthly Meeting   Subsequently she was for a time overseer, and was called to the clerkship of the Quarterly and Yearly Meetings   For this service she had a special gift, being ready in taking and recording the sense of the meeting on any subject, and acting with a dignity and grace that gave a charm to the proceedings   At a time when an unhappy and controversial spirit was occasionally manifest in our Yearly Meeting, Beulah Coates said we had one comfort in the midst of it, " Our clerk is a lady."   Such she truly proved herself to be, always giving to each one respectful attention, never losing her self-poise and calmness   Lovely, too, she looked in the gallery, either as clerk or minister, her noble and serene countenance, erect and well-propor-

* In 1891

tioned figure, her transparent muslin cap and neckerchief, her dress and shawls, rich and soft in material and choice in shade and coloring. She and our father were perfectly matched in personal appearance: tall and symmetrical, every attitude natural and expressive of purity and truthfulness; in their movements celerity without haste or confusion. I wish we could have something more tangible than an imaginary picture to represent them as they stood hand in hand to make their marriage vows in the old Pine Street meeting-house, amidst the somewhat grave and stately friends whose autographs are on their marriage certificate. Our father in his fine broadcloth suit (for he was always careful in his selections), breeches buttoned at the knee, low shoes and silk stockings. Our mother in a rich, glossy, silver-colored dress, low neck, short sleeves, long kid gloves, and neckerchief crossed in front and fastened in the belt of her gown.

One of our dear father's habits was to take a glass of water before breakfast; and as he never could think any water, however pure, as sweet as the spring from which he drank in childhood, in winter or summer he would walk down the hill to fill his glass there. Perhaps this was partly an excuse to have a nearer look at the old home. As long as my grandmother lived he went to see her every day, consulted her in all matters of importance, and generally made another call in the evening before she went to bed. These daily visits he continued as long as my uncle George was there to greet him.

Our literary instruction claimed early attention, and our parents succeeded in bringing an attractive young lady as governess to our house. I remember the first morning at school distinctly. I was about six years old, my sister Deborah five, and our brother Joseph nearly four, the three pupils with whom she opened the exercises. The dining-room was in order, the windows were partially shaded as the morning sun shone upon them, and our teacher, her auburn hair nicely braided and a delicate flush on her bright face, was seated by a square mahogany table. I was called upon to read, and I think the lesson was one of Anna Letitia Barbauld's hymns in prose.

Rebecca Allinson's happy sway, however, did not last long.

A hectic bloom told of pulmonary trouble, and she was obliged
to leave us to be under her mother's tender care for the remainder of her brief earthly sojourn.

To replace her came one of maturer age; but she failed to
establish agreeable relations with her charge, and, being evidently unfit for the care of children, her tutelage ended with the
first winter.

She was succeeded by a very different character, a native of
Ireland, although educated chiefly in our Pennsylvania schools.
Her warm Irish nature quickly drew us to her, and her methods
of instruction were thorough and successful; besides which she
was a valuable aid to our mother in her many cares, faithfully
supplying in her absence from home a salutary oversight in the
household.

Our mother never shrank from responsibility, and with her
wonted liberality shared the benefits of our well-lighted school-
room and the abilities of our teacher with some of our neighbors, allowing their children a place in the classes. This continued several years until the Friends of our meeting, seeing
the need of larger opportunities for the increasing number of
children belonging to it, established a select school on the meeting-house premises at Springfield.

With great sorrow we parted with Ann Magill, who took
charge of a school near Chester, and we were sent to the new
one, a mile from our home. There, with the facility of childhood, we soon became contented and made fair progress till,
one by one, we were thought to be old enough to enter the
boarding-school at Westtown.

A fine element in our education was the company drawn to
our house and cheerfully entertained by our father and mother.
They were particular in choosing companionship; but for a
country residence it included a wide range.

The numerous members of our family connection were expected and welcomed as often as they could come, and many
and varied were the guests beyond the line of kindred and of
country, and the social influences thus brought into our home
were refining and elevating.

Besides the oversight of the farm and whetstone quarries, our father's business as a manufacturer obliged him to make frequent visits to Philadelphia and sometimes to other cities. Sometimes he was called from home on religious service as companion to ministers who were out on gospel missions.

His business trips to Philadelphia were frequently made on horseback in his early life; and I well remember the boots and spurs and saddle-bags that were used on such occasions, and how we learned to look for some little treat of fruit, or confectionery, or toys, to be drawn from the saddle-bags on his return.

I have before me a letter written by my mother in one of his longer absences, and addressed to Joseph Rhoads, care of Abigail Robinson, Newport, R.I.

"MARPLE: Sixth mo. 14th 1824.

"MY DEAR HUSBAND,—I expect this will find thee at Newport, and probably will be the only letter I shall write, as it is uncertain whether another would reach thee after leaving that place.

"Thou art much the companion of my thoughts, and I have been so accustomed to thy returning home (when absent) by evening, that the impression is often felt that I shall see thee in the course of a few hours, but as many letters as thou canst write must suffice till the proper time arises for thy restoration to us. I would by no means awaken one anxious thought respecting home, as we are, I believe, getting along as comfortably as we can expect without thee.

"I heard from thee at New York by brother William's letter; it was pleasant to find you had got safely there, and had the prospect of agreeable company the remainder of the journey.

"I staid in Philadelphia after thou left me until the next day, not finding any suitable person from our neighborhood to accompany me. J. Scattergood, Jr., came out with me in the chair.

"We stopped at H. Jackson's to inquire of A. Bunting if she would be willing to go to father's to assist sister Mary in her heavy charge.* She was not at home, but I since hear there is

* I believe the serious illness of my grandmother.

a probability they will get her awhile   Mother Rhoads is much
as when thou saw her, the other branches of their family, with
ours, are well

"Brother Joel and sister Hannah were here last Fifth-day
Elizabeth and Sidney Lownes, and Abraham, Jr , and Hannah
Pennell paid me a visit on Seventh-day, all great strangers, but
particularly the latter   We have called at their father's so often
on our way from Concord, that I was pleased with the opportunity of returning some attention to any of the family.

"I suppose thou wilt have a more exact account of mother's
situation by father's letter than I can give, it is really a great
comfort to hear she has been so much relieved from extreme
suffering

"Please give my love to brothers, should wish to write to
Thomas, but can scarcely get at liberty from the children so
as to be able to address thee, am now writing with Hannah
on my lap, and the others in the room with me   Mary and
Deborah say send their love to father

"If thou canst write me when thou wilt be likely to get to
Philadelphia, perhaps I can meet thee there, or send some of
our folks to furnish thee with a conveyance home

"From thy loving wife,   ·

"H RHOADS"

Alike as our father and mother were in their chief characteristics, there were marked differences in minor traits admirably
supplementing each other   Their lives were guided by habitual
attention and obedience to the leading of the Holy Spirit, and
constant dependence on our Father in heaven, keeping their
eyes on the example and precepts of the Lord Jesus   This
gave them a stability and calmness that never seemed to be
shaken by the changes and shocks of time

Peace-makers they were in the truest sense, endeavoring to
avoid prejudice, and neither repeating nor listening to detrac-
tions, slow to take offence, and unsuspicious, they could labor
with others who were estranged from a friend or neighbor and
harmonize conflicting elements

Our father had by nature and long cultivation so nice a sense of propriety that he seemed to avoid intuitively in remarks or conversation the remotest allusion to anything that could wound or be unpleasant to those about him. Yet he was careful never to extenuate error while throwing the veil of charity over the erring. Our mother was almost as perfect in this respect, although her quickness might sometimes bring her near the danger-line. Both were free from any little personal habit that could annoy the most sensitive. They spoke English in its purity with unaffected clearness and simplicity, free from provincialisms and exclamations.

Liberal they both were to the extent of their ability in providing for their family, in all their intercourse with their relations and friends, in their service and contributions in the church, and in help and consideration for the poor and afflicted.

One of my earliest recollections is of a winter day when my mother and governess took me with them in a walk across the fields to carry some supplies to the cottage of a laborer on an adjoining farm, where twins had just been added to an already large family of children.

Shortly after my last coming home from boarding-school, my mother asked me to write on her behalf to several of our friends of Springfield Meeting, to request their co-operation in opening a school on First-day afternoons for the instruction of colored women in our neighborhood who were refugees from slavery.

The appeal was promptly responded to, and a school was opened on the meeting-house premises, where classes were regularly taught by the ladies interested in the work.

Such practical lessons were given by our parents when occasion arose, making life-long impressions on the minds of their children. Many might be mentioned, but I will relate only two more illustrations of their methods. One night my brother James, who was sleeping in a little bed near our mother's side, awoke in pain and called on her for relief. Always prompt and efficient in applying remedies, in this instance she appears to have been guided a little out of her usual course, and instead of rising, said to the child, " Ask thy heavenly Father to cure thee." In childlike faith the prayer was immediately made and answered, and thus a belief in the value and practice of prayer was firmly implanted in her boy's mind

In our school-days there were some remarkable snow-storms, when fences were buried in the drifts and roads were impassable On such a morning our father came up to the house from his business about nine o'clock, and seeing James and Charles lingering about home, said, " Boys, why are you not at school ?" They replied that the storm was so great that they could not walk there. Father told them to go to the stable, take Fan, mount her, and ride on to school The little fellows did as they were bidden, and were soon floundering through the drifts. About half-way they reached the house of our neighbor Samuel Pancoast, and then the horse could push on no farther Samuel Pancoast came out and called, " Boys what are you about ?" " Going to school," was the reply, to which he rejoined, " Turn around and go straight home !" Seeing they could not proceed, they took the kind advice, but never forgot their father's lesson, that perseverance in the line of duty is a rule of life

With us the habit of obedience had been established in infancy, as it was our mother's conviction that it should be so before a child was three years old. How she accomplished it I do not know, but we never thought of going counter to her expressed wishes, and there was so much tenderness and love in the paternal sway that fear was unknown in our relations to the dear father and mother The boys used to laugh at father's custom, when calling them to rise in the mornings, of going into their room and tucking them snugly in as if for another nap

How pleasant were the long drives with him to the city, and with both parents to our Monthly and Quarterly Meetings at Middletown and Concord, and when visiting our friends and kindred at Newtown, Chester, and the Great Valley ! No matter how difficult the roads, nor how dark the nights on the homeward stretch, we felt secure in our father's guardianship, and fearlessly trusted him to guide safely even when the horses were invisible through the gloom

Moderation in all things preserved his fine physical powers in vigor; and almost to the last day of his stay on earth his step was quick and firm, his hand steady, sight and hearing equal to all demands, his voice well modulated and clear.

At table his appetite was discriminative without fastidiousness, and he partook slowly and very temperately of what was before him, always observing the same limit, even in his favorite beverage, coffee. Fresh air and pure water were his hygienic aids, combined with a sufficiency of exercise; and habitual cheerfulness was maintained by keeping a clear conscience and always having worthy objects to employ his talents and energy.

He had a taste for literature, and in his brief hours of leisure acquired much useful information. The political state of his own country and of Europe, the progress of arts and science, the condition of the peoples, and the aspects of civilization and of nature in different parts of the world interested him, and he read with such purpose that he kept up an intelligent knowledge on those subjects in his day. His acquaintance with works of imagination was limited, but he enjoyed some of the graver poets and essayists, especially those of the seventeenth and eighteenth centuries, and often used some sententious quotation to express an opinion, or give force to a sentiment that he wished to emphasize. He read more to gain wisdom than to accumulate knowledge, and what was gleaned in this way he assimilated in his life and transfused into action.

This was particularly noticeable in relation to his study of the Holy Scriptures, drawing from them rules for the every-day duties of life, and many a text from Proverbs and Ecclesiastes was brought to bear upon ordinary occurrences. In reading aloud his manner was always agreeable, beautifully so when it was the Bible in the family circle, so reverent yet perfectly natural. I recall evenings in his last winter with us, when he sat up late reading Sir George Simpson's "Overland Journey Round the World," and tracing his course on maps.

I have before alluded to the promptness with which he and our mother prepared to attend all their religious meetings far ·and near, whether it required an absence of two hours or several days. After our dear mother was recorded a minister of the gospel, and at times felt herself called to distant places in the performance of her religious duties, she had our father's cordial support and co-operation If he could not go with her himself, he saw that she was provided with suitable companions and the means for travelling, and patiently bore the deprivation of her society for the time   In 1850–1851 she was drawn in the love of Christ to visit Great Britain and Ireland, and for about one year was separated from her family   Our father went with her to New York, saw her comfortably aboard a vessel sailing for Liverpool, and by his sympathy and spiritual unity helped to sustain her in her service of devotion, cheerfully bearing his part of the sacrifice in abiding amidst the cares of home   A joyful reunion was granted to them when that labor of love was completed, and the beloved wife and mother was brought safely back to her native shore, enriched by the experience she had gained and the friendships she had formed, which were liberally shared with those who "abode by the stuff."

Our mother so carefully followed the guidance of the Good Shepherd in such missions that her path was made signally plain. One instance may be briefly mentioned here   It occurred in 1840, when she went to Ohio through the northern part of Maryland and southwestern corner of Pennsylvania, purposing to return so as to visit the meetings of Friends in Dunning's Creek, Bellefonte, and Muncy   The journey was made in her own carriage with her sister-in-law, Grace Evans, and their friend Enos Sharpless, and required many weeks for its accomplishment

In the mean time our father was taken seriously ill, and there seemed little probability of his recovery   Communication by mail was then slow and difficult, and our kind neighbor, George B Allen, volunteered to proceed to Muncy on horseback, where he might possibly intercept the travelling party and hasten their return, that the wife might once more see the dearest object of her affections before the closing hour of his precious life

But "a swifter messenger" met our mother the night she reached Bellefonte, and the "still, small voice" bade her return immediately to her home   Acquainting her companions early next morning with her decision, they approved it, and all three set off for Delaware County Without apprehension they nearly completed the long drive over the mountains and into the southern counties, and only when about to stop for the night near West Chester did they learn of the anxiety at home Hughes Bell was at the door of the Friend's house where they proposed staying till morning, and when asked by the travellers for information respecting their families, gave our mother the first intelligence she received of her husband's illness. A conveyance was ready for a drive to Westtown, but Hughes Bell, appreciating the emergency, kindly asked our mother to take a seat beside him, and brought her directly to Chestnut Bank, which they reached about nine o'clock She was much overcome by the shock, but in a few hours was able to give her skilful and efficient attendance in the sick-chamber, and from that time our father began to revive, and slowly, though steadily, regained his wonted health

Late in the summer of 1846 the dear parents went together to Muncy, attending the meetings of Friends in that part of our State, thus fulfilling the commission given six years previously to our mother. The time for this visit to the family* at Wolf Run was peculiarly appropriate They took with them their stricken daughter and her orphan child, the sorrow shared by all bound the two families more closely together, and they found comfort and strength in loving Christian intercourse

In 1848 they made their last long tour on religious service, driving in their own carriage to Richmond, Indiana, attending the Yearly Meeting there, and other meetings on the route going and returning

My father not only gave freely of his time and means to help his wife in gospel labors, but was equally liberal in assisting other ministers in their missions. In comparatively early life he travelled with Isaac Stevenson, of England, and afterwards with others from that country, and as late as 1843 he went with Rachel Priestman and Isabel Casson through the Western Quarterly Meeting

His house was open to all the Lord's messengers, and in those days they were many Ministers frequently came from

* Of Jacob Haines, Muncy

England, and with scarcely an exception they were welcomed and entertained at Chestnut Bank and forwarded on their way. Both father and mother were truly courteous on such occasions, and I have a pleasant recollection of a fine summer day when our father drove over to Merion to escort Joseph John Gurney to our house, of the cordial reception given by our mother, the handsome dinner, and her enjoyment in his interesting conversation. A meeting appointed for him that afternoon at Springfield was attended by a large number of Friends and neighbors.

A more perfect example of brotherly love could not be found than was seen in the life-long intercourse of our father and his elder brother, George. Born in the same house, and living there together for thirty years, then side by side on adjoining farms, partners in business, and all their interests closely interwoven, there was always entire harmony, and affection ever fresh and lively in mind and heart. This beautiful bond was sealed on the dying bed of our dear uncle, when father uttered the fervent prayer, " Lord be with him !" as his spirit ascended to the eternal home.

With his usual calmness and habitual acquiescence in the Divine will our father bore this bereavement, and faithfully carried out the wishes of his departed brother in the settlement of his affairs.

The old home was finally closed, and the world could never be the same again to him who had almost daily entered its doors for more than seventy years and sat with the beloved ones by its hearth-stone. But the race was nearly run, and soon there would be no more partings.

On Fourth-day, the 9th of First month, 1861, our dear father set off in his carriage as usual to attend to some business in the city. Soon after he left it began to snow, and continued all day to be very inclement. Our thoughts frequently turned towards him with anxiety, knowing how much he felt such wintry weather of later times.

As night drew on we became impatient to see him, and our hearts were relieved soon after the lamps were lighted by his arrival. He brought our friend Anna Potts, and they did not appear to have suffered on their way home; the storm blowing on the back of the carriage, they were sheltered from its severity.

He was less lively than common on his return, but did not complain, only acknowledged, on being questioned, that he had some headache. On Fifth-day morning he started alone before the hour for meeting, wishing to visit one of the workmen who was ill, and who lived a little beyond the meeting-house. This kept him rather late, and I think we were all seated when he came in. I looked at him occasionally during the time for worship, according to my custom, wholly unconscious that it was the last time I should see his honored form in the attitude of reverential waiting upon God in humble devotion and deep introversion of spirit.

The meeting was shorter than usual, at which he felt some concern, but we repressed any thought about it, remarking that our meetings were often long. My sister Deborah rode home with him. Of that afternoon and the next day I have no particular recollection except that he was out much of the time driving or walking.

On Sixth-day evening as we sat round the centre-table with our books and work, my brother Joseph and I were on the sofa and father had his arm-chair near my right hand. Joseph made some remark from which I dissented, and both expressed ourselves positively. Father looked up with a smile and gave one of his gentle rebukes, the propriety of which was at once felt.

The next morning I prepared to leave home, expecting to make a visit of two or three weeks to my uncle William Evans's family and to my brothers in Philadelphia. As I went to the carriage father walked by my side, looking not so well as usual, but giving no other indication of ill health. I expressed some regret in leaving home, to which he replied, " We shall not want to spare thee so long." I then kissed him and bade him farewell, tried to name a time when I should see him in the following week in the city, but could not, and said, " I hope I shall see thee some time next week."

That day it snowed again and the cold increased, the walking was slippery and continued so for several days. I was anxious

about my father, fearing he might fall and receive an injury that
would give him a long time of suffering

On First-day he was at meeting, and after its close talked
affectionately with some of our friends   It was throughout a
quiet, pleasant day to him   In the afternoon he read and had
his accustomed nap on the sofa   Towards evening, according
to long habit, he set off on a solitary walk, this time going no
farther than to our brother Jonathan's

On Second-day snow was falling again, but a sense of duty
seemed to urge our dear father forward, and he went to see his
sisters in Upper Darby   Our aunt Phebe could not persuade
him to stay and dine with them, but he went up to see our aunt
Rebecca, who was confined to her bed at the time, and tried to
make her sensible of his love and his presence by gently stroking
her face   His little grandson George was ill, and he drove
to Dr Anderson's, which was near our uncle Isaac Garrett's
house, to ask him to see the child   The doctor's wife remarked
that it was a rough day for him to be out ; he said yes, but if he
could keep his feet warm he got along pretty well   As he sat
by the fire a dog * came up to him   Julia Anderson observed
that father moved away from it, and she sent the dog out of
the room , her little daughter then went to him and father laid
his hand on her head.

When he reached home the family were at the table , he
joined them pretty directly, and my mother sat by him, helping
him to the dinner that had been kept hot for him

He had an engagement to meet our uncle Joseph Evans that
afternoon and visit a young man who was a member of Springfield Meeting   My brother Joseph asked that he might go and
tell his uncle that it was too cold for him to be out again that
day, but our father had a decided choice in keeping the appoint-
ment, and our brother Jonathan went down with him till he met
with our uncle, and then they two went on together to Stephen
Ogden's   They had a good deal of conversation as they passed
along, and the last interview of these long-proved and faithful
friends was full of consolation to the survivor   With Stephen

---

* He disliked the breath of a dog near his face, and when any of us patted a
dog would send us to wash our hands

Ogden father's remarks were tender and impressive, encouraging him to the faithful performance of the highest duties, saying before he left him, " It is very important to fulfil our part in life so as to obtain peace in the end "

He coughed frequently, and my uncle drew around him the fur robes, and asked him more than once if he felt the cold, to which my father replied in such a way as showed that he was not quite comfortable   After they parted at the meeting-house my father drove home, stopping on his way to talk with Mary Brown, a colored woman who often worked in our house, and who had lately been sorrowing over the removal of a daughter by death.

Before taking a seat at home, he walked down to our brother Jonathan's house, and this last loving ministry accomplished, slowly ascended the well-worn path up the hill, and about five o'clock sat down in his favorite arm-chair in the midst of his family around the parlor fire.   He soon became drowsy and his breathing somewhat unnatural, and lying down upon the sofa, fell asleep.   When supper was announced he did not incline to go to the table, and my sister Deborah carried his tea into the parlor and placed it on a stand near him, our mother sitting by him as he drank it

Near nine o'clock, with some assistance, he went up to his room.   He had evidently taken cold from exposure, and every remedy that affection and our mother's skill could suggest was applied for his relief.   As the night was stormy and the doctor's residence several miles away, the family hesitated about sending for him immediately, and all retired to rest except our mother, who lay down by his side.   He continued so ill that our mother called my brother Joseph at midnight, and a man was despatched for Dr. Anderson.   Father answered the doctor's questions clearly, and remarked that he would like to get over this illness a little, which seemed to have reference to some affairs of business that he wished to see settled   Before the doctor left it was decided to call in Dr. Charles Evans or our brother, Dr James E Rhoads

Accordingly, my brother Jonathan set off early for Germantown with the understanding that he was to return through

Philadelphia, let Charles know of our father's illness, and bring me home in the afternoon.

Throughout the morning he grew worse, frequently dozing for a little while and then arousing with expressions of " Oh, dear !" " Oh, yes !" or ejaculating " Oh, Lord !" indicative of bodily distress. Mother asked, very tenderly, whether anything was upon his mind. He answered, in a cheerful, natural tone, " Oh, no ; I guess not much," and signified that he knew each one around him.

Towards noon a messenger was sent to Westtown for our sister Elizabeth and my daughter Hannah, who were at the school there. The day seemed long to those who were watching the dear invalid while waiting for the arrival of those who had been summoned ; but our sister Rebecca G. Rhoads came to them both morning and afternoon, giving them the comfort of her presence, and near six o'clock our brother James came and promptly made some applications that afforded temporary relief.

Anna Potts returned to the city that morning and came at once to see me. Although careful not to excite alarm, the seriousness of her countenance conveyed her impressions. I was speedily ready to go home, but had to wait for my brother Jonathan, so that it was near five o'clock when we left Union Street, and then had to call at our brother Charles's house. Our drive on that cloudy winter evening was solemn, those lines of Cowper's frequently passing through my mind,—

> " God moves in a mysterious way
> His wonders to perform,
> He plants His footsteps in the sea
> And rides upon the storm."

On our arrival I went directly up-stairs and found my precious father lying apparently unconscious of the presence of any one about him, and breathing heavily. Dr. Anderson was then in consultation with my brother James, and both considered him critically ill with congestion of the lungs. As I looked at him the pressure of disease seemed too great to be thrown off, and I prayed earnestly that our heavenly Father would make all his bed in sickness, and be very merciful in sustaining

him through every trial   The promises in the forty-first Psalm
came with comforting assurance to my mind: " Blessed is he
that considereth the poor. the Lord will deliver him in time of
trouble   The Lord will preserve him, and keep him alive; and
he shall be blessed upon the earth "—" The Lord will strengthen
him upon the bed of languishing: thou wilt make all his bed
in his sickness." I knew that our dear father had tenderly and
faithfully considered the poor and afflicted, and, while I did not
expect him to be restored to physical health, I believed that he
would be safely carried through " the valley of the shadow," and
have the victory over death.

About half an hour later our sister Elizabeth and my dear
Hannah came in, and we were all gathered around him except
our brother Charles, who would not arrive till early next morning   We were told that once during the day our dear father
had said to our mother, " Do not mourn too much," and that
he had expressed a wish to see me.

Between eight and nine o'clock James applied cups to the
back of the chest, Jonathan and myself assisting. This relieved the brain so that he soon aroused, and his mind seemed
quite clear.   He asked whether the doctors thought his condition critical   I replied that he had taken a heavy cold, but
that we hoped he would be better before long.   He then wished
to know what the disease was, to which I answered that his
lungs were affected   He remarked, " I cannot expect to continue very long."

His perceptions now became very quick, and his tones very
sweet and natural   Some water was handed him to drink, on
tasting he remarked it was not very nice,—he was always particular about water being fresh and cool,—so immediately
another pitcher of iced water was brought   Some time after he
was induced to take wine whey, and distinguished the wine as
being of different flavor from another kind that was in the house,
and again, on taking some chicken tea, had salt added to it.

Our mother was not well, and weary from the previous night's
watching, and now retired to another room for a little rest
Deborah and Joseph also went to lie down, and about eleven
o'clock our brother James left the chamber, telling us to call

him at two. Elizabeth, Jonathan, and I stood constantly near
the bed. Our dear father was calm, undismayed by the coming
of the great change, much nearer than we were aware of. He
frequently ejaculated, " Lord, help me!" and once, " Forsake
me not in the time of old age !"

As the night wore on I became apprehensive that the end
was drawing near, and anxious to be certain that he knew that
Elizabeth and I were by him, asked him if he knew us.   " Oh,
yes," he said, and wanted to know how Elizabeth got home.*
My heart was bursting with the mingled tenderness of love and
the remembrance of times when my impetuosity must have
wounded his gentle, affectionate spirit, and I bent over him in
deep emotion, and assuring him that I had always loved him
ardently, begged him to forgive everything that I had ever done
to grieve him.   In heavenly tones he answered, " As I hope to
be forgiven." Some other expressions passed between us that
helped to relieve my breaking heart.   My father continued to
utter at times short prayers for help and mercy, and Jonathan
heard him softly say, " Happy, happy, happy!"

We called my brother James at one o'clock, and soon after
our poor dear mother, Deborah, and Joseph were summoned.
Mother came to his side as quickly as she could, and we all
surrounded the bed, but he had ceased to speak, and lay with
his head supported by pillows, in calm repose, yet conscious.
Mother kissed him, saying, " Thy Saviour, whom thee has
loved and served all thy life, is with thee." I stood close to
him on one side, James on the other, occasionally moistening
his lips with water. No damps of death were on his brow,
his skin was warm and natural, and like one falling asleep in
peaceful quiet, he passed from earth to heaven near five o'clock
in the morning.

In solemn silence we drew around the fire and sat near his
bed for some hours. Messengers had been despatched for our
uncle William Rhoads, uncles Joseph and Joel Evans, and
brother Charles. One after another they arrived, and freely

* He spoke of my brother Charles, and wished to see him; and once said,
" Brother George!" probably with the thought that they would soon be reunited
forever.

mingled their tears with ours Our father's beloved form still
lay almost as if in life, where he fell asleep in Jesus, until they
all came.

Our dear mother maintained her wonted calmness, but the
blow prostrated her, and for many days we did not know whether
the time was at hand for us to part with her, too

On the following First-day morning, the twentieth of the
First month, we saw for the last time the beautiful, manly form
of the tenderest of fathers Many friends and acquaintances,
near and far, came to accompany us to the resting-place of the
earthly tabernacle Our dear mother could not rise from her
bed, and I felt it a privilege to be, as it were, the next one to
him, his eldest child My eyes were fixed upon the coffin as
we followed it on that clear winter morning, and even when
deposited in its lowly bed, and gladly would I have exchanged
places with him, so completely did I realize that for him death
had no sting and the grave no victory

Peaceful as the sunshine pouring into the tomb was the
assurance that his happy spirit was then and forever in full
possession of life, light, and glory, through Him who had
washed him in the fountain of His own blood and crowned
him with salvation and immortality

Many testimonies came to us of impressions made by our
beloved father's blameless life and loving Christian service in
his daily walk

On hearing of his sudden removal, a neighboring proprietor
of mills where he had frequent business remarked that it must
have been well with him, for he lived a life of prayer.

A man whom he employed in the quarries for many years
said to George Allen, "I was never so hurt in my life as I was
one day by Joseph Rhoads." "How was that?" "I had been
drinking and went to his house, when he met me he said,
'Oh, John!'"

John Ogden was driving on the West Chester road one day
that winter, and had occasion to stop at a blacksmith's shop a few
miles from our house Something was said about the decease
of Joseph Rhoads, when the blacksmith, expressing surprise,
added, "Had I known of it I would have gone to the funeral

if I had been obliged to make my way there on my hands and knees: he cured me of swearing." John Ogden asked him how it was, and the smith replied that Joseph Rhoads had stopped there once in passing to have a shoe fitted to his horse. The smith was busy at the time shoeing an unruly animal, and, losing his patience while Joseph Rhoads was standing by him awaiting his turn, used very profane language. This brought a sigh so deep and sorrowful from our father that the smith's conscience was smitten and he was enabled to give up the sinful habit from that hour.

I have before me some observations of my brother Charles's, written years ago, which show how his inner life at home impressed a close witness, and also its effect in the conflicting circumstances that sometimes arise unavoidably in proper attention to business.

" My father was the most extraordinary instance of Christian purity of character that I ever knew. Long at the head of Springfield Meeting as its presiding elder, and holding many other stations of high trust in the Society of Friends, he was untiring in the performance of his religious duties. His meekness and gentleness were proverbial. I have seen him under the strongest provocation, but never knew him to lose his temper.

" Andrew D. Cash, my preceptor in the conveyancing business, whose opportunities for observing character in the line of his profession were equal to most, and whose ripe and unbiassed judgment gave great weight to his opinion, in commenting upon my father's conduct in the course of some legal business which he transacted for him, and which grew excessively annoying from the protracted litigation arising out of it, remarked to me that he had never seen such patient forbearance exhibited under such circumstances by any other man." *

On the day of his decease my uncle Thomas Evans wrote to my mother-in-law Rachel Haines informing her of the event. Expressing his sense of loss, he says, " Few men, I believe, lived nearer to Christ than did our dear brother. His daily

---

* The business here referred to was in the care of my aunt's property, and was always done as a labor of love by my father.

walk was loud preaching as the example of one perfecting holiness in the fear of God   Loving, gentle, and ever ready to serve others, he endeared himself to us all, even as an own brother, and will go down to his grave honored and beloved by a large circle

"May I—may we all—follow in his footsteps, considering the end of his conversation and walk on earth, even Jesus Christ, the same yesterday, to-day, and forever"

The household left by my dear father continued to reside as before at Chestnut Bank, till the approaching marriage of our elder brother Joseph made some change inevitable

After serious consideration and consultation with some of our near relatives, it seemed best for all concerned that the old home and its surrounding acres should be the residence of the eldest son   My mother and sisters Deborah and Elizabeth, myself and daughter, decided to remove to Germantown, which would bring us near to my brother, Dr. James E Rhoads, and within easy reach of many near relations, beside offering other advantages to a family composed of women

From the time of our father's departure our mother's health was extremely delicate, but her lovely spirit rested in the Divine will, and all her mental powers continued to the last in their wonted strength and brightness   Calmly, and with her usual clear judgment, a house was chosen in Germantown, and she prepared to leave the home of forty-three years of happy married life, endeared to her by its own attractions and the most sacred associations

The autumn of 1862 saw us settled in our new abode, and much as we had to feel in the change, we never doubted that the movement was a right one.   We had already many friends in that part of the city, and their welcome was warm and sincere.   The house was convenient and cheerful, sunshine and flowers and the air of refinement and domestic comfort that our mother always imparted to her surroundings made it satisfactory to our moderate wishes.

Our religious privileges were not diminished, and we enjoyed free intercourse with the most cultured social circle and with spiritually-minded Christians

Frequent visits from her children and from her brothers and sisters soothed our mother's heart, and her influence and judgment in spiritual matters were owned and appreciated. When unable to go out to the meeting of ministers and elders it was sometimes held in her house, and one of them told me of the grace and dignity with which she greeted them as they assembled in her parlor.

The last time she attended public worship was on a beautiful First-day morning in the summer of 1865. Dressed with her accustomed neatness and good taste, her erect figure gave no sign of age, and when she rose to speak it was as of one inspired by a heavenly message of love and earnest desire that every one might be firmly established on the Rock of Ages. Before closing her address she expressed the belief that a special blessing of Divine grace and power was even then beginning to descend on the congregation, but she also added that she feared there were some who, like the lord on whose hand the king of Israel leaned, would see it with their eyes, and yet, for want of faith, would not partake thereof. Words prophetically true in regard to the blessing which did come abundantly, and sadly so in the case of some who did not discern the signs of the times.

Month after month of her more than four years of widowhood rolled on, her active spirit yielding with sweetest grace to the restrictions of lessening physical powers, but all alive to the interests of her family, her friends, her country, the whole Christian church, and the world. Her heart was ever expanding in love and her mind enlarging in its views.

Perfectly natural in all her ways, ever ready to acquire fresh knowledge, with undiminished interest in the social, mental, and religious development of her children and grandchildren, she would meet the repeatedly severe attacks of disease, when the moment of departure seemed at hand, with utmost composure and serenest trust.

The warm friend of the colored race, she watched the long struggle of her country in the throes of emancipation with sympathy for all the suffering, but in firm reliance on the Supreme Ruler of nations, and none could have been more devoutly thankful when the bonds of slavery were broken and peace was restored to the brotherhood of States When Lincoln fell a martyr for his country, she felt as if one of her own family had been taken away, and her house was closed at once, as in mourning, till the funeral was over.

In those last few years we conversed together on every topic of interest to us, and the memory of that intimate intercourse is precious Sons and daughters, other near relations and friends, were indefatigable in their affectionate attentions and loving ministrations.

Our sister Deborah had been called to Haddonfield to the care of our brother Charles's children, whose lovely mother was removed to her home above, and that gave to our sister Elizabeth more care of our precious mother and of domestic affairs, as much of my time was occupied in the education of my daughter and three of her young companions

In the eighth month of 1865 Elizabeth needed a change of air and went for a short visit to her friends at Muncy During her absence our brother Charles brought his little daughters Mary and Katharine to see us and stayed all night In the morning, before they left, our mother wished to see the children, and as she did not rise to breakfast, they came to her room She noticed their dresses particularly, and said she wished them to be dressed as their mother's good taste would have directed, and desired that we should purchase some nice material for a frock for each of them, as a present from her

Hannah and I sat in her room most of the morning, Hannah trimming a straw bonnet, in which my mother took her usual interest Her dinner was taken to her on a tray, and although she declined taking any dessert, she seemed to relish a piece of a fine watermelon that I induced her to taste

About three o'clock in the afternoon I left her for a short rest in the adjoining room, hoping she would have also refreshing repose Soon I heard a sound that called me to her side, and I saw that a hemorrhage had come on In allusion to her desire that she might keep as well as usual in my sister Elizabeth's absence, she looked at me and said, " This looks discouraging " I called Hannah immediately, and placing myself on the bed beside her, supported my precious mother in my arms Seeing that I was alarmed, she said, as naturally and as calmly as if in perfect health, "I wish to die quietly" In a moment the happy spirit was gone, free from all bonds, and welcomed by the Saviour, whom she had so long loved and trusted, to the world of light and love and eternal life For hours we sat by her side, her head resting on the pillow as if in sleep, shaded by her soft, waving brown hair, her placid features were majestically beautiful and almost young again

My brother James soon joined us, and then our uncle Thomas Evans and aunt Katharine, who happened to be passing near on the way to their daughter's house on a neighboring street

Loving hearts and tender hands accomplished for her all the last offices, and then the still lovely form was laid beside her husband in the old family burial-ground at Springfield Herself was otherwhere Never do I think of her without seeming to see her in the realms of eternal joy and blessedness, radiant with life and happiness

CHAPTER XIV.

WILLIAM ELLIS HAINES

To HANNAH RHOADS GARRETT

MY DEAR DAUGHTER,—I have long wished to write a memoir of thy beloved father that might give thee a distinct impression of him, but have always been discouraged by a sense of inability to fulfil my desire I need the pen of an angel to portray his character and represent him as he moved among men in his manly vigor

One of my chief pleasures is the contemplation of his virtues and the remembrance of the share I had in his society and affections, together with the assurance that he is now enjoying a far more glorious state of existence

Yes! his early and unexpected removal was only the exchange of a perfected earthly life for immortality in the kingdom where the glory of the celestial is given in place of the glory of the terrestrial

"The memory of the just is blessed," and may his be blessed to us, although his watchful care is removed and his loving voice is hushed Great is our loss, but his parting words, " God will be a Father to the fatherless, and will not forsake the widow," are verified as we put our trust in Him and follow His guidance

Incomplete as I know the following sketch to be, I hope it may have a value in conveying to thee some impressions of him whose name and character are so dear to thee M R H

William Ellis Haines was of honorable descent in the truest sense of the term, as traced through five successive generations to an upright English ancestry All his grandparents were highly-esteemed members of the religious Society of Friends

His grandfather, Jesse Haines, retained the use of a clear, strong understanding and an accurate, retentive memory to the close of his long life, near the end of his hundredth year. His later years were passed chiefly in reading and meditation, cheerful conversation with his friends, and regular attendance at public worship, where he was frequently engaged in preaching the gospel and in vocal prayer

His grandmother, Rachel Haines, deceased about the eightieth year of her age, before I became acquainted with the family. She was honored by her descendants and esteemed by her friends as one of those "elders who have obtained a good report"

William Ellis, for whom this grandson was named, deceased in the meridian of life. His character was marked by persevering energy and unbending integrity, combined with a most generous and benevolent temper His grandmother, Mercy Ellis, cheerfully shared with her husband the cares incident to life in a newly-settled country, and together they were favored to see "the solitary place become glad for them, and the wilderness to rejoice and blossom as the rose" She survived him for the long period of forty-one years, and continued to reside on the estate in the valley of Muncy that bore so many marks of his efficient enterprise

To her is applicable St. Paul's description of a "widow indeed;" she having "brought up children, lodged strangers, washed the saints' feet, relieved the afflicted, and diligently followed every good work."

The memory of his parents, Jacob and Rachel Ellis Haines, is cherished by many who knew them with the love and honor eminently their due.

For nearly eight years after their marriage they resided at Westtown, Chester County, in Pennsylvania, and there he was born on the thirtieth day of the Tenth month, 1816.

His very infancy was marked by a spirit of uncommon energy and sweetness. A little incident foreshadowing presence of mind and prompt action occurred when he was scarcely three years old. He and a baby sister were playing in an upper room where the windows opened down to the floor; the maid left them for an instant to bring something she had forgotten; while absent, the little girl crept to the window-ledge, and was found suspended by her clothing, to which her brother was holding on with all his might, anxiously calling for help.

When but little older, as his father and mother were driving down hill in a chaise, with their boy between them, the horse stumbled and threw them out of the vehicle; alighting on the awkward animal's back, he clung to it till rescued by his father.

It was his delight to examine into the history and foundation of things, and this disposition being properly directed, proved advantageous in later life, when the correctness of his knowledge or of his principles was put to the test.

Another trait, love of order, seemed inherent, when the yet infantile boy, unconsciously obeying one of the commandments (Deuteronomy, xxii. 1) to the ancient Hebrews, marched up to the boarding-school and, saluting the principal, said, "Superintendent, dost thou know that the cattle have broken into the corn-field?"

In the autumn of 1823 the family removed to the valley of Muncy, in Lycoming County. At first they lived on the farm that my mother-in-law inherited from her father. Her brother, William Cox Ellis, having given up the Wolf Run house when he entered on the practice of law, it was occupied for a while by Henry Ecroyd, who in a short time desired to leave it for a place better adapted to his business, which gave my father-in-law, Jacob Haines, an opportunity to purchase the whole property, and it has been the residence of the family ever since

Surrounded by grand and beautiful scenery, blessed with a home and parents that fostered all that is good and noble, William Ellis Haines grew in vigor of mind and body In person he was tall and well formed, lithe and graceful in action; his complexion fair; his countenance full of intelligence, dignity, and sweetness, the mouth and eyes most expressive

His whole bearing was manly and courteous, distinguished by the indefinable charm that springs from native nobility of soul, superior abilities, and a warm, generous, and gentle heart

A lady who resided near his father's house in his childhood, when speaking of him long afterwards, said that in her frequent visits to the family, if she remained till evening, he never allowed her to go home alone, but, if his father were absent, would insist, boy as he was, upon escorting her.

Always his companionship was pleasantness itself, and a playfulness of temper would often glide with lambent light along his conversation, or break into joyous action

The first record of his thoughts in my possession is a little journal of a visit to Philadelphia with his father in the spring of 1831 On this tour they had the agreeable company of Rebecca Singer, afterwards Rebecca Collins, of New York, an active evangelist and philanthropist They attended the Yearly Meeting while there, and at his father's suggestion he noted the subjects that came before it, the friends at whose houses they visited, and gave some account of various objects of interest that he examined, such as the shipping at the wharves, the Mint, Museum, State-House, and several benevolent institutions With his cousin, William E Morris, he crossed the Delaware and walked through Camden He recorded the presence and services of Jonathan and Hannah Backhouse at several meetings and at the funeral of his uncle, Dr Benjamin Ellis, who was taken ill with scarlet fever and deceased while he was in the city, at the age of thirty-two.

Dr. Ellis was a gifted man, of a fine poetical temperament, and was already well known as a rising physician and author of a "Medical Formulary" in use to this day. He was married to Amy, daughter of Ellis Yarnall, a lady of superior character. Few as were their opportunities of being together, Dr. Ellis made a lasting impression on his young nephew. Similarity of mind and taste led him into the same pursuits, and made him a legatee of the uncle, whose will directed that his medical library and a handsomely-bound copy of the "Edinburgh Encyclopædia," in twenty-one volumes, quarto, inherited from his father, William Ellis, should become the property of that one of his nephews who should first take the degree of M.D. in the University of Pennsylvania.

After preliminary instruction partly under the care of his grandfather Jesse Haines, he entered at the fifteenth year of his age on a three years' course at Westtown Boarding-School. There he enjoyed the respect and good-will of teachers and classmates, which they continued to manifest as opportunity offered, and in speaking of him have expressed the high estimation then formed of his character. His lively spirits, habits of observation, and an innocent play of wit made him an agreeable companion among his youthful associates; his steadfast regard to truth and right insured the esteem of both old and young.

Diligently pursuing his studies in the Greek and Latin languages, mathematics, and some other branches of learning, his too close application began to affect his health so as to render a temporary retreat from school advisable.

A few only have been preserved of the many letters to his parents and other members of the family during different periods of absence. In one—dated at Westtown, 6th mo. 18th, 1834—he says, "I have concluded, after a consultation which I suppose lasted five minutes, to write, and have procured apparatus to perform the great and laborious task. We are all here yet, house still standing, and people living in it. Everything seems to enjoy the short time allotted to it here. The boys and the birds and even the locusts may be heard at certain times in the day, but not I. I have taken a great delight in surveying; my time between schools is wholly taken up with it. Possibly Mary* may have mentioned something respecting my having a pain in my breast 'Tis true I have been troubled not a little with it, and it has given me some uneasiness Mary says she thinks if mother should come down this summer she would take me away. I have made up my mind to go through surveying first, if I can stand it I am not as healthy as I have been, but as this will be the last schooling I shall get, I hardly know what to think of it I am convinced it would be the best policy our nurse says she thinks I had better go home. Should you deem it best, I shall expect a little corner in the house next winter (for a study), for I am not going to give myself up as a scholar yet "

Shortly after he relinquished his favorite pursuits for a time, and after spending a few weeks at his uncle William Haines's residence in New Garden, returned to Muncy with his father in the Eighth month

It is clear, by remarks in the letters referred to, that he became very early interested in the religious society with which he was by birthright connected, and it was after careful consideration, and no superficial examination, that he adopted its Christian principles, doctrines, and practices, and was settled in his membership as a Friend Simultaneously the charity that always marked his intercourse with others, of every rank and sect, was taking deep root in his heart No shadow of bigotry or superstition ever tinged his views of the relations existing between man and man, or between man and his Creator.

In thinking of his future career, the medical profession appeared to him to be his true vocation, and accordingly he began special preparation for it under the supervision of Dr James Rankin, a highly-esteemed physician in the town of Muncy.

Residing at Wolf Run, his father's house, in the summers, it was his custom to rise early in the morning, often breakfasting alone before the usual family hour, and walk three miles to the town On the winding road that leads to it over Muncy Creek, he enjoyed the fine scenery of the cultivated valley and tree-

* His sister Mary was a student at Westtown at that time

covered hills blending into the distant Alleghanies; but once arrived at the office of his preceptor, his time and attention were assiduously devoted to study until the approach of evening.

In these morning and evening walks he had to pass the residence of his uncle William Cox Ellis, whose four daughters were noted for their beauty and accomplishments. A momentary chat with these lovely cousins materially enlivened the long hours of study.

Although a close student in hours set apart for that purpose, he entered with cheerfulness into social pleasures, and engaged actively in open-air exercises at proper seasons for relaxation.

Whatever he undertook he did well and quickly. His social privileges gave him ready access to a large circle of attractive young persons, as well as to the society of older friends and acquaintances, whose culture and wisdom he knew how to appreciate.

But even his recreations were subservient to progress in usefulness. Anticipating Ruskin's ideas of turning the student's physical training to good account, he volunteered in one of his vacations to plough a field of twenty acres on the Wolf Run farm. It is a fine piece of ground commanding an extended prospect, so that he had a threefold pleasure as he turned over the brown earth,—intimacy with nature, healthful invigoration, and a sense of adding to the value of the farm. That ploughing was remarked upon for its precision and thoroughness. At another time he built a summer-house in the garden, that he might have a quiet retreat for reading after tea, and this was in later years a favorite resort of his aged grandfather.

Dr. Green, a minister from New England, visited Lycoming County on a missionary tour, and needing a guide among the mountains, the young student was chosen to go with him. They travelled on horseback, and the doctor being an adept in horsemanship, his companion improved the opportunity for taking lessons. He became an accomplished rider, and the graceful ease with which he could in this way travel for hours made it a ready and healthful mode of performing frequent professional tours.

Entering the University of Pennsylvania under the instruction of a corps of able men, including Drs Hare, Gibson, Hodge, Chapman, and George B Wood, his closest attention was given to advancement in his chosen line of study, but he neglected no suitable opportunity for general culture This enabled him to meet others on common ground, and, combined with quick sympathies and ready wit, secured a welcome in the best society

Writing to his father, near the close of lectures in the spring of 1837, he remarks, " The swift hand of Time, even should I remain till they are over, will soon bring round the day for my returning Then, I hope, if I should continue to be blessed with health as I have been thus far, I can return home with the full assurance of having performed my duty so far as application goes, and that is two-thirds at least in getting along in this sublunary sphere . .

" Thou, as well as mother, seems to urge my visiting my, or your, friends in the city rather more than I do I am fully satisfied that it is best for body and mind not to be as secluded as an anchorite, yet the danger of getting upon the other extreme is very great and much more to be dreaded in my estimation I intend paying a visit all round before I leave town

" I was pleased to learn that Sister Mary had gone to Wellsborough, though I hope (selfish) she will be at home when I return I called on Martha Ecroyd the day after she came to town we were speaking of Mary, and some one remarked, ' How lonesome Mary must feel !' I began to think of it and found she had very few associates indeed I just thought what a fine thing it would be if she could spend some time at Lockport, there I leave it "

The letter goes on to mention having purchased Good's " Book of Nature" for his father as an addition to the home library, and enters into some business affairs, particularly agricultural improvements that his father had in view, discussing them carefully and with judgment

Laborious confinement was again beginning to tell upon his strength, but with care he was able to continue his studies until the lectures were ended, and also to pass with much credit a strict examination by the faculty His friends were not ex-

16

pecting him to graduate till the following year, but with his usual earnestness and celerity he had gone so thoroughly over the prescribed course * that some of the professors encouraged him to try for a degree at once. This he determined to do, and wishing his father and mother to feel no anxiety about it, the first intimation they received of it was when he handed them his diploma.

Several of the faculty gave him letters expressing their esteem for his abilities and recommending him with confidence as a physician to any community in which he might conclude to reside.

And now, with a settled determination to occupy fully the talents committed to his trust, in reliance upon his Lord for aid and blessing in his exertions, he assumed the responsible duties of independent manhood.

A few weeks passed at home, and again he crossed the mountains, this time accompanying his grandfather, Jesse Haines, already over fourscore, to Philadelphia. While there, attending the Yearly Meeting, they incidentally heard that a competent physician was needed in Springfield, Delaware County. Having made some inquiry respecting it, Dr. Haines decided to pass through the neighborhood on the homeward route, which accorded well with the inclination of his grandfather, who was an old friend of my grandmother Rhoads and her family. They left Philadelphia on the last morning of the Yearly Meeting week, a day ever after remembered by us both as the first on which we met. It was the spring I was seventeen, and one of the most beautiful I have ever seen.

I had been left mistress at home for the week, and was anxious to have everything in good order and a bright welcome for my father and mother on their return. To give the last touches my little brothers and I had rambled off to meadow and woodland for wild flowers, and had just come in, our hands full of lovely blossoms for ornamenting the rooms, when, hearing a knock at the door, I opened it. "Are Joseph and Hannah Rhoads at home?" was asked, in a pleasant voice. To my

---

* One proof of his thoroughness was that he had prepared and mounted a complete anatomical specimen of the human frame.

prompt rejoinder, "They have not yet come back from the city," the gentleman, with a half-amused expression, replied, that his grandfather, Jesse Haines, was in a carriage at our gate, and had intended calling to see them, bowed, and went away. I was too intent on my own plans to make any effort to detain them, and they drove on to my uncle, George Rhoads's, whose house was in sight and not unknown to Jesse Haines. There they were hospitably welcomed and refreshed, and in the afternoon they proceeded towards Muncy. Brief as was the interview, it left with me the impression of an agreeable countenance and a bearing gracefully courteous and dignified

A physician at Jersey Shore, on the Susquehanna, requested Dr. Haines to supply his place for a few weeks of absence, which he did, and then some of his friends were desirous that he should settle in Williamsport, but that situation not commending itself to his judgment, he concluded to visit Springfield again and ascertain what could be done there.

Turning on Limestone Ridge to take a last look at the paternal mansion, uncertain where his lot might be cast, he felt for the first time, in its full force, that his home could be no longer there, and now success depended on his own energies, under the guidance and blessing of an Almighty Protector

To his sister Mary he wrote from

" PHILADELPHIA, Sixth mo 27th, 1837

" I received a very acceptable letter from thee, my dear sister, to-day, Third-day, after having returned from Springfield I found much more difficulty in obtaining board than I anticipated from the interest evinced for my success by several of the residents of the place, such as Joel Evans and brothers , but it is always necessary for a young man when going to settle in a new neighborhood to have some regard to the character of the family he is about entering Soon after my letter to father was written I went out there and made some inquiry, but was unsuccessful. I then went to West Chester and Westtown and down to Kennet Square, but heard of no place save New London Cross-roads. Not relishing the idea of going there, I returned to Springfield. All reasonable exertions were made in

my absence, but ineffectually. I returned on Seventh-day
through the rain, remained there over First-day, and also attended Monthly Meeting on Second-day. That evening I
mounted Solus with the intention of shaking the dust from my
feet upon their soil, but a friend requested me to call as I went
along at the house of Thomas Rudolph, who lives about half a
mile this side of Springfield meeting-house. I accordingly called
and was somewhat surprised to find them hesitate a little, and
mentioned if they would like to have some time I would give
them till morning, which was agreed to. I returned to Joseph
Lownes's * and this morning called again, and I may say to my
utter surprise they had concluded to take a boarder.

"One might think from the difficulty I had in obtaining
boarding that the prospect was rather dull, but if I can judge
from the expression of those I called upon they were very glad
of the circumstance (of my coming), and had no doubt I would
succeed, though it probably would take time. At all risks I
shall go out there and let them know what I came for, and if
they choose to employ me, well and good, and if not it will be
time enough to think ' what next ?'

" I think I shall go down to New London Cross-roads this
week and call at Westtown on my way and attend to some
matters father and I had some conversation about. Next week
I wish to move into my new habitation."

Thomas Rudolph's occupation brought many business-men
to his house, through whom Dr. Haines became speedily known
in the county. The most influential families applied to him at
once as occasions arose requiring medical advice and assistance,
and he quickly won the confidence of the laboring class ; yet
there was some leisure left for acquisitions in other fields of
knowledge.

He was never one-sided in anything, his interest extending
beyond subjects connected directly with his profession into the

* Joseph Lownes's son William was a schoolmate at Westtown, and always a
firm and faithful friend to Dr. Haines. He was a young man of good understanding, well educated, refined, and rather handsome in appearance, and decidedly a
Christian. He died in early life of pulmonary consumption.

varied domains of science and literature and improvements in agriculture and other arts. He delighted in poetry, had a fine perception of the pure and beautiful in all its forms, and enjoyed a racy bit of wit or humor.

In the winter of 1837–38 he gave a course of lectures at Springfield on chemistry, one or two on optics, and a few on astronomy. They awakened a lively interest in the vicinity, and were well attended by an appreciative audience. It was one of his principles to advance steadily and perseveringly towards a worthy mark, saying none were likely to go higher than their aim; yet it was not personal elevation that he sought, but to take his part in the general uplifting of the whole family of man.

Love of his early home was not diminished by unavoidable absence from it, and his letters often expressed his affectionate solicitude that his younger brother and sisters should press forward in the line of mental and moral improvement.

TO HIS SISTER SARAH.

" Fourth month 29th, 1838.

" In the quiet of a First-day afternoon I have seated myself to write to my dear little sister. It shall not be said that I do not write to thee any longer. I was very glad to receive thy kind little communication, as it gives me an evidence I am not entirely forgotten by thee and affords thee an opportunity of improving in thy letter-writing, which is a great accomplishment in any one's sister.

" I hope by this time you have the company of our dear mother. I was very glad to see her and very sorry to part with her, as I did not, nor did any one else, know how long it would be before I should again enjoy the same pleasure. But I hope we may all be favored to meet many times together, although our places of abode may be many miles apart.

" I received a letter while mother was here from our dear brother Jesse. He appears to be much pleased with his situation and studies, and I hope will improve rapidly. I am very glad that my dear little sisters take so much interest in their books. I hope they will continue to do so, and then they will grow up to be intelligent young women, and everybody whose esteem is worth having will be pleased with them if they only cultivate a quiet, gentle disposition.

"I often think of my dear little sisters at home, and how glad I should be to see them. I was much pleased with thy attempt at letter-writing: it is very well done for a beginner. Endeavor to be particular about thy spelling at the commencement, as nothing looks so badly as a letter badly spelled; it shows at once that a person reads but little, or is careless and does not attend to what he does read. . . .

"I must close to write to father, so as to send by Cousin Martha. Please give my love to dear little sisters Anna, Rebecca, and Rachel, and accept a large share thyself from thy affectionate brother, W. E. HAINES."

To have the advantages of a school in Wellsborough, Jesse and Sarah were kindly received as members of the family in the house of their uncle and aunt Morris, who resided in that town. Writing to them he says,—

"Second month 10th, 1839.

"MY DEAR BROTHER AND SISTER,—It is with peculiar satisfaction I now attempt to hold conversation with you in this silent, but I hope not unacceptable, manner. I have many times as I have been passing up and down the country in the line of my occupation thought of you, who are so much younger than myself, and are so far from the place you were taught to call home.

"Notwithstanding you are deprived of the tender care of our dear mother and the prudent counsel of our affectionate father, you are under the roof of one of the kindest aunts any children were ever blessed with, who takes pleasure in ministering to the wants of those around her.

"Your opportunities are excellent, both for the cultivation and consequent expansion of the mind, and for becoming acquainted with the regulations of a well-organized and wisely-conducted family. How impressive is the manner of the inmates of such! all know their respective tasks, which they go about quietly, speedily, and tastefully. I wish before long you would write to me and let me know how you are getting on with your different pursuits, and also how you continue to like the school   I do not know that I have heard anything from you since I bid you farewell   If I should be able to visit Muncy next summer I hope it may be at such time as you can leave without any disadvantage, or interfering with the prosecution of your studies, so that we may all once more gather round the family table. . . .

"I attended the Philadelphia Quarterly Meeting last Second-day, and had the pleasure of listening to Daniel Wheeler, concerning whose travels in the South Sea Islands you have probably seen some account in *The Friend*   He is an inhabitant of Russia   Please give my love to dear aunt and cousins, and write soon to your affectionate brother,

"Wm E Haines."

Sarah was sent for advanced study to Westtown, where our brother Jesse was also at that time in school, as will be seen in the following extract from a letter to Sarah in 1841 :

"As, if I remember rightly, thou art to leave in the fall, I hope thou wilt embrace every opportunity for improvement   Regard as nothing, or worse than nothing, every gratification or pleasure which will not repay in some substantial nourishment   By having thy mind stored with substantial knowledge thou wilt be enabled to form friendships which will wear those formed at school, unless with persons of a studious, thoughtful bent of mind, are of no value, but tend to sap laudable intentions.   Do not allow thy mind too often to dwell on home and its attractions, but resolve to carry back with thee the rich fruits of a well-spent year, which will stand the test of time   My dear sister, I must now close   Tell Jesse to write and let me know how he succeeds "

Attention to all branches of science connected with his profession, his clear, calm judgment and efficient action, insured a constantly-increasing practice and left little time either for social visiting or miscellaneous reading, but that little was carefully used   Opportunities which his long rides by day and by night afforded for reflection were to him a source of pleasure and improvement. Sometimes he would tell me of special trains of thought that had occupied his mind in those solitary journeys, and express the wish that he could have penned them as they passed before him.

Thomas Rudolph removing with his family to a distant neighborhood, Dr. Haines was obliged to look for another home, and resided for a time in the house of E. W., situated nearer the centre of his practice. This did not prove to be an agreeable change in some respects, but cheerfully acquiescing in what was for the time unavoidable, he resolved to provide a home of his own as soon as prudence would warrant it, George Maris, an elderly Friend, was then boarding at E. W.'s, and became his firm friend, and was particularly kind to him in a severe illness with rheumatic fever in the summer of 1840. After partial recovery he thought it best to leave the scene of his labors for a while and seek rest and renovation amidst his relatives in the bracing air of Lycoming County. A few pleasant weeks there, and his strength gradually increasing, inaction became irksome, he resumed his duties in Delaware County, and finally regained his usual health.

In the autumn of that year his sister Mary was taken ill with typhoid fever. Her recovery seemed, at the crisis, very doubtful, and the prospect of separation by death from one to whom he had been so closely and tenderly united since infancy gave the brother exquisite pain. Difficult as it was to leave his patients, he felt that a higher duty called him to his father's family. At that day typhoid fever was not so well understood as now, and skilful as were his sister's physicians, they had failed to discover the true cause of her protracted suffering. His penetration convinced him that a change in treatment was necessary, and on consultation it was adopted, resulting in ultimate recovery.

As soon as he was satisfied that there was a favorable turn in the condition of his dear sister, he hastened back to his post at Springfield, and his arrival there was none too early, as quickly appeared. He came to Harrisburg by the canal, a cold rain making the journey uncomfortable; but a letter, dated Tenth month 7th, says it was rendered more tolerable by his having the company of Dr. Patterson and his wife, of Philadelphia, and Squire Smith, of Wellsborough. The remainder of the way was by rail, a new mode of travel over that route. His comments on it are: "From Harrisburg came home in style; left there at eight o'clock A.M., and was at home by five o'clock P.M., and visited a patient by six, having stopped to dine on the road; came from Harrisburg to Middletown, a distance of twelve miles, in thirty-six minutes. There is some sense in travelling when you can go at that rate." To one of such warm affections it would have been a great boon to breakfast, as I have been able to, in Philadelphia at seven, and dine at Wolf Run at two on the same day. In the letter referred to above he goes on to write, " On my way to Muncy it seemed as if I could not get on as fast as I should like, but when I saw thee improving it seemed as if I should be home again in order to be in my right place.

" When I got in the neighborhood I learned of the illness of Joseph Rhoads. As soon as I came I was applied to and still continue to attend him. He is much better, and I am in hope will gradually regain his former state of health."

That autumn my mother, accompanied by my aunt Grace Evans and our friend Enos Sharpless, was engaged in a religious visit to the western parts of Pennsylvania and eastern Ohio. It was during this absence that my father was taken ill and was brought so low that for a few days neither himself nor those of his family around him expected him to continue long with us. Another extract from the letter quoted above shows how his watchful and sagacious physician viewed the circumstances in connection with the return of our dear mother at this crisis. Alluding to her absence, he says, " It made it very trying for his family. As the disease kept on apace, they were so much alarmed as to start a messenger * in pursuit of her. But, my dear sister, where the concern is a right one, there is no necessity for making ' much ado about nothing.' The same Power which ordered His servant to leave all for the sake of the gospel would not

* George B. Allen, ever a most kind neighbor, went on horseback to Muncy to meet my mother. According to her proposed plan of travel she would be there by the time he could arrive.

leave her destitute if the eye was kept singly turned to His holy self; that is the difficult point. But here is an individual whose mission is from the only true and safe source, far from home; her family do not know where to find her when her husband is taken very ill; they send letters and a messenger where she expected to be, in the hope of hastening her return, in order, as they feared, to take her last leave of him she loved most in this world. But a messenger far more fleet than the wind, in whose career space is entirely annihilated, had already done what was necessary. He told her she might be released from further service at present and return home to her family.

"They accordingly left Bellefonte on Third-day morning and came home as directly as they could. Hannah Rhoads heard not a word of the state of her family until Seventh-day evening when they came to Charles Lippincott's, near West Chester. Hughes Bell, who keeps the farm-house at Westtown, was there with his wife, and had the horse put to the chair to go home when they drove up. The first question Hannah Rhoads put was, had they heard from her family. They then told her. She got out of their carriage into Hughes's chair, and he kindly brought her home by nine o'clock that night, so she was spared all the anxiety she would have felt had she known it sooner, for I doubt whether she could have borne up under it. She could not speak when she entered the house at first; those present looked as cheerful as they could; she then exclaimed, 'I see he is living!' Joseph was decidedly better when Hannah came home. . . .

"George B. Allen arrived last evening, by whom I received three lines and a half from father, telling me thee had not got well yet. I think thee is slow. What has thee been about? I could get sick and well, too, half a dozen times since I left you. Come, buckle to afresh. I want father and mother to come down this fall, as every six months mother puts off coming the angle of her jaw will become more and more obtuse.

"As my dear sister is yet weak, I do not wish to be the means, directly or indirectly, of fatiguing her; with my best wishes attending thee, I hope there will not for long be the like necessity there was [for a visit to Muncy as] when I came last."

His own serious illness in the summer, and the anxiety occasioned by his sister's afterwards, made a lasting impression on his character. It was a season of taking deeper root in spiritual life, and of entire surrender and dedication to the will of his Lord, with earnest prayer to be firmly established on the only sure foundation, the Rock of Ages. From this period his walk was that of one who plainly declares that he seeks a better country,—that is, a heavenly.

After consulting with his particular friends, my uncles William Rhoads and Joel Evans, in the winter of 1840–41 he purchased a convenient piece of land, pleasantly situated, containing about fifteen acres, on which were three dwelling-houses. Writing to his father of the transaction, he playfully remarked that most young men would be satisfied with one house, but that his ambitious son had bought three. Choosing one for his residence, he immediately set about such alterations and improvements that by the end of the following summer he had for his own accommodation a cheerful, ample home, with a neat stable and carriage-house, and two good dwellings to let.

On a beautiful morning, the seventh day of the Tenth month, 1841, in the venerable meeting-house at Springfield, surrounded by a large assembly of relatives and friends, we were united in marriage. The next week we entered our home together, our hearts filled with happiness and not a cloud on our horizon.

It was Dr. Haines's intention that we should make a tour northward immediately after our wedding, and spend some time with his relations in Lycoming County. With this in view he purchased a comfortable four-seated carriage, which, with his lively bay horses, made an attractive outfit ("very bridish," a groomsman remarked). But severe illness among his patients bound him to Delaware County, and we cheerfully began our new mode of life without that gratification.

Some slight circumstance, some glimpse of beauty, will often remain impressed upon the memory without our being able to account for it. One such among the many recurs to me at this moment. It was near the close of a delightful October day; the balmy air, clear sky, richly-tinted autumn flowers, and the varied hues of our magnificent woodlands threw an exquisite

charm ovei the departing year   Returning from his daily circuit, his attention was caught by the brilliant glow over the
landscape from the westering sun.   Spurring his horse, in a few
moments he was at my side, and together we watched the glory
of day fading into the soft gray of twilight

There is little of incident to record   A steady growth in
knowledge and wisdom, an increasing sphere of usefulness in
his own rank and largely among the laboring class and the
poor, marked each succeeding year   Blessed with a wide circle
of relatives and friends most kindly interested in our welfare,
and whose society was at once improving and animating, our
own wishes and tastes thoroughly congenial, the days seemed
gliding on in the sunshine of prosperity, only now and then
interrupted by circumstances that, when safely passed, made us
more appreciative of the many favors we enjoyed.

Early in 1842, George Maris, who had so truly befriended
Dr Haines in his severe illness two years before, was taken
with typhoid fever   He was not altogether comfortable in the
family with whom he was residing, and, with his native generosity, Dr Haines brought him to our house and took care of
him like a son   George Maris recovered, but each one of our
household was in succession seized with the fever, which was
rife in the county that season   Many weeks passed and life
and death seemed to vibrate in the balance   Our friends were
lavish in their kindness and attention, till finally health again
reigned in our dwelling

In reviewing the past, it has often comforted me to remember
that we recognized with a degree of thankfulness the blessings
so richly showered on our path   Dr Haines was often clothed
with gratitude to the Author of every good and perfect gift, but
he did not allow the pleasant things of this life to draw him
away from the consideration of important duties   In the ful-
filment of these resulted his highest enjoyment, and I recollect
his replying one day to a worldly remark of mine, " I have great
pleasure in a daily performance of my duty "

His temperament was ardent, but his spirit was admirably
regulated and controlled, and his influence over others checked
any improper expression in his presence, even among the rude

and careless with whom he was at times necessarily brought in contact.

His friends were received with genial hospitality, and it gave him peculiar satisfaction to welcome our parents, our brothers and sisters, or any of our kindred to our home, and to make their visits as agreeable to them as possible. Previous to our marriage he made several visits to Muncy; once, as before alluded to, in consequence of his own ill health, and twice owing to the extreme illness of his early companion and beloved sister Mary, whose recovery was greatly aided by his advice. As responsibilities increased he was seldom able to leave home, and then only for brief intervals. Several times I was obliged to go to recruit my health; the first for a few weeks at Muncy, afterwards to Philadelphia, and once to Cape May; but these separations were painful to both, and nothing but the hope that change of air would give more strength to minister to the comfort of my dear husband and attend to household cares could have reconciled me to them. When favored to meet again, we felt, as he was accustomed to express it, " that our cup of happiness was full."

In the autumn of 1844 he felt at liberty to indulge the strong desire to visit his father and mother and his aged grandparents. On a sunny morning in the Ninth month we left home, going by way of Harrisburg. Our short journey was charming, especially after entering the Susquehanna Canal. Fine weather allowed us to sit on deck and enjoy the scenery, as, following the winding river, picturesque views were continually unfolded, glowing in the soft light and gorgeous tints of autumn.

The venerable Elizabeth Hall was among the few passengers, a sudden death in her family having called her to return alone to her home at Muncy; this circumstance gave Dr. Haines an opportunity to look after the comfort of an old friend of his grandmother Ellis.

At Wolf Run house they did not know of our coming, and of course there was no one to meet us at Hall's Landing. We walked to a cottage, where I rested while he went on to Henry Ecroyd's, and asking for help, their lively son James, our future brother-in-law, kindly brought a carriage and drove over to the old home, giving them a happy surprise. A few delightful days at Wolf Run with our kindred, and we had again to turn our faces southward.

A most generous offer had been made to us that our sister Rebecca should go with us and spend the winter at Springfield. His father and sister Mary brought us to Selin's Grove in their carriage, and from thence we came by canal and railroad home. In the spring our dear sister Rebecca left us to enter school at Westtown, but we were kindly allowed to have the company of another sister, Sarah, for two months. Before the end of her acceptable visit a great blessing was bestowed upon us in the gift of a little daughter, the delight and darling of her father.

Exposure and fatigue inseparable from a practice extending over a large country district often suggested the propriety of seeking another field where full occupation might be had within smaller limits, and we had reason to hope that such would open. Those among whom he labored regarded him as a friend and brother; his abilities and medical skill inspired them with confidence and respect, his warm sympathies and genial manners won their love.

I often noticed that even the rude or erring seemed to refine and soften in his presence, something in his nature calling out the noblest and most amiable traits in those around him. He appeared to be fairly launched in a happy course that would insure his own advancement and prove a blessing to all who were connected with him. Leisure moments were not wasted, and, in addition to other means for improvement, we began together the study of French, in which he had made some progress previously.

In the autumn of 1845 he began some alterations in his property with a view to our ultimate removal to Philadelphia as a place of residence. But He whose ways are higher than our ways was preparing for him a service and a home in the City that has no need of the sun, neither of the moon, to shine in it, for the glory of God enlightens it, and the Lamb is the light thereof.

One First-day afternoon he was returning from a visit to

some patients in Providence Ascending a hill near Crum Creek, his horse was startled by boys rushing out from a hiding-place behind some trees, he was thrown upon the ground and his head wounded by the blow Quickly recovering himself, he caught the horse and drove slowly home. I was looking for him, and, with our darling in my arms, was standing at the window when he reached the gate and, without alighting, beckoned to have it opened. As soon as he came in I hastened to dress the wound and apply such remedies as he suggested to prevent inflammation Though still suffering from the bruises, he felt best satisfied to see some of his patients the next day I had sent for my father and mother, and as we were all anxious about him, my brother Joseph kindly went with him the two days following the injury

To me this was an alarming accident, but he seemed to recover from it so entirely that I well recollect being in the garden at sunset some time afterwards, and as I watched the sky, beautiful with changing hues and the soft light of the evening star, my thoughts turned to a young man whose sweet wife had just been removed by death, and contrasting his fate with my own, my heart overflowed with joy and gratitude that I had been spared a similar bereavement.

At this time he was closely occupied, and successfully performed some delicate and difficult surgical operations. But it was too much, and on Seventh-day the 7th of Second month he was riding nearly all day in the rain, and was called out again in the night He had taken cold, and before going to bed had a warm foot-bath It was past midnight when a man came up from Lewis's factory, I went to the window and tried to persuade him to wait till daylight, but he insisted on immediate attention.

The desire of Dr. Haines to do his whole duty to those who placed themselves in his care overcame his prudence, and he rose and prepared to go. I went down-stairs, had some tea and toast for him, walked beside him to the gate, and bade him farewell as I usually did It was the last time I saw him mount his horse and ride away from our door.

Dearest William, how often I watched thy graceful form till

it vanished over a hill, and then joyfully welcomed the most distant glimpse of thy return!

When he came back at noon, having completed his morning round, he seemed really ill. That afternoon he read some and played with his little daughter, but at night rheumatic fever had a firm hold upon him. The next day Dr. Thomas, of Darby, was called in, who continued to attend him, assisted by my uncle, Dr. Charles Evans.

From the beginning of the illness he was seriously impressed with the belief that he should not recover, remarking, " I wish to have my mind quiet; at such a time as this it is very necessary." As I sat silently by him on the morning of the 13th, I observed his lips moving, and heard him say, " Six, seven, yes, this is the eighth time. I cannot ask to be spared longer; I only ask for mercy." He was evidently thinking of the many times when he had been brought near to death. He shed some tears, but was calm and very quiet. Soon after he said, " I have been thinking much of our Saviour's crucifixion," and then asked me to read about it. I read the account in the gospel of Luke; he lay very still in deep thought. After a while he said, " I want thee, dear Mary, to trust in the Lord, and not only trust Him, but rely upon Him, depend upon Him. Thee will be enabled to lead our little one in the right way with the Divine blessing; I know thee will, as that is attended to. It would have been pleasant, very pleasant, to enjoy thy society longer, but I do not expect it." Severe pain coming on, he was much exhausted, and as I was wiping his face, he alluded to what had been read, saying, " He sweat drops of blood."

As time went on our dear parents on both sides, our brothers and sisters who were near enough, our uncles and aunts, and some warmly-attached friends came to us continually and assisted in waiting upon him by day and night. Kind neighbors were anxious to do all in their power to relieve, and to bring anything that could be agreeable or refreshing. This I accepted, not only as proofs of their love, for he seemed to have won all hearts, but as the tender loving-kindnesses of our heavenly Father. His chamber often seemed like a Bethel, and this feeling pervaded the house; love abounded and a deep sense that an Almighty Hand was at work. Of some days I have no distinct recollection; my feelings were so intense that the changes of day and night were scarcely noticed.*

As the fever and pain abated there seemed to be some improvement. Dear William conversed cheerfully with his physicians, and all thought him better but himself. Sitting with him alone one morning, I observed a change in his countenance, and soon perceived that a slight attack of paralysis had come on. In a short time he was able to make me understand that there was congestion at the base of the brain, and indicated some remedies that were immediately applied. His sister Anna was with us and my uncle Thomas Evans quickly came. Our physicians were sent for, and our uncles Dr. Evans and Charles Ellis set off together the evening of the same day to come to us. A furious snow-storm was raging, and the man who drove the carriage refused to come beyond the Market Street bridge over the Schuylkill, although they made him a liberal offer, and they were obliged to wait till morning.

Again there was a rallying to some extent, and one afternoon he asked me to bring up our dear little daughter. I placed her by him on the bed, and he talked with us for some time. But, oh, the anguish of my heart! he, too, felt the struggle, but not the bitterness of being left behind. He was glad to see the dear child, said she might learn to lisp his name, but would never know, in this world, him to whom it applied; desired me to trust in the Lord, adding, "He will make a way for thee better than I can, and will help thee to bring up that dear little babe in the fear of the Lord, if thee attend to His pointings. I desire to commit myself into the Lord's hands, and thee, too."

The following night the storm raged again. He observed it, and remarked, "What a night to round Cape Horn! What should I do if I were like some of those young men off in South America?" No doubt alluding to what he had once told me, that when about to leave Springfield because there seemed no suitable opening for a home there, he thought of going to South America to live.

He was frequently engaged in prayer, and in a night of great

17

suffering, when his uncle Charles Ellis was watching by him, he said, " O heavenly Father, be pleased to have compassion on me, a poor unworthy creature ! Gracious Lord, enable me to bear with patience whatever it may seem meet to Thee to put upon me. Do, O Lord !" He had full faith in the power of God to heal him, even were he in the last extremity, but he was never heard to ask for that, only for grace and strength to endure; desiring that this affliction might be a blessing to us all, and expressing the wish that all our brothers and sisters would look upon it as a dispensation of Providence, saying, that " when He sees meet to cut down a young and thrifty plant, He can do it in a moment." He asked me to read the account of the man who was healed of the palsy, and I think I selected the second chapter in St. Mark. He made no remark at the time, but afterwards expressed his entire confidence in the Divine Power to raise him up again, and his perfect resignation to the will of God, whether it were for life or for death. A gradual amelioration of suffering and increase of strength again revived my hopes, but in a moment he was again partially paralyzed, and they were almost extinguished. To the astonishment of all, a third time he appeared to be recovering, and improved so far that in a few weeks he could sit up, and with help went down-stairs.

All through his illness he was thoughtful about the comfort of those who were so kindly giving us their sympathy and aid, and would ask me if I had procured such and such things for their refreshment. Once I replied that I left those things with my mother and devoted myself to him alone. He said, " That will not do. While we have a house we must provide for it;" and this accorded with his example when in health, for he left no duty unfulfilled, neither undervaluing nor neglecting any.

He was not unmindful of interests beyond the immediate circle of his relatives and friends. Being from deliberate choice a Friend in religious connection, he was one with the most enlightened Christians in advanced views of the brotherhood of man, and of the means that should be used for the improvement and elevation of our race. All philanthropic efforts had his sympathy, and to the extent of his ability his co-operation. The poor he befriended in his capacity as physician ; and being often called upon to attend those who fled from slavery to take refuge in our neighborhood, he met them so as to make them look to him as a brother. The abolition of slavery, the education of all classes, the promulgation of peace among all nations, and the advance of temperance everywhere were bound up with his principles as a Christian.

He spoke with deep concern of his solicitude for the religious Society of Friends as a part of the one Catholic Church, especially in regard to those occupying conspicuous and responsible stations in it, desiring that none might be drawn aside through unwatchfulness from the true foundation and what they had once known of the truth as it is in Jesus, saying, " Ours is a high and holy profession," and that if he were raised up from that bed of illness he hoped he should lead a life of greater circumspection, and be more diligent in attending meetings. He remarked that he had been desirous to attend meetings faithfully, but business sometimes prevented him. I do not see how he could have been more exemplary in this respect, for he often rose early on days set apart for Divine worship and rode many miles before the hour, that he might join his friends in their devotions.

In the preceding autumn some changes had been made in the house we occupied, in anticipation of our final removal from the neighborhood. We thought another house belonging to him on the same premises could be fitted up to advantage, giving us more space for a pretty lawn and garden. Consequently the one in which we were living had been let, and the time was near for the new tenant to take possession. Our plans had been suspended by the uncertainty before us and the impossibility of going forward with the alterations designed. In these circumstances my dear father and mother proposed that we should go to their house, where we could have the assistance and attentions of their large family, in addition to others who were with us in our own. Our friends approved this proposal, and altogether it seemed the only one practicable at the time. My hope was that my dear husband would gradually improve, and that by the following summer a few months' residence in Ly-

coming County would restore him to comparative health. Such
were my fond anticipations, and no one undeceived me.

When the subject was mentioned to my dear William, the
thought of leaving our own pleasant home appeared to trouble
him; but with the patience and meekness he had learned so
thoroughly, he acquiesced in the arrangement.

On First-day, the 22d of the Third month, my uncle Dr.
Evans came to see us. I remember the morning well: it was
the last day we lived in a house of our own. But then *he* has
a mansion, eternal in the heavens.

My uncle thought him better: he was sitting up and conversed cheerfully, and it was decided that the next fine day he
should take a drive. In the afternoon dear William came down
and sat in the parlor; some of our brothers and sisters came in
and took tea with us. All looked pleasant, but sadness was in
my heart.

The morrow was a beautiful day and William wished to go
out. It was arranged that we should drive up to my father's
house, only a mile distant. At eleven o'clock he was lifted into
the carriage, both our fathers and I accompanying him, our
mothers following with the little daughter. Solicitude on his
account, and thankfulness that I did not leave that house a
widow, overcame every other emotion. How we are enabled by
an unseen Helper to pass through the very depths of the sea!

On arriving at Chestnut Bank, my beloved one spoke cheerfully of having borne the drive well, and lay down to rest while
a room was being prepared for him. The west parlor was given
to us as being most roomy and quiet, our own furniture and
books were put in it, and everything was done by our dear relatives to make it home-like and agreeable for its occupant, and
he seemed well satisfied with the change.

At this time he saw most of his friends who called upon us,
and almost every day passed a few hours in the south parlor.
Often he sat in silence, his mind appearing to be withdrawn
from every earthly object, yet a peaceful cheerfulness marked
his manner, and the heavenly expression of his countenance
drew still closer the hearts of those around him.

On the 27th his father left us, but before going took us a

short drive. The following Second-day William expressed a wish to go out, and my mother, always prompt in having everything done that he proposed, soon had the carriage ready and one of my brothers to accompany us. William said that he would like to see how a willow that he had planted was doing, and we went down and stopped for a few moments in front of our house. He observed that the tree was growing nicely, and I felt encouraged to hope we might have many such little excursions. The day was warm, and although he enjoyed the change of air and scene, it was not invigorating; and this was the last time he went beyond the door.

On Third-day, the 31st, we had the company of John Allen, of Liskeard, England, and of our uncles and aunts, William and Elizabeth Evans and Thomas and Catharine Evans. Two of them saw dear William in his own room, and my aunt Elizabeth spoke to him comfortingly and encouragingly, desiring him not to allow a thought that might be presented to his mind to induce him to look upon himself, while in this state of physical weakness, as a cumberer of the ground, and said that the whole house might be blessed for his sake; that such as he sometimes drew down the blessings of heaven upon a family.

Three days after this he asked his mother for pen and paper, and wrote a short letter to his father that he might cheer him with an evidence of increasing strength. Assisted by my brothers, he still came into the south parlor and dining-room. On First-day, the 12th, I brought him some flowers from the garden, and then read to him for some time in the Bible. In the afternoon an old school-mate came to see him. He conversed with him, and we drew his chair towards the window that he might see how the landscape was changing under the influence of spring. Presently a snow-squall blew up, quickly succeeded by sunshine, and he remarked, "What a beautiful storm!" When we were alone again, our little daughter playing near us on the floor, he looked at her lovingly and said, "She seems like a bright spot in our horizon." His tender care for her was frequently expressed. At one time previous to this he said to me, "Thy next husband must be the Lord.

Thee must wed the Lord. He will make a way where there appears to be no way, and carry thee smoothly over rough places. He will enable thee to bring up that dear little babe in the way she should go, and when she is old she will not depart from it, so that she may be a blessing to thee."

On the 14th of Fourth month he came into the south parlor and dining-room for the last time. As his friend was taking leave of him that morning, and told him that he found him better than he had expected to, and hoped he would continue to improve in health, William replied, "That is not very probable."

The next day he was distressed with nausea, and from that time it was very difficult for him to take any nourishment except once, when I brought a cup of tea and a small piece of toasted brown bread, which he ate, and for a while seemed more comfortable. I opened a window near the bed, and looking up the hill beyond, he said that it reminded him of the Schuylkill Narrows, a place we pass in driving to and from Muncy. All that morning I sat by him, occasionally reading to him from a collection of religious poetry. One of the hymns, a favorite of William's, was that written by Robert Grant, governor-general of India, beginning "O Saviour, whose mercy, severe in its kindness." Another was on the seventeenth verse of the fourth chapter of First Thessalonians, "Forever with the Lord."

My uncle Thomas Evans called to see him on Fourth-day morning. To some remark of uncle's when he was about to leave, William replied, "I have for some time seen the necessity of having my dependence weaned from man. I know that I have a kind and merciful Father in heaven to deal with, and if it be His will to take me away now, all will be right." Frequent ejaculatory prayers told where his confidence was placed, and several times he said, "If it be the will of the Lord to take me now, the will of the Lord be done." One night, being in great pain, he said, "I ought to be willing to suffer; my sufferings are light in comparison with His who died for us. He sweat drops of blood and groaned till the heavens noticed it." At another time, "We have a merciful High-Priest, touched with a feeling of our infirmities, ascended to the right hand of the Majesty on high, continually making intercession for us "

A night near the last my mother, sister Deborah, and brother Joseph, with myself, were sitting by him He addressed my brother Joseph, encouraging him to make the Lord his friend while he was young, saying that it was the only thing that could support him in such a time On another occasion he requested Joseph not to exact too much from himself, adding, "I believe I have done more than it was ever intended I should do " Love for all his relations seemed to grow stronger as he felt the hour approaching when he must leave them for a little while Turning to me with his own affectionate manner, he said, "My lot has been a highly favored one ever since I became acquainted with thee I believe our union was a right one" And as I expressed my sorrow for having ever given him one unkind word or look, he replied, "I never saw them " Often he would look around upon us and say, "Bless you! bless you all !'" and seeing that some were weeping, he seemed troubled, and said to me, "Wipe those dear eyes Will thee have some water for thy face ? Mary dear, do not worry thyself"

He was anxious to see his father once more before his departure, and told me he firmly believed he should, although to us it did not seem possible After returning from meeting on Fifth-day, my uncle George Rhoads came into his room William called him by name, asking how he was , but my kind uncle, who loved him much, could only reply with tears In the afternoon our uncles Joel and Dr Evans came to see him, and being near the bedside, he raised his eyes appealingly and said, "Cannot you comfort your poor niece ? Uncle Charles, I feel very tenderly for that dear niece of thine " To which uncle answered, "I do not doubt it " Then trying to lessen my grief, he said, "Mary dear, do not worry thyself. If we both do as we ought to, we shall meet again in heaven perhaps " He had expressed a wish to see my cousin Abby Evans, and she arrived that evening. She said to him, "Cousin William, thee has always felt like a brother to me," and he replied, "Allow me to reciprocate that feeling "

In the night he talked of many of our connections, and

remarked, " I should like to say farewell in an audible voice to all my dear relations," and particularly mentioned his "dear grandparents, faithful servants in their day and generation," and his brother: "Will not Jesse shed tears for me?" On Sixth-day it was difficult for him to recall the words he wanted to express his thoughts. He intimated that he might be able to drink some tea, and when I handed him a cup he asked, "Will I not want that beyond tea?" I answered, "Yes, my dear, thee will want the palm branch and the harp." To which he at once rejoined, " Is not the time almost come? Is not the time almost come?" He was still suffering much pain and languor, and I repeated the text, "What are these which are arrayed in white robes? and whence came they? And he said to me, These are they which came out of great tribulation, and have washed their robes, and made them white in the blood of the Lamb." He answered, "Yes!"

After this he tried to speak several times, but failed to do so clearly. My mother, who was close by him, divined his meaning and assisted him. He was thinking of the beggar who was carried by angels to rest in Abraham's bosom, and the great necessity of having an interest in Christ. He wanted to see our little daughter, but could not pronounce her name, and asked for "beautiful little blue-eyes." She was brought to him; he kissed her and looked at her with his own sweet, loving smile.

That morning his uncle Charles Ellis and cousin Rachel W. Morris drove out from the city, and he was much pleased to see them. About two o'clock his father arrived and observed immediately an unexpected change in his beloved son. William recognized him quickly, and turning to me, said, "I told thee so," alluding to the belief he had expressed that he should see him again with mortal eye. He called his father's attention to our daughter, so soon to become an orphan, and was assured by his father that she should be well taken care of. Then he mentioned our servant-girl Letty, and the last earthly care was attended to.

After this he was partly unconscious of what was surrounding him, and when his sister Mary arrived it was doubtful whether he was fully aware of her presence, but he frequently mentioned our names, and his father would say, "We are all around thee ; we are here by thee." For the last few hours there seemed to be little pain, and his last words, as I kissed his pale cheek, were an emphatic assurance that my love was still dear to him.

The earthly life slowly ebbed, and at half-past two o'clock on the morning of the 18th of Fourth month, 1846, he passed into that fuller life above, where he was welcomed into the presence of his God and Saviour whom he so ardently longed to serve in perfect holiness.

The funeral was on the afternoon of Second-day, the 20th. Many sorrowing relations and friends assembled to testify by their presence their love and their share in the general loss. As they surrounded the sacred spot under the old oaks at Springfield, my uncle Thomas Evans spoke from the text, "The voice said, Cry. And he said, What shall I cry? All flesh is grass, and all the goodliness thereof is as the flower of the field : The grass withereth, the flower fadeth ; because the spirit of the Lord bloweth upon it : surely the people is grass. The grass withereth, the flower fadeth : but the word of our God shall stand for ever."

Then we left the beloved form in His keeping who rose triumphant from the tomb, believing that so surely as Jesus died and rose again, so, also, them that sleep in Jesus will God bring with Him. Thanks be to God who giveth us the victory through our Lord Jesus Christ !

Second month 2d, 1891.

> When all my fond desires combined
>   To ask for thee in fervent prayer
> That God would shield thy life from ill
>   And make thee " His peculiar care,"
> Sought I one boon more richly blent
> With love than those He freely sent ?
>
> I would have prayed for length of days
>   From pain and sorrow free,
> That Time his cold and withering hand
>   Might lightly lay on thee.
> But Love divine, in realms of truth,
> Has clothed thee with eternal youth.

I wished that ample recompense
　Thy anxious toils might gain,
And honors fair in future days
　Thy gifted mind obtain.
And now, where hosts angelic shine,
A crown of light and life is thine.

I would have asked that Friendship's voice
　Might cheer thy upward way,
And pure Affection's sweetest tones
　Make glad each passing day.
Now songs of everlasting love
Surround thee in thy home above.

I would have prayed that heavenly grace
　On thee might still be poured,
That thou might ever stand prepared
　On earth to serve the Lord.
But He has said, " Enough ! well done !
Come share the joy thy Lord has won."

Then let me bow beneath the stroke
　That falls on me alone !
O help me, Lord, in truth to say,
　" Thy will, not mine, be done !"
Thy parting words shall hope sustain,
" We yet may meet in heaven again."

Sixth month, 1846.

CHAPTER XV.

THE OLD HOMESTEAD IN MARPLE.

WHILE reading a recent *résumé* of the archæology of America, I was impressed with the superiority of written records as compared with other works of art in conveying a knowledge of existing races to later generations of mankind. The one gives shadows of the past, the other brings us into communication with the people themselves, telling us their thoughts and feelings with the freshness of life.

For this reason a simple story of what is passing before the narrator in time becomes valuable as a telegram from a former age, and, possibly, some one in the future may become interested in what it gives me pleasure to recall a few slight sketches of rural life in the southeastern counties of Pennsylvania during the earlier half of the nineteenth century I will give them as they rise before me, photographed in memory.

One of the most distinct of my early recollections is that of being seated on a low chair at the feet of my grandmother, who was occupying her accustomed place in the corner of the sitting-room by a bright wood-fire. She was an invalid, unable to walk alone, or to use her hands for any more difficult purpose than to move her pocket-handkerchief or turn the leaf of a book Rheumatism had fettered her once active limbs, but had left her serene spirit and sound judgment unclouded By her side was a small round table, upon which, after breakfast was removed, was duly laid by one of her faithful daughters the large family Bible.

I still seem to hear the reverential tones of her voice as she read to me the history of Joseph, St. Paul's speech before King Agrippa, and similar passages from the Old and New Testaments.

Two cupboards answered as the most useful of closets in this small yet ample apartment The low windows were filled with roses, pinks, geraniums, and gillyflowers, and a large daphne indicum bore its wealth of fragrance in front of the ancient clock that ticked with almost unvarying accuracy in the farthest corner. All the furniture was plain yet substantial, and an American-made carpet covered the floor; but comfort and cheerfulness seemed to abide there, and what more was needed ?

The house was built of stone quarried on the place, and was the work of three successive generations, each one beginning at the foundation and completing its portion as far as it extended It stood on the southern slope of a gentle hill, and being in the shape of an L, enclosed two sides of the court-yard The short part of the L, towards the southeast, contained the afore-mentioned sitting-room and the kitchen, attached to the angle was a "shed-room" in which was a pantry, beyond were the parlor and "middle-room," and then came the "far-house," which had been occupied by my great-grandmother in the days of her widowhood, and whose deserted rooms and large lighted closets made charming play-places for the children of my day.

A long stone-floored porch ran along the front of the parlor, "middle-room," and "far-house;" honeysuckles, daily, "champagne," and multiflora roses wound around its pillars and climbed about the windows. A stone horse-block at the west end of the porch was a frequent resort on summer evenings, that we might see from thence the sky at sundown, or pet the horses as they trotted up the lane from the fields to their stables, patting their necks while they licked up the contents of a large pewter salt-cellar brought by eager hands from the kitchen dresser. Weeping willows and majestic buttonwood and walnut trees cast their friendly shade about the house.

Divided from the front yard by a whitewashed paling covered with morning-glories, passion-vines, sweet-peas, and nasturtiums, a garden dropped by two or three terraces down the hill slope. My aunts were amateur florists, and the upper part of the garden was gay with flowers, from the earliest crocuses and hyacinths till the last asters and French marigolds bowed to the frost. A clump of box trees and cedars with tangled grape-vines filled a part of the garden, but left room enough for vegetables and raspberries. In the meadow below stood a group of tall pear trees, beautiful in early spring with masses of white bloom, and busy little feet danced with delight among the daffodils that opened their golden bells in profusion around their roots when robins and bluebirds came to build in their branches.

Another favorite haunt was the yard into which the north doors of the old mansion opened: two box trees grew near the parlor door, enclosing with their shining foliage rustic seats, where, secure from sunshine and interruption, we might talk over our plans and read our story-books. The yard was nearly filled with lilacs, snow-balls, sweet-scented shrubs, and large crimson roses, growing luxuriantly among trees that bore luscious greengages and apricots. In those days the insect enemies of fruit had not reached our longitude, and the lane running back to the barn was an avenue of plum, pear, and cherry trees. The barn itself was flanked by two apple orchards, while an enclosure for currants lay between it and the kitchen yard, where the wood-pile was reared for winter fuel.

Hydraulic rams had not then been thought of, and the supply of water for household use was brought by a stream through the garden, or carried up from the spring-house that stood in a line with the "dip-hole" and the smoke-house below the kitchen door. Nearly all supplies for the table were drawn by the hand of industry from the farm. Barrels of cider and vinegar from the press in the orchard, and of grape and currant wines, were stored in the cellar; the last russets and pippins did not vanish till strawberries and gooseberries again made their appearance; poultry clamored about the barn doors and swam in the brooks, and the cool dairy furnished sweetest cream and butter and the daintiest curds. Gleeful were the nutting excursions on crisp autumn days, when a band of boys and girls, with one strong man to shake the trees, would set off to gather the glossy treasures of the grand old chestnuts that stood like patriarchs about the fields.

To fill the barns and make the hay-stacks required five or six weeks of labor, but it was relieved by many of those sweet pictures of rural life, as dear to the sunburned laborer as to the poet who sings of them in easy retirement. The steady march of reapers along the hill-side, the "sweep of scythe in morning dew," the luncheon partaken of in shady hedge-rows, and the merry harvest suppers were all accompanied by a cheerfulness, the natural result of sunshine and fresh air, healthful exercise and innocent employments.

Hard work and stormy days did sometimes come together, it is true, when wearied workman and tired horse came home shivering with drizzling rain or driving snow. On such evenings it was my delight to slip out into my grandmother's kitchen; her heart sympathized with every one, and so well was the law of kindness understood in her household that warmer cheer always greeted the men on such nights when they came in from their daily labor.

How delightful it was to stand in a corner of the great fire-place, see the blaze stretching upward, and watch the sparks as they eddied up the chimney and went out among the stars that looked down upon us through its wide tunnel as the storm rolled away! And how nice were the slices of brown toast, broken hot and crisp into the porringers of cold milk set on the men's supper-table! so nice that I often lost my appetite before tea was ready in the sitting-room

Early hours were the rule in this primitive abode, and generally before ten o'clock lights down-stairs were extinguished: profound stillness brooded over all, undisturbed except by the baying of dogs in the distance and the crowing of cocks on their midnight perch, until the rising sunbeams glinted on frosty window-panes or the twitter of summer birds and dewy perfume floated in through open casement.

GEORGE RHOADS.

" The sun was trembling on the sea,
     Winds were low and clouds were high,
And one bird sang in the old oak tree,
     When Lindsay laid him down to die
It sang a song of early days,
Rich, rich with childhood's fairy lays
The robin sang on the linden bough
In the home of his youth as it sung to him now ·
'Twas a song of heaven it chanted him then,
And the self-same song it was chanting again "

The above lines of Ernest Jones have mingled themselves with my memories of my uncle George till they seem to belong to him. His whole life was passed under the same roof that sheltered his infancy, the same songs welcomed the morning of his birth that ushered in the early dawn when his "soul to Him who gave it rose," and each succeeding year of his more than threescore and ten found him contentedly fulfilling the daily allotment of duty in his native vale, accepting its joys with gratitude and its trials with patience

He inherited steadiness of purpose and a love of home from his English ancestry, for it was not so much the spirit of adventure as the desire of religious freedom that led them across the sea towards the westering sun

In Penn's new province they found a land much like the

one they had left in its swelling hills 'and grassy glades, its abundant springs of water, spreading trees, ferny banks, and flowery dells

Choosing a fair portion between two fine creeks, they reared their roof-tree on a southern slope, built their solid walls of gray stone from their own quarries, and soon made their ample hearths glow with coals of hickory and oak as the flames crackled and the smoke curled upward and out of the wide chimneys to the sky   Along with fruit trees and ornamental shrubs and flowers they transplanted from the old country names of places dear to them, and while the garden, dropping down from the flag pavement of the long front porch, renewed the bloom and fragrance of transatlantic days, the ear was soothed by sounds of familiar words

Thus, amidst customs and traditions of the ancestral land mingling with the life and freshness of the new, Uncle George's childhood and youth glided into manhood   Our memory of him begins when silver threads were already gleaming here and there in the dark locks that shaded his fair forehead, and he was left the only son in the house for his widowed mother to lean upon

Two brothers had founded homesteads of their own on separate portions of the paternal estates, and a group of rosy children prattled round the fireside in each

Now shone out the true characteristic of Uncle George,—his crystalline unselfishness, and when the honored mother, too, had taken her place among the "shining ones," his heart, his house, his all, were ready to serve the brothers and sisters who were left.

All were dear to him, but between himself and the brother next in age there was always a peculiar bond of love.   As boys they joined in the same sports, as young men they shared together in the cares and toil of business, everything was held in common; less demand for expenditure on one side counterbalanced by greater energy and enterprise on the other, and perfect integrity in both justifying their repose in unbounded confidence

Together the brothers worshipped in the way of their fathers, together they took sweet counsel touching things temporal and eternal

The children entered Uncle George's house as a second home, romped in the "far-house," played in the large, light closets, and climbed the fruit trees in lanes and orchards. A kind welcome ever beamed from those clear gray eyes, and a loving smile lit up the manly face.

With him the word neighbor found its meaning in the tenth chapter of St. Luke, and a true neighbor he was to all about him, not even a beggar was ever turned away empty-handed. His life demonstrated the problem of the growth of true social harmony, that it flourishes in those hearts where the love of God has rooted out all selfishness.

Was he never imposed upon? Sometimes, perhaps, but he also proved one other truth, that with what measure ye mete it shall be measured to you again.

There came a day when he was unable to rise and join the family at breakfast At once he recognized his failing strength as the call to a better world, and so expressed himself to a niece when she entered his room that morning.

For one week his brothers and sisters and his thirteen nieces and nephews were allowed to minister to his relief and comfort him by their love, as he was placidly, even cheerfully, laying off mortality.

"I have had a pleasant life," he said, as he seemed to be looking back over the seventy-three years of his pilgrimage "We must act fairly every way," was his rejoinder to one who asked him about a transaction requiring immediate attention

He had long loved the Bible as the best of books, and his hope of salvation was in the Lord Jesus Christ, and now he appeared to have nothing to do but to wait The last night I was watching beside him, occasionally giving him some nourishment Once he said, "I don't know how I should have got through the night without thee," then he lay still a long while, and when some slight motion showed that he was awake, I asked him if he had been asleep. "Just waiting for the morning," was his reply

To him it was the morning of an eternal day. Turning his

head on the pillow, he exclaimed, as if seeing a vision, " Lord
God Almighty!" His eyes closed, his brother, that other self
as it were, quickly took a seat by him, and as he gently breathed
his life away, bowed his head in prayer, saying, " Lord be with
him !"

The birds were chanting their matins in the old trees that
sheltered the windows of that quiet room, and the dim light of
an early spring dawn was tipping the eastern horizon as our
" Uncle George" passed from his first, his only, home on earth
to the mansion incorruptible,—

> " Where glory, glory dwelleth
> In Immanuel s land "

OUR AUNTS AND UNCLE WILLIAM RHOADS

Our aunts Rebecca and Elizabeth never married   Kind,
loving, actively useful in their home, faithful in religious duties,
and unambitious of worldly honors, they filled their sphere of
domestic and social life with that propriety and completeness
that their refined, gentle, and industrious natures must have
inevitably achieved   Each had her special line of service.

Aunt Elizabeth was a reader and the family chronometer
and almanac ; she kept the steady clock true to time, and could
tell about the changes of the seasons, the rising and setting of
stars, and the age of the moon   She also had the oversight of
their dairy, and never was table supplied with more luscious
cream and curds or sweeter butter than that cool spring-house
produced, and our childish whims were often gratified by small
pats of golden hue moulded expressly for our own use at their
hospitable board   In family emergencies, at home or at her
brother's, she was the one to be summoned

At fifty-five she succumbed to an attack of typhoid fever. It
was my privilege to be with her occasionally in her illness , she
was just the same pleasant " Aunt Elizabeth," liked her room to
be kept light and cheerful, and when she was evidently passing
away from us, looked up with a most natural smile as she made
some remark on the stimulant administered in the hope of
reviving her

18

Aunt Rebecca was devoted to the children of her brothers, and I fear was sometimes imposed upon by them. She survived the closing of the old home, and passed a few quiet years with her married sister Phebe in Upper Darby, and then she, too, was gathered unto her people in the First month, 1861, just two weeks after her brother Joseph whom she loved so well. One of her last expressions was, " It is a great thing to be right in the Divine sight."

Aunt Phebe, youngest of the sisters, was perhaps more aspiring, possessing all the native refinement and gentleness inherent in the family, with a tinge of timidity. She loved beauty, and her gratification of this taste came through nature and the execution of the more delicate arts in household economy. She was successful in the cultivation of flowers and in floral decorations for their apartments. She also travelled farther than her sisters, and some of the objects gathered in her journeys were wonders in our childhood's estimation.

Her courage did not rise to the point of marriage till after long years of courtship: there was no doubt of mutual attachment, but on her part a fear of making a misstep in such an important change. When the engagement was finally settled, some of the next generation were old enough to enjoy the lively side of progress towards the wedding ceremonies, and especially the ardent devotion of the groom elect, full of humor and playfulness as he naturally was, and therefore a contrast to our aunt, who was always so guarded in her words. She, poor dear, was taken ill some weeks before the important day we were anticipating, and at the crisis her strength was so reduced that her nephew George was despatched with a message to our future uncle. George performed his part promptly and, waiting for the gentleman to accompany him on his return, witnessed the alacrity with which the summons was obeyed, and when the steed, ready saddled, was brought to the door, the lover, in his haste to mount, sprang completely over the horse. A second attempt was successful, and my cousin came back with his prize and a story that raised many a healthy laugh among his young comrades.

Happily, our aunt soon recovered, and, the marriage rites

duly solemnized, my sister and I, in our light silk dresses and capes of *crêpe lisse*, made our unconventional *début* at the large wedding-party Our new uncle, Isaac Price Garrett, took his bride to the pleasant home prepared for her on his inherited land in Upper Darby It became a favorite resort for a large number of nephews and nieces, who delighted in the freedom, warmth, and genial mirthfulness that pervaded its premises, and who were always welcomed with affectionate generosity.

Both uncle and aunt were earnest in their religious life, most faithful to every call of duty, and the divine charity of their spirits diffused an influence for good to all around them.

Our aunt's taste for flowers made her second home always bright and fragrant, as had been her first. To me she was most loving and indulgent, and my heart always expands when I think of her.

The dear uncle passed away from earth on the 24th of First month, 1869, and on the 1st of Second month, in 1871, our aunt rejoined him Their kindness followed us beyond the bounds of their mortal existence; niece and nephew, great-niece and great-nephew, were remembered in their wills. With all her natural timidity, Aunt Phebe was not dismayed when she knew that the end of this life was rapidly approaching , her frequent prayers for the Divine presence and support were graciously answered, and she expressed her belief that a mansion was prepared for her in heaven

It only remains to mention the youngest of that band of brothers and sisters before coming to the fuller account of our immediate ancestor At twelve, Uncle William was deprived of the guardianship of his father, but the loss was in some degree supplied by the affectionate care of his brother Joseph. The three brothers—George, Joseph, and William—were always bound together in unity,—civil, social, and religious. Uncle William inherited from his father land in Newtown, and soon after his majority made it his residence for the rest of his days Early in life he married the one woman best fitted every way to promote his highest and lasting happiness. Anne P. Levis became Anne P Rhoads in 1822, bringing additional strength, comfort, and pleasure to the whole family circle.

Two sons and four daughters grew up around them, and with their seven cousins at Chestnut Bank formed life-long intimacies and attachments.

Uncle William was tall and graceful in person, had a very agreeable voice and pleasant smile, was remarkably neat and methodical in his habits, and in manners, as my father-in-law, Jacob Haines, used to say, the true gentleman. Between his family and that of his brother-in-law, James R. Greeves, there was an intimate association, the latter spending much of the summers at Ashley, and Uncle William and Aunt Anne often staying for weeks in the winter at the home of James R. Greeves on Chestnut and Seventeenth Streets, Philadelphia. Uncle frequently went out for exercise in the open air, and his rather striking figure in the becoming Friendly costume was a well-known personality in that part of the city, and recognized as an interesting feature in a morning walk.

Aunt Anne was of medium height and well-rounded proportions, her countenance full of intelligence and feminine grace; even the simplicity of her sectarian dress could not abolish an air of style in her appearance. Both were firm in their adherence to the Christian principles of the Society of Friends and active in their support, and for many years filled the office of overseers in Chester Monthly Meeting. Uncle lived nearly to the completion of the sixty-sixth year of his age, and aunt to her eighty-ninth.

CHAPTER XVI.

COUNTRY RAMBLES, RIDES, AND DRIVES.

ALTHOUGH the old farm-house always welcomed the grandchildren to its hospitable doors and contributed in every way to their vivacious happiness, it was not the home to which they properly belonged.

The sons of the ancestral abode, true to the family instincts, reared independent dwellings, in somewhat similar fashion, on distinct portions of the paternal estates. With wise forethought,

my father planted a large and well-selected orchard on an opposite slope, behind the site which he had chosen for his buildings   Taking from his quarries the same gray stone that had
proved its excellence in the preceding century, he erected a
substantial house with liberal views in regard to sunlight and
fresh air, and set it about with shade and fruit trees, preparatory to bringing home his bride from the city of Penn and
Franklin

Here began the life of a group of healthy children, who were
allowed to partake largely of " Free Nature's grace "

Our first experience in rambling was gained in a meadow
where mint and sweet vernal grass grew in abundance   Drawing on our shoes and stockings after paddling in the burn that
sparkled over warm sand, we chased butterflies among daisies
and scarlet-painted cups * that almost reached our shoulders.
It was a dear delight to follow the brooks that flow through the
farm.   Sometimes we lingered about a little bridge under the
willows, watching the tortoises in shining mail of gold and
ebony as they crept in and out from their hiding-places, and
tadpoles swimming round and round in shallow pools, and then
gazing in admiration mingled with awe on splendid dragon-flies
that flashed in the sunshine and hovered mysteriously over the
water.   Here the boys built dams and water-wheels to send
crystal drops flying into the air

Lower down its borders we strolled (in our childish estimation) through brakes of calamus and prairies of quaker-ladies †
to jungles of alder and hazel, where swamp blackbirds ‡ qua-
vered their mellow notes, and darting from thicket to thicket, dis-
played their jetty coats and scarlet epaulets   Here the brook
glided into a wood.

And this wood !   Did ever Greek or Druid approach sacred
grove or forest with such pure delight as we this enchanted
ground ?   It was entered by two wide grassy paths that soon
united and ran parallel with the rivulet, as nearly as the gently-
curving lines marked out by feet of woodman can with those

---

* Castilleia coccinea (Gray)
† Houstonia cerulea (Gray)
‡ Agelaius phœniceus of Wood, probably

drawn by Nature for the channels of her aqueous bounty. Each turn had its own domain of beauty; in one grew robin-run-the-hedge,* for Christmas wreaths; in another, wild geraniums and the pyrola and chimaphila tribes, with their waxen umbels and delicate odors; far up on the right were two other lycopodiums, the ground-pine and a congener, prized for winter bouquets. At the top of a little hill began a fernery of various species, whose graceful fronds clustered about the tree roots and sides of the path, spreading farther on over a rather open space, where one might lie and see the fleecy clouds sailing in blue ether above the lofty net-work of foliage woven in airy patterns by tops of forest trees.

Here I was first surprised by the notes of a hermit-thrush, that verily seemed to be singing "at heaven's gate," so sweet and unworldly was the song.

For mosses, lichens, and gay-colored fungi we turned aside to the brook, where through miniature rocks it idled and slept, or "made a sudden sally." Here also we came for early flowers; gathering in its cool recesses fragrant orchis, lily-shaped bells of erythronium, so delicately shaded in brown and straw color, spring beauties, and violets. A tiny peninsula, formed by the roots of a tall tree in a quiet part of the stream, was daintily covered with anemones; but these were too sacred to be touched, and only such as grew scattered through the wood were plucked for our decorations.

These rambles were by no means confined to the children of the family, nor to the period of their childhood; it was an habitual pleasure in which all shared,—father and mother, young men and maidens, guests who were staying with us from town or country, and sometimes from foreign shores. Our county lying along the Delaware, intersected by several large creeks with intervening hilly ranges, and watered in every part by streamlets springing pure and cold in its sloping meadows, presented for a lowland country an unusual variety of scenery. Sometimes broad views over an undulating surface of cultivated fields and intermingling forest, studded with comfortable homes and fruitful orchards, and the blue river and its white sails near

* Lycopodium complanatum (Gray).

the distant horizon, then a lonely dell where the sunbeams seemed to sleep in its grassy bosom, or some rocky glen dark with hemlock and draped with kalmia, mitchella repens,* and trailing arbutus   in ride or walk, one was ever coming upon some new turn or unexpected beauty

Our wood-path came out amidst some old whetstone quarries and into a winding road that led through one of those dells   The brook, turning and issuing from its covert near the same spot, pursued its way upon the right, joined by a rill that trickled from a rustic spring-house gleaming in the edge of a copse   Fine oaks and chestnuts threw their shadows down the hill-side and extended their friendly shelter to an ancient farm-house   Near the head of the glen a grape-vine, supported by cedars, made a leafy bower, and two cottages, one above and the other below, gave the warmth of human interest to its seclusion   On the left was a hedge-row of tulip trees, oaks, ash, and cedars, with a wealth of wild vines and shrubbery twining about their trunks and many a fern and blossom at their roots

Beyond the second cottage the road, making a sudden curve, passed a pond and saw-mill, and then by a one-arched stone bridge crossed the creek just where our brook falls into it over the edge of a dam   This was frequently the terminus of our walks in that direction   Passing below the bridge, we rested on cushions of trailing plants and mosses, watching the flicker of sunbeams on the flowing water, or the silvery touches of moonlight through overarching boughs, according to the time of day we had chosen for our stroll   From the adjacent banks we went home in early summer with our hands filled with clusters of pink kalmia, or in the autumn with the highly-prized fringed gentian, Bryant's blossom,—

> " Bright with autumn dew
> And colored with the heaven's own blue "

A few years had sufficed to bring around our father's roof-tree the shelter of pine and willow, fir and hemlock, and partly to cover its walls with Virginia creeper and ivy   Often, when tea was over on summer evenings, we turned westward from

* Partridge-berry vine

the piazza and crossed the lawn to opposite fields, that we might have unconfined views of the azure vault, where masses of rose and amber clouds were floating off in detachments from the golden gates of departing day.

How lovingly our eyes rested on the familiar scenes around, softened in the evening light! blue smoke curling upward from chimney-tops half hidden among the trees; herds slowly returning from the dairies to clover-fields; loaded wagons carrying the last fragrant hay-cocks to the barns, or gathering up the yellow wheat-sheaves.

Roaming through these same western fields in autumn days, when the invigorating air made even mid-day sun a not unwelcome heat, we came to a "bushy dell" where, through "alley green" to "bosky bourne," late-blooming flowers and frost-tipped leaves vied with each other in brilliancy. Well I remember the exclamation of pleasure with which a sweet English lady in one of our strolling parties bent over a rich bed of maiden-hair growing there, thinking it scarcely possible that the elegant fronds she had only known as pets of the greenhouse had sprung spontaneously in that wild spot; and how, after we had wandered some miles over the breezy hills, gay with asters and golden-rod, she recited in her musical tones "The Monk and the Bird," as we rested in the edge of a wood.

Sometimes our young friends from the city would accompany us to this dell and grow rapturous with delight as they came upon the haunts of fringed gentians and spied tall racemes of cardinalis glowing in damp recesses. Splendid bouquets were carried home on such occasions, and pleasantly shone the windows with reflected golden light as we returned to chat around the fire on the parlor hearth till called to partake of the season's bounty at the table, where conversation lasted long into the evening.

More distant expeditions were occasionally made on horseback: a saunter in the long twilight of a hot day; a canter along some quiet road, where autumn leaves were falling in the cool, still air; or some rider, bolder than the rest, would dash up a creek and make a cross-cut through the country. But oftener, when friends were staying with us, we would drive to some chosen locality and, alighting, pursue our explorations on foot.

Hills on the Schuylkill near Norristown give fine views of that picturesque region, and possess historical interest in connection with the old camp-ground at Valley Forge; and a road that used to follow the edge of a pond in a pretty vale had special charms when overhanging trees, shading from crimson to brown and from saffron to straw color, were doubled in its watery mirror.

In some seasons of the year Bartram's garden and Buist's hot-houses formed the ostensible objects of a drive, and presented attractions that might have repaid a trip affording less pleasure in itself than our devious roads furnished. Throughout the county the creeks are turned to purposes of utility, but in many places without destroying their natural beauty; indeed, often enhancing it by forming little lakes amidst the hills, where the water is dammed up to turn mills below. A romantic portion of the banks of Crum Creek belonged to some of our relatives, and two of these sheets of water were near it; the lower one, lying in open meadows, entered beneath a bridge on the Baltimore turnpike, was the scene of many a pull in boats where the oars kept time to the song and flute of the rowers.

Higher up is a paper-mill where we often stopped to look at the huge cylinders rolling up the pulpy sheets and to chat with its frank and gay-hearted proprietor, and then continued our way along a path among steep rocks shaded by hemlock and kalmia and carpeted with trailing arbutus, partridge-berry, and moss. In sunnier parts of this wood grew lupines and columbine, and ground-squirrels and marmots burrowed along its borders.

The upper lakelet lay in a basin, formed on one side by abrupt hills covered with deciduous trees intermingled with evergreens, on the other by clover-blossomed slopes and the retired dwellings of their owners. Here we might row for a mile or two in silence, broken only by our own voices and the dip of the oar as the image of the cloud-flecked dome trembled and parted before the gliding boat. In winter, when an icy crust glistened on the snow, and "every pointed thorn seemed

wrought in glass," a brilliant morning would suggest a sleigh-
ride to some distant meeting that it was our duty and privilege
to attend, or else to the house of a friend whose hospitable welcome kept us till moon or stars should light our homeward
way.

But whatever object took us beyond its bounds, home was
the centre of attraction.   There our hearts were drawn to a
realizing belief that

> "One spirit—His
> Who wore the platted thorns with bleeding brows—
> Rules universal nature. . . .
> Happy who walks with Him! Whom what he finds
> Of flavor or of scent in fruit or flower,
> Or what he views of beautiful or grand
> In nature, from the broad majestic oak
> To the green blade that twinkles in the sun,
> Prompts with remembrance of a present God.
> His presence, who made all so fair, perceived
> Makes all still fairer."

CHAPTER XVII.

HOME OCCUPATIONS AND MENTAL PLEASURES—AN AFTERNOON
OF LONG AGO.

To fulfil the duties and keep everything in order about the
home of a large family in the country allows little time for idleness, that mother of mischief and destroyer of happiness.

The wisdom comprised in the texts, " See then that ye walk
circumspectly, not as fools, but as wise, redeeming the time,"
and " Whatsoever thy hand findeth to do, do it with thy might,"
was practically taught us from infancy.   And most conclusively
did we prove the beneficence of our Father in heaven in so
mitigating the sentence against fallen man as to attach to all
well-directed labor of body or mind an inseparable reward.

Our earliest school-days were passed first under the care of
governesses living in the family, and afterwards of teachers about
a mile from home, the hours being so appropriated as to allow

ample time for play and a share in some light occupation within
doors or without. As these little duties were expected from us
with regularity, they formed an admirable system of calisthen-
ics, so that I do not remember ever growing weary over a lesson, or suffering from those stupefying headaches that so often
afflict the pupils of the present day.

As we grew older and left home for higher schools, of course
these employments had to be dropped, but the foundation of
good health and active habits was already laid.

When a family of children is once separated to be sent from
the paternal roof to school and college, it is seldom they are
long together again in the old home. The girls come back, it
is true, and stay till some other home claims them, and the
boys have it as a rallying-point while pursuing their studies and
preparing for business, and it is still *home* to them all ; and no
period is more filled with interest and energy than that in which
the powers of the young and the training of the parents are
manifesting themselves in the nearly-fledged group.

Confining myself chiefly to feminine branches of industry, I
may remark that by the end of the first quarter of this century,
hatchels and reels, spinning-wheels and cards, had been doomed
to banishment from kitchen and balcony to out-house and loft.
Yet I can faintly recall the vision of an old German woman
spinning flax in the sunny corner of my mother's kitchen, and
also the pleasant hum of a large wheel mingling with the buzz
of summer flies in the " far-house" at my grandmother's, as
the yarn for winter knitting was spun from long white rolls of
wool, while a child sat near making knotty threads on a small
implement of the same kind that had been given her for a
plaything.

Although spinning and weaving lost their title as handicrafts,
and fell into the power of the subtle yet mighty worker, steam,
the wife and daughters in country households found employment enough for the healthful exercise of their physical energies in supplying the multiplicity of wants that refined and
intelligent people are sure to have.

The more arduous domestic labors were largely performed
by refugees from south of Mason and Dixon's line, and very

faithful and efficient they generally proved themselves to be. While profiting by their industry, we learned, from the history of their silent suffering and hardships in the past and their continued liability to be torn away from their new homes by the relentless slave-hunter, to sympathize with their fellow-bondsmen and to abhor a system that entailed such degradation and woe on its victims.

Sometimes the occupations necessary to supplement the service of our colored helpers seemed to interfere with mental culture and work in higher spheres, but it was only seeming, perhaps, for in intervals of leisure the mind could seize upon and assimilate with greater rapidity the intellectual treasures within its reach; labor gave zest to repose; the calm majesty of Nature became more impressive, contrasted with busy hours, and in the performance of many humble duties we were brought into familiarity with some of her loveliest appearances.

Occasionally rising with the dawn of a summer morning, that our share in the handiwork might be completed before the heat of the day, my sister and I have watched those magnificent displays of growing light that can only be witnessed when the dewy earth, awaking with "charm of earliest birds," catches on tree and hill-top the first rosy gleam of day, and as Venus hides in the luminous glory, islets of gold and crimson, detached from the eastern horizon, float up and melt into the long bars of purple and saffron that divide coming morn from the flitting shades of night.

Sometimes choosing the hour before breakfast for making the semi-weekly supply of cakes and pastry, I have carried my materials to a rustic porch at the kitchen door. There, shaded by "large leaves of the sycamore," before me blooming sprays of Carolina rose trained over a whitewashed smoke-house in the garden, a bit of hedge-row at the orchard's end, and a glimpse into ripening wheat-fields beyond, I have rolled and moulded my prandial compounds to the lively tune of Bob White as it was blithely whistled in a neighboring croft.

Going to the spring-house at mid-day for a pitcher of cream, the walk has been beguiled—I might almost say hallowed—by the glory and stillness of the hour: the earth steeped in radiance beneath, skies of intensest blue above. How tranquillizing to rest under the stately chestnut on the hill and let the eye follow those piles of white clouds slowly wafted onward in that sapphire ocean, revealing through their rifts still deeper and deeper abysses of blue!

Many cares came with the spring-time of the year. As faint red rays struggled through the mist into which subsiding rains dissolve at the close of mild March days, the piping of frogs in thawing meadows gave the signal for new labors. Farm and garden called for tillage, fences and out-buildings were to be repaired, and every corner and closet of the house from roof to cellar to be emptied and cleaned.

True, the fitful weather gave us days of enforced leisure, when books and pen and needle resumed their importance; still, the active days preponderated, not, however, without their peculiar charms. It was pleasant through the wide-opened windows to watch the steady march of April showers from distant delicately-tinted woods across the young green of wheat and clover and the rich brown of newly-ploughed fields, and while rearranging the well-cleaned apartments to inhale the sweet winds

> " wafting through the rooms
> The snow-flakes of the cherry-blooms."

The various employments of the day being ended and the " cheerfu' supper done," the circle wide broke away from the tea-table and disposed itself anew in the vine-covered portico. Peace seemed to fall on them with the twilight, as stars came twinkling in the purplish-gray dome above and returned swallows skimmed the air, uttering now and then a quick chirp. Low voices mingled in conversation or recitation; the father would make some kind inquiry as to how the day had sped, and give news from the great world lying beyond their little domain; the mother interpose from her loved Psalmist some of those " strains that once did sweet in Zion glide," expressive of thankfulness for all the goodness and mercy that surrounded them.

A small, well-selected library formed by an association of

Friends in the neighborhood, in addition to books on our own shelves, furnished a wholesome variety of instructive and entertaining reading. That our library was small was probably an advantage, as in choosing a volume from its stores we felt none of that hopeless bewilderment with which one is apt to survey those vast collections, overwhelming in a sense of the unattainable.

The current literature of the day, including poetry, formed the staple of our summer reading, more systematic studies being kept in reserve till the bracing air and less interrupted hours of late autumn and winter gave greater tone and freedom to the mind. At all times one Book was placed before us, first in consideration and regard. The customs, habits, history of the people and nations recorded in its pages, and the geography and natural history of the lands where they dwelt, were made interesting subjects of inquiry, and its all-important truths were reverently impressed upon our hearts.

Morning by morning was wisdom drawn from its wells of inspiration for our help and direction through the day, and often were its songs of thanksgiving rehearsed to kindle our gratitude and awaken devotion. Regularly, also, on First-day afternoons or evenings we were assembled to listen to some of its chapters, and in connection with them were read biographies of holy men and women of later days, or memoirs of children who, having given themselves early to the Saviour, had been carried to those happy mansions that He prepares for His own. Sweetly solemn were these occasions when all were drawn together to the One Great Fountain of love.

With the nineteenth century began an era of extraordinary activity in art, science, and literature; every year was marked by new inventions and discoveries. Steam and electricity have been knitting the nations together; the press has become " one of the three mightiest." History was beginning to be understood; great research and critical acumen were brought to bear upon its authenticity; and, no longer gliding from peak to peak on which kings and heroes sit enthroned, the condition of the masses of mankind has been studied,—their every-day life, their mental and moral development. The laws that govern the rise and fall of nations were sought, together with the relations of great events and changes of empire to the ultimate welfare of the human race. Of those whose names were familiar to us fifty years ago, Mackintosh, Hallam, Mahon, Nugent, and Arnold were elaborating their works in Great Britain; Niebuhr, Neander, Ranke, Sismondi, and D'Aubigné, in Germany, Switzerland, and Italy; Guizot and Thiers, in France. Our own Irving, Prescott, and Bancroft were illustrating the history of the western continent, and portions of the one that colonized it; the Herschels, Lord Rosse, and Ehrenberg opened new worlds to view in the vast and the minute; and the genius of Humboldt produced the "Cosmos."

Travellers in every part of the world were making its scenery, peoples, and productions familiar to the fireside tourist and bringing countless treasures into the halls of science. Chemistry has been daily disclosing the beauty and simplicity of materials that give variety to the earth's surface and minister to the wants of its inhabitants. To us Murchison, Lyell, and Hugh Miller were unfolding the stony leaves of its history and tracing backward its chronology; De Candolle and Gray displaying the arrangement of the Divine Artist in the structure of plants, from the vegetable dust that floats in the air to the monarch of the Yosemite; Cuvier, Audubon, Agassiz, Wood, and Gosse were leading into familiarity with the forms, relations, and habits of the denizens of flood, field, and forest. In the hands of Somerville, Guyot, and Maury, geography became a science full of life and reality.

Men of clear thought and close observation and reasoning laid open the human intellect and exhibited the moral nature of man with their wonderful growth and dependencies.

The literature of our country, rapidly increasing, was improving, too, in force, depth, and sweetness. Bryant, Longfellow, Whittier, and Lowell took their places among our household friends.

But none of the writers of our early days contributed more to our pleasure than the galaxy of British essayists and reviewers then in the zenith of their splendor. Brougham, grave and stately; deep-thinking Foster; Sydney Smith, of pungent wit; Jeffrey, clear, calm, and lordly; the hilarious humor and heathery freshness of Christopher North, the genial author of "Friends in Council;" and Macaulay, with his pen of fire, blackening or illuminating whom he would, yet taking up the marble statuary of other authors and sending it forth instinct with life, grasping the floating films of men's thoughts and weaving them into rich banners; these, and others of kindred genius, touched our little world with their magnetic power, and kept it in motion and progress with the large one lying around it.

Among living poets whose tones were wafted across the Atlantic, Tennyson was pre-eminently a favorite. Dwellers in the country, we greatly enjoyed his exquisite perception of all that is beautiful, graceful, and impressive in Nature; the notice of those minute touches that only a lover's eye can distinguish, and his nice blending of the peculiarities of thought and feeling, as affected by the advance of science and art in this century, with those underlying depths that remain ever the same.

No words could better paint than his some of those "all-golden afternoons," when trees had "counterchanged the floor of our flat lawn of dusk and bright," and friends and brothers from neighboring city came to mix in our simple sports and shake "to all the liberal air the dust and din and steam of town."

All-golden afternoons they truly were to us, whether to mark from our shady covert "the landscape winking through the heat," to watch "the gust that round the garden flew, and tumbled half the mellowing pears," or whether, all in circle drawn about one of the group, we listened as he lay and read some favorite poet on the lawn.

> " Nor less it pleased in livelier moods
> Beyond the bounding hill to stray,
> And break the life-long summer day
> With banquet in the distant woods;

> " Whereat we glanced from theme to theme,
> Discuss'd the books to love or hate,
> Or touched the changes of the state,
> Or threaded some Socratic dream.

> *   *   *   *   *   *   *

" By night we linger'd on the lawn,
   For under foot the herb was dry;
   And genial warmth; and o'er the sky
   The silvery haze of summer drawn;

" And calm that let the tapers burn
   Unwavering: not a cricket chirr'd:
   The brook alone far off was heard,
   And on the board the fluttering urn:

" And bats went round in fragrant skies,
   And wheel'd or lit the filmy shapes
   That haunt the dusk, with ermine capes
   And woolly breasts and beaded eyes;

" While now we sang old songs that peal'd
   From knoll to knoll, where, couch'd at ease,
   The white kine glimmer'd, and the trees
   Laid their dark arms about the field."

But it is not only the flushing dawns, glowing noons, and resplendent evenings of the milder months that bring peculiar charms and joys to the country home. The depths of winter are full of them, and from the first day when November winds make us sensible of the exceeding coziness of a warm fireside till spring suns and showers open the blue eyes of violets and hepaticas, they beckon us onward in ceaseless succession.

Daily occupations assume greater regularity; and literary pursuits become more systematic. Even while the arts of housewifery proceed the latter are not wholly interdicted, and I vividly recall happy hours when mother and daughters have been surprised by twilight, as with busy fingers and minds intent they have followed the narrative of some far-off time or traveller, perchance that of Eusebius in the early Christian church, or of some explorer in tropic zone or arctic circle.

Wild work often goes on o' winter nights, and clouds are busy while men sleep. Pleasant, then, is the wakening to faint sounds of rural melody in the pauses of the wind, as

" From sheds new-roofed with Carrara
   Comes chanticleer's muffled crow,
   And stiff rails are softened to swan's-down
   As still flutters down the snow."

19

Besieged by the storm, the whole family are hemmed in for the day. How interesting in our warm citadel to watch the fleecy descent! The little dale takes upon it a new aspect and seems to be some Alpine valley, and neighboring farm-house and cottage, acquiring turret and bastion, look more distant through the feathery shower, and become fitting location for legend and romance. When every object is enveloped in snow, and the curling drifts, pearl atop and amethyst beneath, are piled round wall and porch, the winds gradually subside, parting western clouds open a pathway for the sunbeams, and a flood of crimson glory streaming across the fields, glances in through the callas and geraniums in the windows, tips with radiance the many-hued shells on the mantel over the blazing hickory logs, and gleams along the ceiling in rose-colored light.

On such an afternoon two of our friends set out from the city, ignorant of the force of the obstacles in their road. For hours they plunged through snow-banks, or tried to outflank them, till their plucky horse seemed half ready to give it up, but, full of enthusiasm, they at last neared the friendly gate-way; then one more push through the opposing whiteness, a sprinkle from loaded vines, and they reached the open door. If they enjoyed the welcome and shelter within, we did most truly their society and the comic story of their drive and its marvellous beauty.

Occasionally such a snow-fall is succeeded by a few hours of rain, just enough in the freezing temperature to form a thick coating of ice. I cannot forget one night after such an occurrence. I had gone up-stairs to see whether everything was made comfortable for some guests who were staying with us, and with only the dim fire-light in one of the rooms, my eye was caught by the splendor without. The moon was at full and just risen over the eastern woods; it shone on crystalline shrub and evergreen, a flood of silver glittered through the orchard, and long diamond pendants flashed from the eaves. I lingered first at one window, then at another, to make the scene of magic shadows and lustrous lights my own, and joined the circle below feeling that I had come into possession of one more rare treasure.

Time with us had hebdomadal tides that culminated on Seventh-day afternoons and remained at flood for the next twenty-four hours. As sunset approached the week's cares and labors folded themselves away,—the house had been made as tidy and bright as could be, the tea-table furnished with more than usual care, absent members of the family returned, and, fresh and cheerful, all assembled for the evening repast. Conversation soon became animated, every one contributing his share. Incidents of the passing week were related, social hours with other friends lived over again, new books were criticised; one told of some new invention; another of a discovery in science; some new theory in physics or philosophy would lead into lively discussion; and so the hours sped till the tall clock in the corner of the dining-room warned us that it was time to prepare for the peaceful sleep dispensed by our Gracious Guardian with those healthful breezes and quiet nights on the hillside.

It always seemed to me that Nature had a look of reverential attention on First-days, let the season of the year be what it might. There was the waiting attitude on a winter's morning, as if she were biding the hour when the fiat should go forth for renewing the face of the earth; the rejoicing in the Creator's smile on a glad spring day; the thank-offering of summer harvest fields, and the solemn splendor of perfected autumn.

The morning meal, the Bible-reading, and the few minutes for silent prayer ended, we dispersed from the sunny breakfast-room to collect again at an early hour for the short drive to meeting. It was pleasant as we approached our simple place of worship to see friends and neighbors wending their way along the roads that converge where it stands, and many a time of instruction and edification did we experience when gathered there. Sometimes the service was vocal, sometimes only the still, small voice was heard; but never were we without the blessed presence of Him who died that we might live. With hearts renewedly warmed by love, the assembly broke up, and exchanging friendly greetings, all went homewards.

Dinner on that day was a particularly genial occasion; the conversational mood of the previous evening stole in upon us again, and, regulated by the spirit of the morning, the stream of talk flowed in grave or sprightly vein as might be, till it seemed right to remember those who waited for our adjournment before their hours of leisure could fully begin.

Those members of the household were never forgotten, but as far as possible they were incorporated with the family, and their eternal interests as well as their temporal welfare were considered and promoted.

Blessed is the memory of such homes! May they be multiplied throughout the land.

AN AFTERNOON OF LONG AGO.

SOME things I have seen which I would "not willingly let die," the remembrance of which should cheer me even when I press with tottering steps the last sands in life's journey.

I have seen a pleasant parlor with windows opening to the west, unobscured except by one luxuriant calla unfolding its imperial flower in the clear light of heaven; a window on the southern side was filled with pots of pinks and roses, and upon the mantel were a few treasures from the "blue, lone sea" to remind the inmates that even where the eye of man can never penetrate are lavished beauties from the abundance of His riches by the unsparing hand of the Creator.

There, many a long afternoon, when winter, tardily yielding to spring, began to own the warm influences of a brighter sun, have I seen them grouped together. The mother whose pale brow showed that her noon was past, yet in her bosom time had only mellowed all the rich affections of woman. There were three sisters: the face of the eldest could never tell what her heart had known and still felt of dear, deep joys and desolating sorrow; the next with placid countenance beaming with touches of His love who giveth grace to the humble; and the youngest, whose mantling cheek and clear blue eye spoke of youthful hope and happiness. Dancing before the bright wood fire, or roguishly hiding in the corners of the sofa, was the rosy, fair-haired, laughter-loving grandchild. She was a stream of sunlight to all; her little heart quickly swelled at the tale of distress, but "she did not love such sorrowful things;" some "lively little piece" was ever her choice, and, neglecting her inanimate toys, she longed only for kittens and " live dolls that could run about and do mischief."

The well-filled work-baskets and busy fingers gave witness to the habits of industry in which the older members of the family had been trained, and books scattered round also evinced that mental culture was not neglected. While some were rapidly converting snowy linen into articles of use for the loved absent ones and another making "auld claes look amaist as weel's the new," one read aloud an essay from some master-spirit of the age, some sweet or lofty poem, or traced the graphic story of wanderers in the classic East, stirring West, or among the spicy isles of the South. As day declined employ-ments were laid aside for the unrestrained enjoyment of social converse, and the mingling of all rich and glorious hues in the western sky gradually fading into the clear emerald of a winter sunset and the mild radiance of the evening star prepared them to meet with gratitude and love the father and brothers who were gathering around the cheerful hearth.

I

APPENDIX.

WHEREAS Jesse Haines of Middletown Township Chester County in Pennsylvania, Son of Isaac Haines and Mary his Wife; and Rachel Otley, daughter of James Otley (Deceased) and Ann his Wife, having declared their Intentions of Marriage with each other before several Monthly Meetings of the People called Quakers at Concord in the County aforesaid according to the good order used amongst them, and having consent of Parents and Relations concerned, their said proposal of Marriage was allowed of by the said Meeting. Now these are to Certify whom it may concern, that for the full accomplishment of their said Intentions this sixth day of the tenth Month, in the year of our Lord one Thousand seven hundred and Eighty five, They the said Jesse Haines and Rachel Otley appeared in a public Meeting of the said people at Middletown aforesaid, and the said Jesse Haines taking the said Rachel Otley by the Hand, did in a solemn manner openly declare, that he took her the said Rachel Otley to be his Wife, promising through divine assistance to be unto her a faithful and loving Husband until Death shall separate them, (or Words to that effect) and then and there in the same Assembly, the said Rachel Otley, did in like manner declare, that she took the said Jesse Haines to be her Husband, promising through divine Assistance to be unto him a faithful and loving Wife until Death shall separate them, (or Words to the same effect.) And Moreover, They the said Jesse Haines and Rachel Otley (she according to the Custom of Marriage assuming the name of her Husband,) as a further Confirmation thereof, did then, and there to these presents set their Hands. And we whose names are hereunder Subscribed, being present also at the Solemnization of the said Marriage and Sub-

287

scription in manner aforesaid, do as Witnesses thereunto set our Hands the day and year above written.

JESSE HAINES
RACHEL HAINES.

Joseph Talbot	Agness Minshall	Isaac Haines Jur.	Thomas Evans
Samuel Sharples	Martha Sharples	Abel Otley	Jane Evans
Andrew Moore	Priscilla Yarnall	Ann Otley	Cadwalader Evans
Jacob Minshall	Phebe Emlen	Jacob Haines	John Cox Evans
Abram Pennell	Joel Sharples	Martha Haines	Eli Yarnall
William Yarnall	Thomas Sharples	Abner Otley	Elizabeth Otley
John Hill	Margaret Minshall	William Otley	Lydia Haines
Dell Pennell	Phebe Yarnall	Sarah Waln	Mary Cox
Caleb Yarnall	Mary Minshall	Martha Haines	Elizabeth Peirce
Robert Pennell	James Emlen	John Cox Evans	
Isa Yarnall	Francis Townsend	Caleb Peirce	
John Sharples	Rose Pilkington	Abram Sharples	
Elizabeth Painter			
Jane Painter			

MARRIAGE CERTIFICATE OF WILLIAM ELLIS AND MERCY COX.

WHEREAS William Ellis son of Benjamin and Ann Ellis deceased of Chester County Pennsylvania, and Mercy Cox daughter of William Cox deceased, and Mary Cox of Harford County Maryland, having declared their Intentions of Marriage with each other before two Monthly Meetings of the people called Quakers at Deer creek in Harford County aforesaid, and having the allowance of Parents and Relations concerned their said proposals were allowed of by the said Meeting. And Moreover the said William Ellis and Mercy Cox appeared in a public Meeting at Deer creek in Harford County aforesaid, and the said William Ellis taking the said Mercy Cox by the hand did in solemn manner openly declare that he took her the said Mercy Cox to be his wife, promising to be unto her a loving and faithful Husband until death should separate them, and then and there in the said Assembly the said Mercy Cox declared that she took the said William Ellis to be her Husband, promising to be unto him a loving and faithful wife until death should separate them (or words to such Import). And for a further confirmation thereof the said William Ellis and Mercy Cox, she

according to the custom of Marriage assuming the Name of her Husband, did then and there to these presents set their hands this tenth day of Ye second month in the year of our Lord One thousand seven hundred and Eighty five. And we whose Names are also hereunto subscribed being present at the Solemnization thereof have as witnesses set our hands the day and date above written.   WILLIAM ELLIS
    MERCY ELLIS.

Frances Young Wilson	Gerrard Hopkins	Robert Gover	Mary Cox
Sarah Day	Samuel Hopkins	Joseph Husband	John Cox
John Forwood	Joseph Harris	Mary Husband	Rachel Cox Jur.
Mordecai Warner	Jesse Morgan	Elizabeth Hopkins	Israel Cox
Joshua Husband	Isaac Coale	John Wilson	Mary Cox Jur.
Sarah Husband	John Harris	Alissama Wilson	Sarah Richardson
Mary Ann McCaskey	Sarah Worthington	Ann Willits	Ann Harris
Hannah McCaskey	Elizabeth Hopkins	William Hopkins	Margaret Harris
Thos R Rodgers	Ann Coale	Anna Rigbie	Elizabeth Coale
	Freeborn Brown	Sarah Coale	Margaret Churchman
	Joseph Hopkins	Margaret Dallam	
	Micajah Churchman	Ruth Carter	
		Philip Coale	
		Cassandra Coale	
		Sarah Morgan	

MARRIAGE CERTIFICATE OF JACOB HAINES AND RACHEL ELLIS.

WHEREAS Jacob Haines of West Town Township Chester County in the State of Pennsylvania, son of Jesse Haines and Rachel his Wife, of Concord Delaware County, and state aforesaid, and Rachel Ellis Daughter of William Ellis and Mercy his Wife (the former deceased) of Muncy Township Lycoming County and state of Pennsylvania, having declared their intentions of marriage with each other, before a Monthly Meeting of the people called Quakers, held in Fishing Creek according to the custom used amongst them, and having the consent of surviving Parents, their said proposals were allowed of by the said Meeting. Now THESE are to CERTIFY to whom it may concern, that for the full accomplishing of their said Intentions this twenty fourth day of the eighth Month in the year of our Lord one thousand eight hundred and fifteen; they the said Jacob

Haines and Rachel Ellis appeared in a public Meeting of the
said People held at their Meeting house in Muncy aforesaid, and
the said Jacob Haines taking the said Rachel Ellis by the hand,
did upon this solemn occasion, openly declare, that he took her
the said Rachel Ellis to be his Wife, promising with Divine assistance to be unto her a true and affectionate Husband, until
Death should separate them.   And then in the same Assembly
the said Rachel Ellis did in like manner declare that she took
him, the said Jacob Haines to be her Husband, promising with
Divine assistance to be unto him a true and affectionate Wife,
until Death should separate them.   MOREOVER they, the said
Jacob Haines and Rachel Ellis (she according to the custom of
Marriage assuming the name of her Husband,) did as a further
confirmation thereof, then and there to these presents set their
hands.   JACOB HAINES
                                    RACHEL E HAINES.

AND WE, whose names are hereunto also subscribed, being
present at the solemnization of said Marriage and subscription
have as Witnesses thereunto set our hands the day and year
above written.

Jonathan Wilson Jur.	James Kitely	James Paxson	Mercy Ellis
Mary Wilson	Mary Haworth	Amy Paxson	Rachel Haines
Benjamin Warner	Mary Hollingsworth	Henry Parker	Sarah Ellis
Deborah Warner	Martha Parker	Samuel Wallis	Reuben Haines
Joseph Whitacre	Sarah Warner	Joel Swayne	Anna Haines
Catharine Whitacre	Robert Hawley	Enos Hawley	Benjamin Ellis
Job McCarty	Joseph Warner	Robert Hawley Jur.	Samuel W Morris
Anne Webb	Eliza S Cox	Martha Tucker	Jesse P Haines
	Rebekah Lewis		Sarah Haines
			Jesse Hartley
			Mary Hartley

WILLIAM ELLIS'S LAST WILL AND TESTAMENT.

Be it remembered that I William Ellis of Muncy in Lycoming County Pennsylvania, being favored with health and usual
soundness of mind and memory, having in view the uncertainty
of human life, do make this my last will and testament as follows, viz,   First I give and bequeath sundry small legacies to

wit, to my Sister Rachel Ellis if she should still continue in the family and have her living there, from ten pounds per year for the purchase of clothes etc but if she should not have her living in the family, Twenty pounds per year to be paid annually during life, but her remaining in the family and her continued affectionate care and attention to my children is my will unless she should of choice decline it—

To my brother Thomas Ellis his residence in and use of the house where he now lives, and the use of the place called Thornberry and Robert Hawley's land during his natural life, with privilege of fire wood from fallen or dead timber, either off of that, or other of my lands adjacent, but with no privilege to sell or cut green timber therefrom, nor to transfer his right in the premises to any other person, or persons, but merely to hold it in his own possession as a home and living for him, or to have it worked for his use while he remains on it or in the neighborhood or County and no longer, still however reverting to him should he be for a time absent and return again, during his natural life as aforesaid.

To Jesse Haines as a remembrance of the friendship that has long subsisted between us, a silver watch (for his son William when he grows up) to be bought of Charles Townsend, of forty, or forty five dollars price, cap^d and jeweld. To Thomas Lightfoot of Maidencreek for the same reasons a Watch of the same kind.

To my niece Ann Tucker of Philadelphia in remembrance of her father and mother, and her own kind attention to me, a watch of the same kind, the caps of these watches to be engraved with this inscription " With wisdom mark the moment as it flies, Think what a moment is to him that dies."

To Sarah Tucker daughter of Thomas Tucker deceased ten pounds in money, to Joseph Tucker of Muncy I give devise and bequeath one hundred acres of land to be laid off at the discretion of my Executors from lands of mine lying on and near the state road north of Moses Wilson's to have one front on the State road of eighty perches to him and his heirs; or lieu thereof if he prefers it, the balance of his accounts which at present appears to be upwards of one hundred pounds.

To Benjamin Warner Jur, and Moses Lukens one hundred
pounds in trust to be paid in two years after my decease, and to
be placed out safely on interest under the care of the Monthly
Meeting of Muncy, for the beginning of a fund to be applied
to the schooling of the children of friends in straitened circumstances, members of Muncy Meeting, or other poor children
not members, at the discretion and direction of the committee
of the said Monthly Meeting for the time being, on the subject
of schools.

To my children herein after named I give, devise and bequeath
the following tracts of land and premises severally to them their
heirs and assigns ; Viz to my son William Cox Ellis two hundred
acres of land to be laid off the lower end of the tract granted
in the name of John Farmer, including the Mansion Buildings,
Mill, Mill races, dams, &c.

To Benjamin Ellis the plains, being the tract where William
Turnback now lives, taken up in the name of Joseph Smith,
containing two hundred and sixty three acres, and allowance
with the appurtenances together with thirty acres of the swamp
tract, to be taken off the lower end adjoining John Hall in such
a form as to injure the remaining tract as little as possible.

To Charles Ellis the tract called Thornberry, where Cæsar
Talbert now farms for me, with the appurtenances, subject however to the incumbrance of the bequest to Thomas Ellis at the
west end of the tract as stated above, containing in the whole
tract about two hundred and fifty two acres and allowance, and
to the said Charles Ellis one equal half of one hundred and
eighty acres of land adjoining the upper end of the pine swamp,
bought of Andrew Carson, on which there is no improvement.

To Henry D. Ellis the place called the Cottage, bought of
Moses Starr containing sixty eight acres and allowance, surveyed
in right of Peter Jones, with the appurtenances, as also the adjoining tract called the red House, with the appurtenances, containing about thirty eight acres and the meadow lot lying south
and adjoining, obtained from John Adlum including the House
where John Eck now lives, making in the three about one hundred and fourteen acres and allowances, as also one other tract
at Jaysburg, mouth of Lycoming Creek where William King

now lives, containing about one hundred acres and allowance with the buildings and appurtenances.

To my Daughter Rachel Ellis one equal half of the tract called in the patent Manchester, on which Judith Rynearson and Moses Lukens now reside, secured in the name of Conrad Hoover, to include the house where Judith Rynearson and family now lives, and the lower half of the tract in two equal halves to be divided, the one half containing one hundred and fifty seven acres and allowance with the appurtenances, and one equal half of ninety one acres which will remain at the upper end of the tract in the name of John Farmer, after William Cox's two hundred acres is taken off as above stated in two equal halves to be divided, but in such way as to best accommodate the two tracts, to which they are intended to be added, making in the two lots just mentioned about two hundred and two acres and allowance with the appurtenances.

To Anna Ellis the other equal half of the two tracts or lots above mentioned including the buildings where Moses Lukens lives and where David Way lives, containing in the two as in last about two hundred and two acres and allowance with the appurtenances.

And to Sarah Ellis the remainder of the tract called the Pine Swamp, where James Paxton now lives named in the patent Mansfield, containing about two hundred and fifty four acres and allowance exclusive of fifty acres which will appear by this will to be otherwise appropriated with the Buildings and appurtenances.

To the said William Cox Ellis, Benjamin Ellis, Charles Ellis, Henry D. Ellis, Rachel Ellis, Anna Ellis, and Sarah Ellis as they severally come of age their respective shares as above described according to the true intent and meaning thereof to each of them in severalty their heirs and assigns forever. To my beloved wife Mercy Ellis I give, devise and bequeath the tract of land now occupied by Jones Hamilton, and the Gardners, called in the patent pine forest survey, in right of Samuel Allinson containing two hundred and eighteen acres and allowance with the appurtenances, and the one equal half of the one hundred and eighty acre tract bought of Andrew Carson in two

equal halves to be divided, the other half being will'd to Charles,
also twenty acres of the pine swamp, to be taken off at the
lower end adjoining John Hall in such a way as to do the least
possible injury to the remaining tract containing in the three
tracts together about three hundred and twenty eight acres and
allowance to the said Mercy Ellis, her heirs and assigns forever.
And further it is my will that she continue in the possession and
use of the income of my Estate as it may be found at my decease
until the eldest surviving child comes of age, (should my life
be taken before that period,) and at all events that she continue
in the uninterrupted possession of my whole Estate and its income for one year after my decease, let it take place when it
may, and also that she continue in the possession of the income
arising from such of the children's share of lands as above willed
until they severally arrive to full age in law, for the purpose of
their maintenance and education.   And before she gives up the
Mansion House let a suitable plain two story stone House of a
price not exceeding five hundred pounds to be built at the Cottage for her retirement, and residence with her children and
family.   From a schedule which will be left with this will, there
appears about eight thousand pounds in bank stock, on Bonds
notes, &c, this I give and bequeath in the following proportions
viz—to the said Mercy Ellis one fourth part and to my several
children the remainder on the rates of one hundred and fifty to
one hundred—to the sons the one hundred and fifty and to the
daughters the one hundred, which admitting the stock to hold
good will stand thus, Mercy Ellis two thousand, each of the
sons one thousand, and each of the daughters six hundred and
sixty six pounds and two thirds.   There appears also on the
Schedule a tract of land lying on the State road north of Moses
Wilson's of three thousand acres, this from the late improvements in that country appears to be worth twelve thousand dollars, this I will to my wife, sons, and daughters, to them and their
heirs severally in the proportion just above stated whether sold
or unsold, having regard however to the one hundred acres
already willed of the same land to Joseph Tucker.   If the remainder is worth twelve thousand dollars, it will then stand
thus, Mercy Ellis three thousand dollars, my sons fifteen hun-

dred dollars each, and my daughters one thousand dollars each, or their proportion of land on that ratio, to them and their heirs as aforesaid—

And there appears on the same schedule the following lands, three thousand acres beech and Maple land being one equal undivided half of six thousand acres lying north of and adjoining the south branch of Tioga held in partnership with Robert Coleman Iron Master as tenants in common lying above Peters Camp—and one thousand or eleven hundred acres of the same property adjoining of my own, and Eleven hundred acres also at the Narrows of the south branch aforesaid above Berreys, all this is rather doubtful property being amongst the Connecticut Intruders. Twenty two hundred acres more or less or thereabouts lying south of the Elk mountain adjoining and on the North of Joshua Guybus land, and two hundred acres on Williamsons road south of the Blue Hill, as also one other body of land lying north of the River Surveys, and south of the Alleghany on the waters of Queeneshikque, Larries Creek, and Lycoming containing between five and six thousand acres, this last is now in the hands of Joseph Williams for sale. All these and all the residuary parts of my Estate real and personal I give, devise and bequeath to my Wife and children as above named, on the ratio and in the proportions as last above described whether sold or unsold at the time of divission, to each of them their respective several shares on the ratio aforesaid to them and their heirs. Should any of the children be removed by Death before they come of age let such share or shares be equally divided amongst the surviving children, but should Henry D. Ellis be removed let his share devolve to his Mother, to her and her heirs—On the presumption that the income of the share now willed to my wife and the income from the settled lands belonging to the children still remaining in their minority may be sufficient for her support and their support, and education, it is hereby declared to be my will that after the first comes of age, and the one year after my decease be elapsed as stated in the fore part of this will, all cash in stock or otherwise accumulated by sales of Back Lands, or otherwise belonging to the children's shares respectively shall be kept at Interest for the benefit of such share—To the said Mercy Ellis and to each of my children as above named I give devise and bequeath an equal share as tenants in common a lot of land obtained of John Hall being a limestone ridge containing about five or six acres, or to have their shares divided as may appear best to them and their heirs; and also an equal privilege of quarrying and using lime stone for their own use from the west end of the said lime stone ridge, being part of the Mansion tract, anything in this will to the contrary notwithstanding.

And lastly I do hereby nominate and appoint my valued friends Thomas Lightfoot of Maiden creek, and Jesse Haines of Elklands Executors to this my last will and testament, committing the whole with myself to the protection of Divine Providence. Given under my hand and seal this fourteenth day of the first month in the year of our Lord one thousand eight hundred and five.

WILLIAM ELLIS { SEAL }

Published and declared to be the testament and last will of the testator in presence of Henry Donald & Thomas Thomas.

HAINES FAMILY.

RICHARD HAINES, of Ainho, or Aynhoe, county of Northampton, England, and his wife, whose name is believed to be Margaret, had five sons, who came to New Jersey and Pennsylvania about 1683. They were:

I. JOHN, *m.* Esther Borton; he *d.* 1728; his wife *d.* 1719.
II. Richard; III. William; IV. Thomas; V. Joseph.

JOHN and ESTHER (BORTON) HAINES had:
    ISAAC, *b.* 1680; *m.* 1714 Katharine David, of Wales, and resided in Goshen, Chester County, Pennsylvania.

ISAAC and KATHARINE (DAVID) HAINES had:

ISAAC, *b.* 1718; *d.* 1790; *m.* 1744 Mary Cox, *b.* 1726–27; *d.* 1773.

ISAAC and MARY (COX) HAINES had:

JESSE, *b.* 1756; *d.* 1856; *m.* 1785 Rachel Otley, *b.* 1756; *d.* 1834, and had:

  I. Mary, *m.* Jesse Hartley. Their descendants are in the Western States as far as California.

  II. JACOB, *b.* 1788; *d.* 1866; *m.* 1815 Rachel Ellis, *b.* 1788; *d.* 1862, and had:

    1. WILLIAM ELLIS, *m.* 1841 Mary Rhoads, and had:

      HANNAH RHOADS, *m.* 1866 John Biddle Garrett, and had:

        MARY RHOADS and FRANCES BIDDLE.

    2. Mary Ellis, *m.* 1866 Edward Marshall; 3. Mercy, *d.* in infancy.

    4. Jesse, *m.* 1852 Mary W. Ecroyd, and had:

      Anna Morris; Henry Ecroyd, *m.* 1888 Anne Morris Wistar; William; Susan Lippincott; Edward; Sarah Ellis; William Ellis.

    5. Sarah Ellis; 6. Anna Morris; 7. Rebecca Ellis.

    8. Rachel, *m.* 1854 James Ecroyd, and had:

      William; Henry, *m.* 1890 Rebekah Ashbridge, and had:

        Henry, *b.* 1892.

      Mary, *m.* 1887 John Shober Kimber; Charles Ellis, *m.* 1891 Laura H. Taylor.

  III. Reuben, *m.* Anna Hawley, and had:

    1. Jesse, *m.* Phebe Lawrence; 2. Emmor, *m.* Ann Moore; 3. George, *m.* Ellen

20

——; 4. Calvin, *m.* Elizabeth Snell.
The daughters' names are unfortu-
nately omitted as unknown by the
compiler.

IV. Jesse Peirce, *m.* Sarah Snell, and had:
    1. William Snell; 2. Thomas, *m.* Julia
    Reed, and had:
        Elizabeth, *m.* Asher Evans, and
        had:
            Florence and William.
    3. Sarah.
    4. Martha M., *m.* William H. Creagh,
    and had:
        William and Richard.
    5. Mary E.
    6. Rachel, *m.* Charles O. Shove, and
    had:
        Ellen Marian; Charles Milton;
        Sarah Elizabeth; Alice; Mary
        Evans; Edward.

V. William Ellis, *m.* Maria Cheney; they
lived in New Garden, Chester County,
Pennsylvania, and had thirteen children.

VI. Thomas, *m.* Mary Edwards, and lived
in Western New York.

ELLIS FAMILY.

THOMAS ELLIS came from Pembrokeshire, Wales, in 1683, to
Pennsylvania. Thomas Ellis and his first wife, who died in
Wales, had:

I. ELLIS, *m.* 1685 Lydia Humphrey; II. Humphrey, *m.* first
Gwen Rees; *m.* secondly Jane David; III. Bridgart, *m.* ——
Jones; IV. Ellinor, *m.* David Lawrence.

ELLIS and LYDIA (HUMPHREY) ELLIS had :
    I. Rachel, *b.* 1686; *d.* 1717; II. Thomas, *b.* 1687; *d.* 1727;
    III. Elizabeth, *b.* 1689; *m.* 1718 Rees Price; IV. Bridget,
    b. 1691; *m.* 1724 John David; V. John, *b.* 1692; VI.
    Joseph, *b.* 1694; VII. Evan, *b.* 1697; *m.* 1726 Sarah
    Yarnall; VIII. William, *b.* 1699; *d.* 1728; IX. BENJAMIN,
    b. 1701; *d.* 1753; *m.* 1735 Ann Swaffer, *b.* 1708–09;
    d. 1777; X. Rebecca, *b.* 1703; *m.* Richard George, of
    Radnor.

BENJAMIN and ANN (SWAFFER) ELLIS had :
    I. Ellis; II. Rebecca, *m.* Henry Reynolds; III. Mary,
    m. Thomas Tucker; IV. Hannah, *m.* Abraham
    Davis; V. Rachel; VI. WILLIAM, *b.* 1751; *d.* 1806;
    m. 1785 Mercy Cox, *b.* 1761; *d.* 1848; VII. Thomas.

WILLIAM and MERCY (COX) ELLIS had :
    I. Mary, *d.* aged 17; II. William Cox, *m.* 1810
    Rebecca Morris; III. John; IV. Charles; V.
    Rebecca; VI. RACHEL, *m.* 1815 Jacob Haines;
    VII. Anna, *m.* Samuel Wells Morris; VIII.
    Sarah, *d.* aged 24; IX. Benjamin, *m.* Amy
    Yarnall; X. Charles, *m.* first Deborah Tyson;
    m. secondly Mary Luke Morris; XI. Henry
    Drinker, *m.* Mary Reynolds.

William Cox and Rebecca (Morris) Ellis had :
    I. Mary; II. William, *m.* first Hannah
    Lownes; *m.* secondly Agnes Boyd; III.
    Richard; IV. Mercy; V. Benjamin Morris,
    m. Elizabeth Masters; VI. Sarah, *m.*
    Edwin N. Lightner; VII. Anna Morris *m.*
    William H. Holstein; VIII. Joshua Alder
    m. first Henrietta Ashmead; *m.* secondly
    Mary Cheney; *m.* thirdly Mrs. Courtney.

RACHEL ELLIS *m.* 1815 JACOB HAINES, and had :
    I. WILLIAM ELLIS, *m.* 1841 Mary Rhoads;
    II. Mary Ellis, *m.* 1866 Edward Marshall;

III. Mercy; IV. Jesse, *m.* 1852 Mary
W. Ecroyd; V. Sarah Ellis; VI. Anna
Morris; VII. Rebecca Ellis; VIII. Rachel,
m. 1854 James Ecroyd.

WILLIAM ELLIS and MARY RHOADS HAINES
had:
    HANNAH RHOADS HAINES, *m.* 1866 John
    Biddle Garrett, and had:
        I. MARY RHOADS; II. FRANCES
        BIDDLE.

Jesse and Mary W. (Ecroyd) Haines had:
    I. Anna Morris; II. Henry Ecroyd, *m.*
    1888 Anne Morris Wistar; III.
    William; IV. Susan Lippincott; V.
    Edward; VI. Sarah Ellis; VII.
    William Ellis.

Rachel Haines *m.* 1854 James Ecroyd, and
had:
    I. William Ellis; II. Henry, *m.* 1890
    Rebekah Ashbridge; III. Mary, *m.*
    1887 John Shober Kimber; IV.
    Charles Ellis, *m.* 1891 Laura H.
    Taylor.
    Henry Ecroyd *m.* 1890 Rebekah
    Ashbridge, and had:
        Henry, *b.* 1892.

Anna Ellis *m.* 1810 Samuel Wells Morris, and
had:
    I. William Ellis, *m.* Mary N. Burnside; II.
    Mary Wells, *m.* James Lowry; III. Sarah
    Ellis, *m.* Joseph P. Morris; IV. Susan
    Marriot, *m.* John W. Guernsey; V.
    Benjamin Wistar, *m.* Hannah Rodney;
    VI. Rachel Wells; VII. Ellen, *m.* Henry
    Booth; VIII. Charles Ellis, *m.* Elizabeth

Amies; IX. Anna Ellis, *m.* George R.
Barker; X. Louisa; XI. Samuel Wells,
m. Charity Paynter.

Charles Ellis *m.* first Deborah Tyson, and had:
  I. Evan Tyson; II. Deborah Tyson.
He *m.* secondly Mary Luke Morris, and had:
  III. Nancy Morris, *m.* William M. Ellicott,
  Jr.

Henry Drinker Ellis *m.* Mary Reynolds, and had:
  I. Benjamin; II. Charles; III. Emily, *m.*
  William Elliot; IV. Elizabeth; V. Regina,
  m. George Everett; VI. Annie, *m.* Reese
  Wall Flower.

Note found in a manuscript book written by William Ellis
respecting his mother, Ann (Swaffer) Ellis.

" Late on the night of twenty seventh of Fourth month 1777
departed this life in the sixty ninth year of her age our dear and
tender mother Ann Ellis, who lived from her childhood a sober,
orderly life, and reaps, I verily trust, the fruits thereof. O, that
I might die the death of the righteous! that my latter end
might be like theirs."

The will of John Roades, of Winegreaves, is copied from one
enclosed with the original letter of administration granted to his
son Joseph and now held among the title-deeds to his property
by Joseph Rhoads, of Marple, Delaware County.

THE WILL OF JOHN ROADES, OF WINEGREAVES, DERBYSHIRE,
ENGLAND, AND AFTERWARDS OF DARBY, COUNTY OF
CHESTER AND PROVINCE OF PENNSYLVANIA.

In the Name of God Amen, this Twentyeth day of the Eighth
month in the yeare of our Lord Christ according to the English
account One Thousand Seven hundred and One, I John Roades
of Darby in the county of Chester and Province of Pennsylvania, Cordwainer, being of sound mind and perfect memory

Prayses to Almighty God for the same, Doe make and Ordain this my present Testament containing herein my last Will In Manner following that is to say First I comitt my soul into the hands of Almighty God my Maker and Redeemer and my body to be buried in such decent place and manner as to my friends and Executors hereafter named shall seem convenient and for that Estate which I have in this World Reall and personall I give as followeth viz. I will that all such Debts as I owe of right to any person or persons be truly paid by my Executors hereafter named without Lett or contradice and after my Debts payd, and funeral Expenses Discharged the remainder of my Estate reall and personall I give as followeth Imp^r. I give and bequeath unto my youngest son Joseph Roades all my land and plantation with Buildings and all manner the appurtenances to the same belonging all which I bought of Rebeckah Hany and Jacob Simcock lieing in Marple Township in the County of Chester I give and bequeath unto my son Joseph Roades and to his heirs and assigns forever Also I give and bequeath unto my said son Joseph Roades the bed and furniture which I now lye upon it being intended for him by his Mother and also some Table napkins and one pewter Dish and one plate one porringer and one Spoone Item I give and bequeath unto my son Jacob Roades twenty pounds, also one Bed and furniture which his Mother left him and also some Table napkins Item I give unto my son John Roades Tenn Shillings over and above what I gave him in the land at White Marsh Item I give unto my son Adam Roades my Bay Mare which I used to Ride upon Item I will that my servant by covenant Charles Robinson shall serve the remainder of his time by covenant to me with my son Joseph Roades or his assigns and I will that att the end of his said time of covenant service my said son Joseph Roades or his assigns shall give to the said Charles as by my Will the Sume of Twenty Shillings Item I will that after my Debts payd funerall expenses and Legacies Discharged the remainder of my Estate I will shall be equally Divided betwixt my sons Adam Roades Jacob Roades and Joseph Roades and my two daughters Mary Maltby and Elizabeth Daws equally amongst them five And I make and ordain my sons Adam Roades and

Joseph Roades my Executors of this my last Will and Testament and I utterly revoke and annull all former Wills Legacies and Bequests etc whatsoever by me heretofore named Willed or Bequeathed.

JOHN ROADES

Subscribed as above ye 20th. 8th. mo. 1701

These being witnesses

JOSIAH GRATTON

JOHN HOOD.

John Moore Gent. Registrar General for probate of Wills and Granting Letters of Administration for the Province of Pennsylvania and Territory. By Virtue of a commission under the honourable William Penn Esqr Proprietor and Governor thereof.

To all to whom these presents shall come Know yee that at Philadelphia in the said Province upon the day of the date hereof was proved approved and insinuated the last Will and Testament of John Roades said deceased (annexed to these presents) Having whilst he lived and at the time of his decease Goods, rights and Creditts in divers places within the said Province and Territories By means whereof the full Disposition of all and Singular the goods rights and Creditts of the said Deceased and the granting the Administration thereof As also the hearing of accounts Calculation or reckoning of the Administration and the finall Discharge and Dismission from the same unto me belongeth and the administration of all and Singular the Goods rights and Creditts of the said John Roades deceased and his last Will and Testament Concerning was granted unto Joseph Roades (Adam Roades his brother renouncing the said Trust) Executor therein named rightly, of well and truly administring the same and of making a true and perfect Inventory and conscionable appraisement of all and singular the Goods rights and Creditts of the said Deceased and exhibiting the same into the Registrar General's Office at or before the 22nd. of February next ensueing and of rendering a true account when thereunto required being solemnly attested. In testimony whereof I have caused the seal of my Office to be hereunto affixed this 22nd. of November 1701.

J. MOORE *Registrar General.*

MARRIAGE CERTIFICATE OF JAMES RHOADS AND ELIZABETH
OWEN.

Whereas James Rhoads Son of Joseph Rhoads Dec^d of Marple in the County of Chester and Province of Pensylvania and Elizabeth Owen Daughter of John Owen of Springfield in the County and Province Afore^d. Having Declared their intentions of Marriage with each other before Several Monthly Meetings of the People called Quakers at Providence in the County afore^d. according to the good order used among them and having Consent of Parents and Relations concerned their s^d proposal of marriage was allowed by the said Meeting   Now these are to certify whom it may concern that for the full accomplishing their s^d intentions this twenty second day of Sixth month in the year of our Lord One thousand seven hundred and forty five they the s^d James Rhoads and Elizabeth Owen appeared in a public meeting of the s^d people at Springfield afore^d and the said James Rhoads taking the said Elizabeth Owen by the Hand did in Solemn Manner openly declare that he took her the s^d Elizabeth Owen to be his Wife promising with the Lord's assistance to be unto her a Loving and faithful Husband Until Death should separate them and then and there in the s^d assembly the s^d Elizabeth Owen did in like manner openly declare that she took the said James Rhoads to be her Husband promising with the Lord's assistance to be unto him a Loving and faithful Wife until Death should separate them   And moreover they the s^d James Rhoads and Elizabeth Owen (she according to the Custom of marriage assuming the name of her Husband) as a farther confirmation thereof Did then and there to these presents set their Hands

JAMES RHOADS
ELIZABETH RHOADS

And we whose names are under written as being present at the solemnization of the s^d marriage and subscription have as witnesses hereunto set our hands the Day and Year above written

James Maris	Grace Lloyd	Bartholomew Coppock	John Owen
Frd. Levis	Jane Hoskins	John Gleave	Hannah Owen
John Lewis	Elizabeth Maris	Robert Williamson	Abigail Roads

Alice Lewis	Joseph Maris	Mord[i] Taylor	John Rhoads
Isaac Howell	Ann Maris	Joseph Yarnall	George Maris
David Ranken	Phebe Coppock	John Coppock	Jane Maris
Dan. Calvert	Eliz[a] Gleave	John Biddle	John Maris
Jacob Howell	Rebecca ffell	Robert Taylor	Robert ———
Joseph Thomas	Hannah Levis	Samuel Levis Jun[r]	Mord[i] Massey
Hannah Massey	Mary Yarnall	Joshua Thompson	George Owen
Elizabeth ———	Katherine Pearson	B. Davis	Mary Powell
Elizabeth Jones	Susanna Cruchshank	Robert Pearson	Katherine Rhoads
	Sarah West	J. W. Hanly	Jane West
	Mary Levis	Joseph Sleight	Elizabeth Rhoads
	Marg[t]. Thompson	John West	Rebekah Massey
		Mary Bartram	George Maris
		James Bartram	Ann ———
		Elizabeth Bartram	Susanna ———

[Some of the names have been obscured by the wear of time.]

[Copy of a marriage certificate brought from Wales by the Owens. It was written on parchment that has shrunk with dampness and age so that some lines are almost illegible. The following has been taken from the original, now in my possession, and is as nearly correct as I can decipher it.—*M. R. Haines, 1893.*]

Be it known by these presents unto all whom it may concern upon the eleventh day of the first month 1678–9 Robert Owen son of Owen ap Evan (deceased) late of Vron Goch in the ——— of Penllin in the county of Merioneth hath taken Rebekah Owen first daughter of Owen Humphrey of Llwyn-du in the Com[t] of Dalybont in the county afore[d] to be his wife and that by the free assent and consent of their parents near relations and friends of truth and that according to the example and practice of primitive Christians followers of the truth. And the said Rebekah in like manere hath taken the said Rob[t] Owen to be her husband the day and year above written in the presence and sight of us the witnesses here under written.

Owen Humphrey her father

Cadd[r] Thomas	John Owen
Rowland Ellis	Joseph Samuel
Hugh Robert	Richard Humphrey
Humphrey Owen	
Rowland Owen	Elizabeth Thomas
	Hannah ———

Edward Vaughan	Ellin Rees
Ellis Rees	Gwen Rees
Evan John	Anne Owen
Rees Owen	Elizabeth Owen
John Thomas	Gainor John
——— Humphrey	Lydia Samuel
Humphrey Reynolds	Rebekah Samuel
John Howell	Gobeithia Samuel
Daniel Samuel	Elizabeth Owen
Rees John	
John William	

MARRIAGE CERTIFICATE OF JOHN OWEN AND HANNAH MARIES

Whereas John Owen son of Robert Owen late of the Township of Merion in the County of Philadelphia in the Province of Pennsylvania Yeoman deceased and Hannah Maries Daughter of George Maries of the township of Springfield in the county of Chester in the said Province Yeoman Having declared their intentions of marriage with Each other before Several Monthly meetings of the People called Quakers at Providence aforesaid, according to the good order used among them Their proceedings therein being with the consent of Parties and Relations concerned and nothing appearing to obstruct were after a deliberate Consideration thereof approved of by the said meetings Now these are to certify all whom it may Concern that for the full accomplishing of their said intentions this two and twentieth day of the Eighth month in the year of our Lord one thousand seven hundred and nineteen They the said John Owen and Hannah Maries appeared at a public meeting for that purpose appointed at Springfield aforesaid and the said John Owen taking the said Hannah Maries by the hand did in solemn manner openly declare that he took her to be his wife promising by God's assistance to be unto her a faithful and Loving Husband until death should separate them and then and there in the said Assembly the said Hannah Maries did likewise declare that she took the said John Owen to be her Husband in like manner promising to be to him a loving and faithful wife till death should them separate and moreover the said John Owen and Hannah Maries, she according to the custom of marriage assuming the name of her husband as a further confirmation thereof did then and there to these presents sett their hands And we whose names are here underwritten being among others present at the solemnization of the said marriage and subscription in manner aforesaid as witnesses thereunto have also to these presents sett our hands the day and year above written.

[Here the parchment has been torn and the names of John and Hannah Owen nearly effaced.]

John Salkeld	Lydia Lancaster	Rowland Ellis Jun.	George Maris
David Lloyd	Elizabeth Rawlinson	Hugh Evans	Jane Maris
Joseph Buckley	Gra. Lloyd	Owen Roberts	Mordecai Maries
John Thomas	Agnes Salkeld	Edward Roberts	Richard Maries
Samuel Blunstone	Deborah West	John Cadwalader	Hooper Maris
Joseph Jones	Margery Pearson	John Acbert	Evan Owen
John Humphreys	Sarah Worrilaw	John Worrilaw	Owen Owen
Reece Price	Elizabeth Hall	Ann Worrilaw	Ann Owen
Samuel Ogden	Mary Smith	John Roberts	Robt Owen
George Lownes	Rebecah Cadwalader	Jacob Simcock	Sus. Owen
George Hall	Jane Schollar	C. Simcock	G. Maris
Thomas Bird	Elizabeth Hallowell	Ben : Simcock	Gainor Jones
John Hall	Sarah Levis	Susanna Maris	David Evans
John David	Margaret Coppock	Alse Maris	Eliz^a Evans
Wm. Way	Jane Lownes	Joseph Taylor	Alice Maris
Nch^a Ogden	Mary Lownes	Wm. Smith	Rowland Ellis
David Jones	Hannah Maris	Samuel Hart	Daniel Humphrey
Jn. Jones	Hannah Simcock	John Stidman	Edward Rees
Jonathan Humphreys	Ester Lownes	Samuel Worthington	Reb:^{a} Rees
George Shiers	Mary Maris	John Gleame	Benjamin Simcock
Lawrance Pearson	John Yarnall	Joseph Harvey	Hannah Humphrey
William West	John Hall	Jonathan Maris	Sam. Humphrey
Walter Worrilaw	Robert Pearson	Job Yarnall	
Thomas Pearson	Thomas Worrilaw		

MARRIAGE CERTIFICATE OF JOSEPH RHOADS AND MARY ASHBRIDGE.

Whereas Joseph Rhoads Son of James Rhoads of the township of Marple in the County of Chester and Province of Pennsylvania (Deceased) and Mary Ashbridge Daughter of George Ashbridge of the township of Goshen in the County and province afforsaid Having declared their intentions of marriage with each other before several monthly meetings of the people called Quakers held at Goshen affors^d according to the good order used amongst them   They having consent of parents and appearing clear of all others their said proposal of marriage was allowed of by the said meetings   Now these may certify whom it may concern that for the full accomplishing of their said intentions This twenty seventh day of the Fifth month in the year of our Lord one thousand seven hundred and seventy nine They the said Joseph Rhoads and Mary Ashbridge appeared in a public meeting of the said people for that purpose appointed at their public meeting house at Goshen afforsaid and the said Joseph Rhoads taking the said Mary Ashbridge by the hand did in a solemn manner openly declare that he took her to be his wife promising through Divine assistance to be unto her a Loving and faithful Husband untill Death should separate them and then and there in the same assembly the said Mary Ashbridge did in Like manner openly declare that she took him the said Joseph Rhoads to be her Husband promising through Divine assistance to be unto him a Loving and faithful wife until death should separate them   And moreover the said Joseph Rhoads and Mary Ashbridge (she according to the custom of marriage assuming the name of her husband) as a further confirmation thereof did then and there to these presents set their hands

JOSEPH RHOADS
MARY RHOADS

And we whose names are hereunto subscribed being present at the solemnization of the said marriage and subscription have as witnesses thereunto set our hands the day and year above written

Mordecai Lawrence	Isaac Garrett	George Ashbridge
Hannah Hunter	Mary Peirce Jhn Griffith	Owen Rhoads
Mary Rhoads	Randal Malin	Hannah Rhoads
Samuel Pancoast	Josiah Garrett	Rebecca Rhoads
John Jones	Mary Garrett	Tacy Rhoads
Jesse Davis	Jesse Garrett	Joseph Malin
Thomas Smedley	Richard Goodwin	Lydia Malin
Nathan Sharples	Lydia Goodwin	Susanna Ashbridge
Wm Townsend Junr	James Peirce	Josiah Hibberd
Joseph Davis	Amey Jones	William Garrett
Ellis Williams	Thomas Smedley	Susanna Hibberd

William Hoopes

Henry Hoopes

Joshua Lawrence

Jos. Ashbridge Junr

Isr^l. Jacobs Junr

Mary Jones

Susanna Hoopes

Christian Hoopes

Abigail Griffith

Deborah Peirce

Mary Davies

Enos Thomas

Sarah Thomas

Owen Maris

Edward Hunter

Benjamin Hickman

Ann Davis

Hannah Townsend

Hannah Ogden

Jane Ashbridge

Priscilla Jones

George Dunn

Massey Lawrence

Jane Massey

Lydia Garrett

Phebe Smedley

Lydia Hoopes

Owen Hibberd

Ann Goodwin

Elizabeth Smedley

Joshua Hoopes

Joshua Ashbridge

Jesse Maris

Jane Maris

Jesse Jones

Thomas Garrett

Hannah Garrett

Wm. Garrett Junr

Debby Garrett

Isaac Massey

Joshua Hoopes

Susanna Hoopes

Isaac Rhoads

Debby Garrett

Amos Yarnall

Sarah Yarnall

MARRIAGE CERTIFICATE OF JOSEPH RHOADS AND HANNAH EVANS.

Whereas Joseph Rhoads of Marple township, Delaware County in the State of Pennsylvania, Tanner, Son of Joseph Rhoads late of the County aforesaid, deceased, and Mary his wife, and Hannah Evans Daughter of Jonathan Evans of the City of Philadelphia in the State aforesaid and Hannah his wife, having declared their intentions of marriage with each other before a Monthly Meeting of the Religious Society of Friends held at Philadelphia for the Southern District, according to the good order used among them; and having consent of the Surviving Parents, their said proposal of marriage was allowed of by the said meeting: Now these are to certify whom it may concern, that for the full accomplishment of their said intentions, this Fourth day of the Eleventh month in the year of our Lord one thousand eight hundred and eighteen, they the said Joseph Rhoads and Hannah Evans appeared in a public meeting of the said people held in their meeting house on Pine street in Philadelphia aforesaid, and the said Joseph Rhoads taking the said Hannah Evans by the hand did, on this solemn occasion, openly declare that he took her the said Hannah Evans to be his Wife, promising with Divine assistance to be unto her a loving and faithful Husband until Death should separate them; and then in the same assembly the said Hannah

Evans did in like manner declare, that she took him the said
Joseph Rhoads to be her Husband promising with Divine as-
sistance to be unto him a loving and faithful Wife until Death
should separate them   And moreover they the said Joseph
Rhoads and Hannah Evans, She according to the custom of
Marriage assuming the name of her Husband, did as a further
confirmation thereof then and there to these presents set their
Hands

JOSEPH RHOADS
HANNAH RHOADS

And we whose names are also hereunto subscribed, being
present at the solemnization of the said marriage and subscription have as witnesses thereto set our Hands the day and year
above written.

Edward Wilson	Catharine W Morris	Margaret Lisle	Mary Rhoads
Benj Martin	Margaret Hutchinson	Ann Wilson	Jon Evans
	(by order)		
Thomas Kimber	Amy Coates	Mary Hughes	Hannah Evans
Earl Shinn	Mary Cresson	Ann Lloyd	William Ashbridge
Samuel Shinn	Anabella Cresson	Gulielma Maria Smith	Thomazin Ashbridge
Isaac Lloyd Jun	Deborah F Wharton	Hannah Townsend	Joseph Bacon
Anthony P Morris	Sarah Fisher	Martha J Hutton	Sarah Bacon
Isaac W Morris	Rachel Smith	Sarah Cresson	T. B Mount
Richard Jordan	Mary Offley	Sarah Waln	Mary Mount
Rebecca Archer	Hannah Fisher Sen	Sarah Hopper	George Rhoads
Sarah Morris	James Rhoads jun	Ann Mifflin	William Rhoads
Geo W Gibbons	Elizabeth H Rhoads	Hannah Lewis	William Evans
Thomas Kite	Elizabeth Lownes	Sarah Humphreys	Elizabeth Rhoads
Joseph Gibbons	Jane Malin	Elizabeth Hutchinson	Phebe Rhoads
Samuel R Fisher	Joseph Malin Jun	Sarah Hopper Jun	Joseph Evans
Jonathan Leedom	William Wharton	Rachel Hopper	Grace Evans
Isaac Lowry	Sarah Leedom	Abigail Hutchinson	Mary Evans
Isaac I Hopper	Erwin J Leedom	Elizabeth Marr	Joel Evans
J Wilson Moore	Lydia Leedom	Mary Price	Thomas Evans
David Bacon	John Townsend	Lydia B Cox	Charles Evans
John Hutchinson Jr	Isaac Lloyd	Mary Fves	Jos R Evans
Henry M Zollickoffer	John Townsend Jr	Abigail Peirce	Margaret Evans
John C Evans	George H Coffee		Sarah Bacon Jun
John Hutchinson			Mary Bacon
George Lloyd			
John Lloyd			

MARRIAGE CERTIFICATE OF JONATHAN EVANS, JR , AND
HANNAH BACON

Whereas Jonathan Evans Junior of the City of Philadelphia
in Pennsylvania House Carpenter Son of Jonathan Evans and
Hannah his Wife of the said City and Hannah Bacon Daughter

of David and Mary Bacon of Philadelphia aforesaid having declared their Intentions of marriage with each other before several monthly meetings of the People called Quakers at Philadelphia aforesaid, according to the good order used amongst them, and having consent of Parents, their said proposals were allowed of by the said Meeting: Now these are to certify whom it may concern, that for the full accomplishing their said Intentions, this Thirteenth day of the Fourth month, in the year of our Lord One Thousand Seven Hundred and Eighty Six; They the said Jonathan Evans junior and Hannah Bacon appeared in a public meeting of the said People at Philadelphia aforesaid and the said Jonathan Evans junior taking the said Hannah Bacon by the Hand, did in a solemn manner openly declare, that he took her the said Hannah Bacon to be his Wife, promising through the Lord's assistance to be unto her a loving and faithful Husband until Death should separate them: and then in the same assembly the said Hannah Bacon did in like manner declare, that she took him the said Jonathan Evans junior to be her Husband, promising through the Lord's assistance to be unto him a loving and faithful Wife until Death should separate them. And moreover they the said Jonathan Evans junior and Hannah Bacon (She according to the custom of Marriage assuming the name of her Husband) as a further confirmation thereof, did then and there to these presents set their Hands.

JONATHAN EVANS JUNIOR
HANNAH EVANS

And we whose names are hereunder also subscribed, being present at the solemnization of the said marriage and subscription, have as witnesses thereunto set our hands the day and year above written.

John Field	Rebecca Biddle	David Evans	Jonathan Evans
Charles West	Anne Dawson	Job Bacon	Hannah Evans
James Pemberton	Susanna Head	Mary Bacon	David Bacon
Samuel Emlen	Martha Dorsey	Owen Jones	Mary Bacon
Nicholas Waln	Sarah Dickinson	Susanna Jones	Adam Hubley
Benjamin Hooton	Jane Biddle	Mary Hough	Mary Hubley
John Parrish	Sarah Jervis	Hannah Elfreth	Rebecca Bacon

William Savery	Mary Jervis jun	Mary Armitt (per order)	Benjamin Evans
John Elliott jun^r	Elisha Fisher	Annabella Elliot (per order)	Elizabeth Evans
Owen Biddle	John A. Fitzgerald	Hannah Saunders	Joseph Bacon
William Wilson	Samuel Jervis jun	Dorcas Lillie	John Oldden
Arthur Howell	William Boyce	Elizabeth Drinker	Mary Oldden
John Townsend	John Hutchinson	Ann Hallowell (per order)	Joseph Scattergood
Joseph Budd	Thomas Follett	Mary Savery	Hannah Hubley
Joseph Richardson	Benedt Dorsey	Mary Pleasants	Thomas Scattergood
Joseph Sharpless	Daniel Offley junior	Sarah Cresson	Sarah Scattergood
Charles Williams	Thomas Savery	Mary Cresson	Elizabeth Jervis
Ellis Yarnall	Charles West jun^r	Margaret Elliot (per order)	Mary Jervis
Robert Coe	Rebekah Carmalt	Ann Emlen Junr	Thomas Trotter
Jesse Care	Caleb Carmalt	Hannah Norton	Gulielma Evans
Thomas Harrison	Caleb Atmore	Phebe Poultney	Saml Jervis
Joseph Bringhurst	Richd Humphreys	Hannah Norton jun^r	Dinah Trotter
Jesse Williams	William Waring	Martha Denn	Margaret Trotter (per order)
		Ann Zane	

MARRIAGE CERTIFICATE OF WILLIAM ELLIS HAINES AND MARY RHOADS.

Whereas William E Haines of the Township of Springfield in the County of Delaware in the State of Pennsylvania, Son of Jacob Haines, of the Township of Muncy in Lycoming County and State aforesaid, and Rachel E. his wife, and Mary Rhoads Daughter of Joseph Rhoads of the Township of Marple in Delaware County aforesaid and Hannah his Wife, having declared their intentions of Marriage with each other before a Monthly Meeting of the Religious Society of Friends held at Springfield in the County of Delaware aforesaid according to the good order used among them, and having consent of Parents, their said proposal of marriage was allowed of by the said Meeting Now these are to certify whom it may concern that for the full accomplishment of their said intentions this Seventh day of the Tenth month in the year of our Lord One thousand eight hundred and forty one, they the said William E Haines and Mary Rhoads appeared in a public meeting of the said

People held in their Meeting house at Springfield in the County of Delaware aforesaid, and the said William E. Haines taking the said Mary Rhoads by the hand did on this solemn occasion openly declare that he took her, the said Mary Rhoads to be his Wife promising with Divine assistance to be unto her a loving and faithful Husband until death should separate them : and then in the same assembly the said Mary Rhoads did in like manner declare that she took him the said William E. Haines to be her Husband promising with Divine assistance to be unto him a loving and faithful Wife until death should separate them.

And moreover they the said William E. Haines and Mary Rhoads, she according to the custom of marriage assuming the name of her Husband, did as a further confirmation thereof then and there to these presents set their hands.

WILLIAM E. HAINES
MARY R. HAINES

And we whose names are also hereunto subscribed being present at the solemnization of the said marriage and subscription have as witnesses thereunto set our hands the day and year above written.

James S. Lippincott	Isaac P. Garrett	Jacob Haines
Joseph Liddon Pennock	Phebe R. Garrett	Joseph Rhoads
Charles Jones	Abigail Evans	Hannah Rhoads
John R. Howell	Mary Evans jun.	Mary E. Haines
William C. Longstreth	Ann Evans	Sarah E. Haines
E. R. Edwards	Mary R. Evans	Jesse Haines
Phineas Lownes	George Rhoads Jr.	Deborah Rhoads
Emily L. Lownes	John W. Tatum	Joseph Rhoads jr.
Rachel M. Hampton	Amy Y. Tatum	Elizabeth Rhoads Jr.
Massey Lownes	Lydia P. Garrett	James E. Rhoads
Thomas Rhoads	Esther Levis	Charles Rhoads
William Ogden	George Maris	J. Evans Rhoads
Maris Rhoads	George B. Allen	Mary L. Ellis
James Rhoads	Sidney Allen	Charles Ellis
Caleb Emlen	Mary Emlen	Joseph Evans
Sarah B. Allen	Chalkley Bell	Grace Evans
Hannah Evans	Sarah Palmer	Mary Evans
Garrett Levis	Sidney Lownes	Joel Evans
William Evans	Elizabeth Lownes	Hannah R. Evans

Richard J Allen
Hannah P Lewis
Joshua Allen
R T Ogden
John Evans

Sarah Mahn
Esther Rhoads
Phebe Rhoads
Elizabeth H Rhoads
Susanna Taylor
Lydia T. King
Phebe Emlen
Margaretta F Thatcher

Elizabeth Evans
Thomas Evans
Catharine Evans
Charles Evans
Mary L. Evans
Wm Rhoads
Anna P Rhoads
Elizabeth Rhoads

MARRIAGE CERTIFICATE OF JOHN BIDDLE GARRETT AND HANNAH RHOADS HAINES.

Whereas John Biddle Garrett of Germantown in the city of Philadelphia and State of Pennsylvania, Son of Thomas C Garrett and Frances B his Wife and Hannah R Haines of Germantown in the City and State aforesaid, daughter of William E Haines and Mary R his Wife (the former deceased) having declared their intentions of Marriage with each other before a Monthly Meeting of the Religious Society of Friends held at Germantown in the City and State aforesaid according to the good order used among them, and having consent of their surviving parents their said proposal of marriage was allowed of by the said Meeting

Now these are to certify to whom it may concern, that for the full accomplishment of their said intentions, this Sixth day of the Ninth month in the year of our Lord One thousand eight hundred and Sixty Six, they, the said John B Garrett and Hannah R Haines appeared in a public meeting of the said People held in their Meeting house at Germantown in the City and State aforesaid, and the said John B Garrett taking the said Hannah R Haines by the hand, did, on this solemn occasion, openly declare that he took her, the said Hannah R Haines to be his Wife, promising with Divine assistance, to be unto her a loving and faithful Husband until death should separate them , and then, in the same assembly, the said Hannah R Haines did, in like manner declare, that she took him, the said John B. Garrett to be her Husband promising with Divine assistance to be unto him a loving and faithful Wife until death should separate them

And moreover they, the said John B. Garrett and Hannah R. Haines (she according to the custom of marriage assuming the name of her Husband) did, as a further confirmation thereof, then and there to these presents set their hands.

JOHN B. GARRETT
HANNAH R. GARRETT

And we whose names are hereunto subscribed, being present at the solemnization of the said marriage and subscription, have as witnesses thereto set our hands the day and year above written.

Edward C. Biddle
John Biddle
Samuel Biddle
Rebecca B. Cope
Sarah Biddle
Philip G. Sheppard
Anne E. Sheppard
John E. Sheppard
Margaret G. Sheppard
Rebecca C. Sheppard
Mary M. Sheppard
Thomas McCollin
Wm. Biddle
Deborah Rhoads
Jos. Rhoads
Elizabeth Snowdon Rhoads
Charles Rhoads
Hannah Evans
James B. Cope
Elizabeth Rhoads
Jas. G. McCollin
Edward T. Comfort
Yardley Warner
Hannah A. Warner
Richard Cadbury
Lloyd Mifflin
Charles S. Folwell
James Whitall
Joseph Howell
John Stokes
Hannah Maris Stokes
Charles Jones
John S. Haines

Jonathan E. Rhoads
Rebecca G. Rhoads
Frances Garrett
Philip C. Garrett
Elizabeth W. Garrett
Hetty B. Garrett
Joseph Rhoads Jr.
Nannie M. Ellicott
Mary Anna Cope
Richard D. Wood
Rand. Wood
Rachel W. Morris
J. Wistar Evans
John W. Biddle
Mary H. Biddle
Edward D. Cope
Annie Pim Cope
Francis Stokes
Katharine W. Stokes
Charles Evans
Mary L. Evans
Frances Edge
Samuel Mason
Jane E. Mason
Jane S. Comfort
Harriet M. Rowland
Henry Chapman
Jane H. Chapman
Anne Warner
Rebecca Warner
Sarah Wistar
Katharine J. Wistar
Susanna S. Kite

Thomas C. Garrett
Frances B. Garrett
Mary R. Haines
James E. Rhoads
Margaret E. Rhoads
John W. Cadbury
Hannah B. Evans
William Evans Jr.
Harriet S. Aertsen
Thomas Scattergood
Martha H. Garrett
Jonathan Evans
Elizabeth S. Cope
James M. Aertsen
Harriet R. Aertsen
Minnie Aertsen
Esther P. Aertsen
Alice F. Aertsen
Joel Evans
Mary E. Rhoads
Elizabeth P. Smith
George Jones
James R. Greeves
Elizabeth Greeves
Mary N. Rhoads
Catherine E. Rhoads
Phebe Rhoads
Anna Rhoads
Hannah M. Matlack
Beulah M. Hacker
Sarah Nicholson
Anne E. Howell
Sarah C. Bangs

Reuben Haines
Thos H McCollm
Samuel Emlen
Sarah Emlen
Francis R Cope
Anna S Cope
Hettie N Stokes
Thos P C. Stokes
Eleanor T. Stokes
Rachel R Cope
Essie S Sharpless
Elizabeth M Hacker

Mary Ann Jones
Lydia S Morris
Rachel P. Smith
Louisa T Anderson
Beulah S Morris
Sam¹ Morris
Elliston P Morris
Hugh D Vail
Edward Comfort
Susan L Comfort
Hannah Williams
Howard Comfort

George G Williams
Jerʰ Hacker
Jennie H Bacon
E B Edwards Jun
Jennetta E Johnson
Frances Pleasants
Emma Williams
Sarah Cadbury
John E Carter
E H Bonsall
Annie Mickle
Edith A. Comfort

RHOADS FAMILY

JOHN and ELIZABETH RODES, or ROADES, of Winegreaves,
Derbyshire, England   After the decease of his wife, John
Roades came to Pennsylvania, where he purchased lands, and
lived in Darby   He deceased 27th of Eighth month, 1701
John and Elizabeth Roades had:

I. Adam, *b.* 1660; came to Pennsylvania 1684; *m* 1691
  Catharine Blunstone, who *d* 1733, they had .

  1 John, *b.* 1692, *m* 1736 Elizabeth Bradshaw
  2. Hannah, *b* 1694; *m* 1719 John Thomas; *d.* 1760.
  3. Sarah, *b.* 1696, *m* John Nickerson, *d* 1777.
  4 Elizabeth, *b* 1698, *m.* 1723 William Kirk, *d.* 1745.
  5 Joseph, *b* 1700, *d.* 1763
  6. Adam, *b.* 1703.
  7 Mary, *b.* 1706
  8 Samuel, *b.* 1710, *d.* 1778. *m* 1737 Margaret Thomas,
     and had descendants:

     1 Adam and Sarah Rhoads
        |
     2. Joseph and Naomi Rhoads.
        |
     3 James and Alice Rhoads
        |
     4. Joseph R and Amanda Rhoads
        |
     5. Alice Sellers, *m.* Henry G. Marston; and J Howard
        Rhoads.

II. Mary, *b.* 1662; *m.* 1689 William Maltby.

III. John, *b.* 1664; *m.* 1692 Hannah Wilcox. He inherited lands in White Marsh from his father; *d.* 10th of Tenth mo., 1733. They have had numerous descendants, who intermarried with the Chandler, Conner, Franklin, Pemberton, Pleasants, Howell, Symond, Fisher, and Drinker families. Among those of the later generation are the names of John L. Atlee, M.D.; Major-General William Buel Franklin, of Connecticut; and Rear-Admiral Samuel Rhoads Franklin, of Washington, D.C.

IV. Elizabeth, *b.* 1667; *m.* 1692–93 Edward Dawes.

V. Jacob, *b.* 1670; VI. Abraham, *b.* 1672; VII. Sarah, *b.* 1675; VIII. Hannah, *b.* 1677.

IX. JOSEPH, *b.* 5th of Second mo., 1680; *d.* 1732; resided on his inheritance in Marple; *m.* 1702 Abigail Bonsall, of Darby; *d.* 1750; and had:

> 1. John, *b.* 1703; *m.* Elizabeth Malin; 2. Mary; 3. Elizabeth; 4. Abigail; 5. Joseph, *b.* 1715; 6. Benjamin, *b.* 1719; *m.* Catharine Pugh; 7. JAMES, *b.* 1722; *d.* 1778; *m.* 1745 Elizabeth Owen, *b.* 1722–23; *d.* 1795.

JAMES and ELIZABETH (OWEN) RHOADS had:

> I. Hannah, *b.* 1746; *m.* Nathan Garrett, of Upper Darby.
>
> II. JOSEPH, *b.* 1748; *d.* 1809; *m.* 1779 Mary Ashbridge, *b.* 1758; *d.* 1830.
>
> III. Susanna, *b.* 1751; *d.* 1752.
>
> IV. Rebecca, *b.* 1754 (?); *d.* 1801; *m.* Hugh Lownes, of Springfield, Delaware County, Pennsylvania.
>
> V. Owen, *b.* 1756; *d.* 1838; *m.* Mary Hall.
>
> VI. Tacy, *b.* 1759; *d.* 1804; *m.* Joseph Davis, of Haverford, Delaware County, Pennsylvania.
>
> VII. James, *b.* 1763; *d.* 1770.
>
> VIII. Elizabeth, *b.* 1768; *d.* 1778.

JOSEPH and MARY (ASHBRIDGE) RHOADS had:

> I. James, *b.* 1781; *d.* 1819.
>
> II. George, *b.* 18th of Second mo., 1784; *d.* Third mo., 1858.

III Joseph, *b.* 1787, *d* 1861; *m.* 1818 Hannah Evans, *b.* 1793, *d* 1865

IV. and V. Rebecca and Elizabeth (twins), *b* 29th of Ninth mo, 1789; *d* Elizabeth, 15th of Ninth mo, 1844, *d* Rebecca, 29th of First mo, 1861

VI Phebe, *b* 1793, *d* 1871, *m* 1840 Isaac Price Garrett, *b* 1795, *d.* 24th of First mo, 1869.

VII. William, *b* 2d of Fourth mo, 1797, *d.* 27th of Second mo, 1863, *m* 14th of Third mo, 1822, Anne Pancoast, daughter of William and Esther Levis, *b.* 4th of Eighth mo, 1799, *d* 7th of Ninth mo, 1888

Joseph and Hannah (Evans) Rhoads had.

 I Mary, *m* 1841 William Ellis Haines, and had.

  Hannah Rhoads, *m.* 1866 John Biddle Garrett, and had ·

   Mary Rhoads and Frances Biddle

 II Deborah, *b* 1821, *d* 1892 Lovely and pleasant in her whole life

 III Joseph, *m* 1862 Elizabeth, daughter of Joseph and Hannah Snowdon, and had

  1 Hannah, 2 Jane; 3 Joseph Snowdon; 4 James

 IV. Hannah, *b.* 4th of Second mo, 1824, lived here two years and eight months.

 V Elizabeth, now residing in the paternal home at Marple, honored and beloved

 VI James E., *m.* 1860 Margaret W Ely, of New Hope, Bucks County, Pennsylvania, and had:

  1. Anna Ely, 2 Caroline Newbold, 3. Charles James.

 VII Charles, *m.* first, 1856, Anna H.

Nicholson, of Haddonfield, New Jersey, and had:

    1. Mary Nicholson, *b.* 14th of Eighth mo., 1857; *d.* 12th of Ninth mo., 1867.

    2. Katharine E.

    3. Eleanor, *m.* 1886 William T. Elkinton, and had:

        Anna Nicholson and Thomas W.

    4. Samuel Nicholson.

    5. Anna Nicholson, *m.* 1891 George Guest Williams, and had:

        Charles Rhoads.

He *m.* secondly, 1870, Beulah Sansom Morris, of Germantown, Philadelphia, and had:

    6. Mary Morris, *d.* in infancy.

VIII. Jonathan Evans, *m.* 1856 Rebecca C., daughter of Thomas C. and Frances Biddle Garrett, and had:

    1. Joseph, *m.* 1882 Harriet E. Masters, of Muncy, Lycoming County, Pennsylvania, and had:

        Joseph Edgar.

    2. Thomas Garrett, *d.* 1872, aged about fourteen years.

    3. George Ashbridge, *m.* 1890 Frances Canby Tatum, and had:

        Thomas Garrett and Elizabeth Tatum.

    4. Edward G., *m.* 1892 Margaret Ely Paxson, of New Hope, Bucks County, Pennsylvania.

    5. John Biddle.

    6. Frances.

    7. William E.

    8. Elizabeth.

William and Anne P. (Levis) Rhoads had:

I. George, *m.* first Eliza Letchworth, and
had
Robert, who died in boyhood
He *m* secondly Abby Braddock, and had
Anna P., William B ; George E ,
Gertrude; Helen E.
II William, *m* Mary R Evans, and had
Mary, *b* 1850; *d* 1867
He *m* secondly Hannah Scattergood; *m.*
thirdly Susanna C S Culin.
III Esther, *m.* Nathan Garrett.
IV. Phebe.
V Mary Ashbridge, *m* Hibberd Yarnall,
and had ·
Elsie Rhoads; Edgar, Mary E ; Ernest
Rhoads, Stanley Rhoads.
VI Anna.

The bit of history contained in the following account of the
Rhoads family in Lincolnshire and Derbyshire, England, however remotely connected with ours of the present day, is interesting in itself

We claim no merit in such relationship, believing that " It is
only noble to be good," and are also well aware of the truth
of the adage, " Thy ancestors' virtues are not thine," unless
made so by cultivation and practice

I am kindly allowed to copy the story from " Memorials of
our Ancestors and their Descendants," belonging to Joseph R.
Rhoads, of Overbrook, Philadelphia.

The sources of information referred to in it are Monthly
Meeting records of Friends; family records, Proud's " History
of Pennsylvania," Smith's " History of Delaware County, Pennsylvania ," facts given by Spencer Bonsall and Gilbert Cope, of
the Pennsylvania Historical Society, Burke's " Extinct and Dor-
mant Baronetcies ;" and Burke's " Commoners of Great Britain "

As previously stated, the name has been variously spelled,
sometimes in the same document, as De Rodes, Rodes, Roads,
Roades, Rhoades, Rhodes, and Rhoads.

" The family of Rodes, or Rhodes, is one of great antiquity, having flourished for several centuries in the counties of Nottingham, Lincoln, York, and Derby, successively.

" The first settler on record, in England, of this family is Gerard de Rodes, a feudal baron, the capital seat of whose barony was Horn Castle, in Lincolnshire. Camden says, ' Horn Castle was a Soke, or seigniory of thirteen lordships.' Gerard de Rodes was, consequently, one of the greater barons ; his absence as ambassador will account for his name not occurring on the Roll of Magna Charta, he having been sent by King John, 29th March, in the ninth year of his reign, ambassador to foreign parts.

" Gerard de Rodes lived in the reigns of Henry II., Richard I., John, and Henry III., from all of whom he received great favors.

" It is not known when the baronetcy became extinct, but the lands of Horn Castle were lost in the reign of Richard II. Froissart mentions two families of Rodes, or Rhodes : one, the Counts d'Armagnach and Rhodes, who came from Normandy with Henry II. and Margaret, his mother; the other, De Rhodes, hereditary knight of Flanders. It is not known to which family Gerard belonged, though Burke says probably to the one first mentioned.

" William de Rhodes, a lineal descendant of Gerard de Rodes, married Anne, daughter and heiress of John Cachehorse, of Stavely Woodthorpe, in Derbyshire, and thus founded the Derbyshire branch of the family.

" John Rodes, a lineal descendant of William de Rhodes, was high sheriff for Derbyshire in 1591.

" Francis Rodes, son of the above John, was one of the justices of the Common Pleas in the time of Elizabeth. He married Catharine, third daughter of Marmaduke, Constable of Holderness, in York. In 1583 he built Barlborough Hall. Barlborough, or Balborough, Hall is in the northeastern part of Derbyshire, northeast of Chesterfield and southeast of Sheffield. It was described by James Pilkington, in ' View of the Present State of Derbyshire,' 1789, as 'a handsome mansion of the age of Elizabeth.' The principal front of this house

retained its original appearance, having projecting bows ter-
minating in octagonal embattled turrets and large transom
windows; the inside has been modernized, but in one of the
lower chambers is a very magnificent stone chimney-piece out
of the great chamber; it is enriched with fluted Doric pillars,
supporting statues of Justice and Religion and coats of arms
and various articles in bas-relief. In the upper part are the
arms of the Rodes family, with this inscription: 'Francis
Rodes Serviens suæ Reginæ ad legem A.D. 1584 ætatis suæ 50.'
In the lower part are two shields of the arms of Rodes, with
different empalements, the one supported by a judge on the
dexter and a lady on the sinister side; at the bottom is this
inscription: 'Constitutus Justiciarius in Banco Communi 30
Eliz.' On the sides are inscriptions describing his two wives
and their issues. The buff coat and sword of Sir Francis
Rodes, worn in the time of Charles I., are preserved in this
house; they are engraved in Grose's 'Ancient Armor,' Plate
XXXIX.

"Godfrey Rodes, son of Francis Rodes, of Barlborough Hall,
was knighted 13th July, 1615.

"Sir Edward Rodes, knight of Great Houghton, son of Sir
Godfrey Rodes, was one of the two dissenters among the gentry
of Yorkshire; he served under Cromwell at the battle of Preston;
he had a colonel's commission from Cromwell in 1654, and was
one of his Privy Council; he was much in Scotland during the
Protectorate, and was returned member to one of Cromwell's
Parliaments for the shire of Perth at the same time that his
son was returned for Linlithgow. The last male heir of this
branch, William Rodes, of Great Houghton, died unmarried in
1740; the property passed to descendants of the female line,
and the title became extinct.

"John Rodes, eldest son of Francis Rodes, of Barlborough
Hall, was knighted at the Tower, 15th March, 1603; was high
sheriff of Derbyshire 36 Elizabeth; he sold the estates of Stavely
Woodthorpe, and resided permanently at Barlborough Hall.

"He was married three times and had a number of children;
he disinherited his eldest son, John, who founded the Devonshire branch of the family.

" Francis Rodes, second son of John Rodes,* and the thirteenth generation from Gerard de Rodes, inherited Barlborough
Hall and was knighted at Whitehall, 9th August, 1641 ; was
created a baronet 14th of the same month. He married Elizabeth, daughter and sole heiress of Sir George Lascelles, knight,
of Sturton and Gateford, Nottingham ; they had several daughters and five sons; three of the latter married,—Francis, the
heir ; Clifford, the second son ; and the fifth son, John of Sturton,
who married Elizabeth, daughter of Simon Jessop, Esq. It is
stated that John Rodes and Elizabeth Jessop had a number of
children, of whom two sons married in America; but no dates
are given, nor the names of any of their children, excepting
that of their eldest son, John, who, it is said, married, in England, Mary, daughter of William Tigh, son of Tigh of Carlby,
in Lincolnshire.

" The barony became extinct by the death of Sir John Rodes,
unmarried, in 1743, at Barlborough Hall, the estates passing
to his grandnephew, Cornelius Heathcote, who assumed the
name of Rodes. He, in his turn, dying unmarried, was succeeded by his nephew, Cornelius Heathcote Reaston, who
assumed the name of Rodes in 1825. . . .

" It would appear from the following quotation by Sir Walter
Scott, from ' Old Ballads,' that the family had at one time a
seat either in Scotland or nearer the border than Horn Castle,
Lincolnshire :

" ' THE HOUSE OF THE RHODES ON THE HILL.

" ' The Gordon then his bugle blew,
And said, " Awa, awa,
The house of Rhodes is all on fire ;
I hold it time to ga." '

" In Besse's ' Sufferings of the Quakers' we find the following :
' For attending meetings at the house of Thomas Fowkes and
other meetings at Tupton and Bilfley, in the months called July
and August 1670, was taken from John Rhodes £20.' ' In 1689
Taken for Tithes in corn and other goods from Lady Rhodes

* Eldest son of Francis Rodes.

£22. in Derbyshire.' 'Cithe Rhoads was sent to prison for absence from his parish church and for being met with others for religious worship in the house of John Elliot of Callumpton. 1661,' 'For attendance at a meeting in Yorkshire in 1683 Thomas Roads and Joseph Roads were sent to prison.' These extracts show that a number of persons of the name were early convinced of the truth of Friends' principles, and no doubt it was the hope of enjoying religious liberty which led John Roades and his sons to leave their Derbyshire home and seek the wilderness of Pennsylvania."

"WAYSIDE, OVERBROOK P.O., Third month 4th, 1893.

"DEAR FRIEND, AND COUSIN, THOUGH IT BE IN A REMOTE DEGREE,—I am very glad the examination of our 'Memorials' seems to have given thee so much pleasure. The book is indeed a beautiful one, but none too beautiful to lend, especially to one who has evidently so thoroughly appreciated it. It was a work of love on the part of two nieces of my father, one of them, who illuminated the letters and drew the pictures of the 'Old Homestead' and of the 'Old Chestnut Tree,' being something of an artist. He prized it greatly in his old age, and was always happy to show it to any one interested in the Rhoads family. I can remember with what interest he used to call attention to the fact that *five* of my ancestors came over in the John and Sarah—I think that was the prosaic name of our Mayflower—in 1681, the year before William Penn came.

"While it is very true, as Whittier says,

> ' Nor honored less than he who heirs
> Is he who founds a line,'

yet so many more of us can enjoy and accomplish the 'heiring' of a line than the 'founding,' that it must always be the more general satisfaction to look back to worthy ancestors rather than forward to distinguished descendants whom we shall never hear of.

"None of our ancestors seem to have been very brilliant or distinguished men, but they seem to have been substantial, respectable, intelligent, and 'good' citizens, of more 'gentle' strain than might have been expected from the descendants of a Norman knight, or of the 'fair ladie' who defended the 'house of the Rhodes' and

> ' Stude upon her castle wall
> And let twa bullets flee :
> She missed the bluidy butcher's hea
> And only grazed his knee.'

"See Porter & Coates's edition of 'Percy's Reliques,' at pages 90 and 91, Ballad of Edom O'Gorman.

" I have great faith 'in gentle blood and good breeding' in the best sense, but I am sure that in a certain sense there is a great deal of humbug about the craving for aristocratic lineage. John G. Saxe very sharply says,

> ' A thing for laughter, sneers, and jeers
> Is American aristocracy,'

and when I read of the dreadful moral degeneracy of some of the present scions of great houses and the present bearers of great and noble names, I sometimes fear it may not be many generations, even in dear old England, before the children of many noble families may dread to hear the true story of their ancestors. Saxe also says,—

> ' You'd best beware, my snobbish friend !
> Your family thread you can't ascend
> Without great danger to apprehend
> You may find it waxed at the farther end
>   By some plebeian vocation. . . .
> Or else it may end in a rope of stronger twine
> That plagued some unworthy relation.'

" My daughter Alice and I visited Barlboro' when we were in England some years since, and drove by the old hall, which is in an excellent state of preservation. . . .

" I did not think to write so long a letter, but the subject, being 'ourselves' and 'our ancestors,' is, of course, an interesting one to us, and I have almost forgotten the real object of my writing, which was to say to thee that I have not the slightest objection to thy having any portion of the ' Memorials' printed with thy family memoirs, and should there be a spare copy of the memoirs, would be much pleased to have it.

"Does it not seem curious that the apostolic name of James should have come into both branches of our family,—in thy great-grandfather and thy worthy brother, and in my dear father, Professor James Rhoads? My father's first cousin, Samuel Rhoads, for many years editor of *Friends' Review*, was, I think, a friend of thy brother.

"Excuse my inflicting upon thee so long a letter.

"Sincerely thy friend,

"Jos. R. Rhoads."

ASHBRIDGE FAMILY.

George Ashbridge, of Yorkshire, England, came to Pennsylvania to reside, arriving at Philadelphia 5th of Fifth month, 1698. In 1701 he was living at Edgemont, in what was then known as Chester County. He married Mary Malin, of Upper Providence, on the 23d of Eighth month, 1701, at Providence Meeting of Friends.

Their children were as follows:

John, *b.* 1702; *m.* Hannah Davies 1732.

George, *b.* 1703–04; *m.* Jane Hoopes 1730.

Jonathan, *b.* 1705. Was lost or killed in a wood near Lancaster.

Elizabeth, *b.* 1708; *m.* John Sharpless.

Mary, *b.* 1710; *m.* Amos Yarnall.

Aaron, *b.* 1712–13; *m.* Sarah Davies 1737.

Hannah, *b.* 1715; *m.* Joshua Hoopes.

Phebe, *b.* 1717; *m.* Richard Thomas; second marriage, William Trimble.

Lydia, *b.* 1719–20; *m.* Ellis Davies; died 1792.

Joseph, *b.* 1723; *m.* Priscilla Davies 1749.

John and Hannah (Davies) Ashbridge had eight children, viz.:
Jane, Jonathan, Elizabeth, John, Amos, Hannah, David, and

LINEAGE OF ELIZABETH OWEN, WIFE OF JAMES RHOADS, OF MARPLE.

It may interest some of the descendants of James and Elizabeth Rhoads, of Marple, Delaware County, Pennsylvania, to have the genealogy of my great-grandmother, Elizabeth Rhoads. As far back as her great-grandfathers, Owen ap Evan and Owen Humphrey, of Wales, it is drawn from the original marriage certificates in my possession and copied in this Appendix. Beyond that the record is taken from "Americans of Royal Descent, through Legitimate Issue of Kings," by Charles H. Browning, member of the American Historical Association.   M. R. H.

1. Alfred the Great m. Ethelbith, daughter of Earl Ethelan.

2. Edward the Elder m. his third wife.

3. Princess Edgiva m. secondly, Henry, Count de Vermandois.

4. Hubert, Count de Vermandois and Troyes, m. ———.

5. Lady Adela de Vermandois m. Hugh Magnus, of France, grandson of Henry I. of France.

6. Lady Isabel de Vermandois m. Robert, Earl of Mellent.

7. Lady Mabel de Bellemont m. William de Redvers de Vernon, Earl of Devon.

8. Lady Joane de Vernon m. William, Baron de Briwere by tenure and Lord of Torboy.

9. Lady Margaret de Briwere m. William, Baron de la Ferte.

10. William, Baron de la Ferte, m. ———.

11. Lady Gundred de la Ferte m. Pain, third Baron de Chaworth or Cadurcis, of Little Brittany.

12. Patrick, fourth Baron Chaworth, Lord of Ogmore and Kidwelly, Wales, d. 1257, m. Lady Hawyse, of Kidwelly.

13. Patrick de Chaworth m. Lady Isabel, dau. of William, Baron de Beauchamp, created Earl of Warwick.

14. Lady Maud de Chaworth m. Henry Plantagenet, third Earl of Lancaster.

15. Lady Eleanor Plantagenet m. secondly, and his second wife, Sir Richard Fitz-Alan, Earl of Arundel and Surrey.

16. Sir Richard Fitz-Alan, K.G., Earl of Arundel, m. first Lady Elizabeth de Bohun.

17. Lady Elizabeth Fitz-Alan m. thirdly, Sir Robert Gonshill, Knt., of Hault Hucknall Manor, Derby.

18. Lady Joan Goushill m. Sir Thomas Stanley, installed May 14, 1457, K.G., Lord Stanley.

19. Lady Margaret Stanley, sister of Sir William Stanley, of Bosworth Field, m. secondly, Sir William Troutbeck, Knt., of Prynes Castle, Werrall, Cheshire.

20. Lady Jane Troutbeck m. secondly, Sir William Griffith, K.B., of Penrhyn Castle, Carnarvonshire, Wales.

21. Sir William Griffith, Knt., of Penrhyn, m. secondly, Jane, daughter of John Puleston, of Carnarvon.

22. Lady Sibill Griffith m. Owen ap Hugh, of Bodeon, Anglesey, High Sheriff of Anglesey, 1563, 1580.

23. Jane Owen m. Hugh Gwyn, of Penarth, High Sheriff of Carnarvonshire, 1600.

24. Sibill Gwyn m. John Powell, of Llanwddwn, Montgomeryshire, Wales.

25. Elizabeth Powell m. Humphrey ap Hugh ap David ap Howel ap Grono ap Einion, of Merionethshire, Wales.

26. Owen Humphrey, of Llwyn-du, a justice under Cromwell, m. Jane ———.

27. Rebecca Owen Humphrey m., 1678–79, Robert Owen, of Vron Goch, Merionethshire, Wales. He was born in 1657, came to Pennsylvania 1690, was Justice of the Peace for Merion Township and member of the Provincial Assembly. He died 1697.

28. John Owen m. 1719, Hannah Maries, dau. of George Maries, of Chester, Provincial Councillor. John Owen was Sheriff of Chester County and member of the Provincial Assembly. He was born 1692; died 1752.

29. Elizabeth Owen m. 1745, James Rhoads, of Marple, Delaware County, Pennsylvania.

30. Joseph Rhoads m. 1779, Mary Ashbridge, daughter of George Ashbridge, of Goshen, Chester County, Pennsylvania.

31. Joseph Rhoads m. 1818, Hannah Evans, daughter of Jonathan Evans, of Philadelphia. (See charts of Rhoads and Evans.)

32. Mary Rhoads m. 1841, William Ellis Haines, son of Jacob and Rachel Ellis Haines.

33. Hannah Rhoads Haines m. 1866, John Biddle Garrett, son of Thomas C. and Frances Biddle Garrett.

34. Mary Rhoads Garrett.   Frances Biddle Garrett.

Aaron. Aaron's son Aaron *m.* Sarah Ware; they had three children: David W., Ann Frith, and S. Howell Ashbridge.

John Ashbridge died 1747; his wife in 1771.

GEORGE ASHBRIDGE II. and JANE (HOOPES) ASHBRIDGE had five daughters and four sons:

Mary, *b.* 1731; *m.* Jesse Jones; *d.* 1765.

GEORGE, *b.* 1732–33; *m.* Rebekah Garrett 1754; *d.* 1785.

William, *b.* 1734–35; *m.* Elizabeth Fletcher; *d.* 1775.

Susanna, *b.* 1737; *m.* William Gibbons; *d.* 1820.'

Phebe, *b.* 1739; *m.* Isaac Massey; *d.* 1774.

Jane, *b.* 1742; *m.* Jesse Maris; his second wife; *d.* 1834.

Daniel, *b.* 1744; *m.* Hannah Paul; *d.* 1771.

Joshua, *b.* 1746; *m.* Mary Davis; *d.* 1820.

Lydia, *b.* 1749; *d.* 1752.

GEORGE ASHBRIDGE III. and REBEKAH (GARRETT) ASHBRIDGE had five daughters and two sons:

   I. Lydia, *b.* 1755; *m.* Joseph Malin. They had two sons, George and Joseph, and two daughters, Mary and Jane. George married Margaret Garrett; they left no children. Joseph married Amy Hoopes and left several sons and daughters. Mary and Jane never married.

  II. MARY, *b.* 1758; *m.* Joseph Rhoads, of Marple. Their children were: 1. James; 2. George; 3. JOSEPH; 4. Rebecca; 5. Elizabeth; 6. Phebe; and 7. William. James, George, Rebecca, and Elizabeth never married. Joseph married Hannah Evans. Their children were eight: MARY, Deborah, Joseph, Hannah, Elizabeth, James E., Charles, and Jonathan Evans.

     Phebe married Isaac Price Garrett, of Upper Darby. They had no children.

     William married Anne P. Levis. They had two sons and four daughters: George, William, Esther, Mary, Phebe, and Anna.

     For further particulars, see accounts of the Rhoads family.

III. Susanna, *b* 1761, *m* John Fairlamb, 20th of Fifth month,
1784 They had five daughters and three sons, viz..
1. Rebekah, *b.* 1785, *m* —— Darlington, a judge in
Chester County, 2. George, *b.* 1787; 3 Charles, *b.*
1789; 4 Susan, *b* 1792; 5. Harriet, *b* 1794, *m.*
John Roberts, 6 Samuel, *b.* 1797, 7. Eleanor, *b.*
1800, *d* 1801, and 8 Lydia, *b* 1802, *m.* Bond
Valentine and lived in Bellefonte, Pennsylvania They
had one son, Robert, who was twice married.

IV Jane, *b* 1764, *m* Samuel Downing and lived in Down-
ingtown for a number of years They had one son,
George, who never married, and in his very advanced
age was kindly cared for by Richard Ashbridge, who
gave him a home in his house at Whiteland

V. Phebe, *b.* 1767, *m* George Valentine They left no
children

VI. George Garrett, *b.* 1770; *d.* 1843, *m* Rachel Valentine,
daughter of Abraham and Phebe Sharples His
wife was born 1786 and died 1858 Their children
were: 1. Phebe, 2 George, 3 Rebecca, 4 Abram S;
and 5. Rachel Phebe died aged about sixteen
George lived to early manhood and died unmarried.
Rebecca married Jacob M Zook They had five chil-
dren. Mary T., Rachel, Elizabeth, Jacob, and Jane D.
Jane *m* Philip Chase; has one daughter named Mary
Ashbridge
  Abram S., the second son of George G and Rachel
V. Ashbridge, married Elizabeth Sharpless They
had George, who passed from earth in boyhood;
Mary, Rebekah, Richard, Abram S, Joseph, Eliza-
beth, and Eleanor. Mary married John Douglas
Perkins, and has two children, John Douglas and
Joseph Ashbridge Rebekah married Dr Henry
Ecroyd, they live in Newport and have one son,
Henry, *b.* 1892

VII William, the youngest child of George and Rebekah
Ashbridge, *b.* 1773, married Thomazine, daughter
of Colonel Richard Thomas They lived in Phila-

delphia, on Arch Street near Ninth   They had two
sons, William and Richard, two daughters, Mary
and Jane. William, Mary, and Jane never married   Richard married Mary B. James. Their
home is in Whiteland, Chester County, Pennsylvania   Their children were William, John, George,
Richard, Thomazine, Hannah, and Charles.

AARON ASHBRIDGE.

He was the fourth son of George Ashbridge I. and his wife,
Mary Malin Ashbridge, and was born 1712–13 ; married Sarah
Davies in 1737. Some time after her decease he married, in
1746, Elizabeth Sullivan   He was a prominent citizen, and his
wife Elizabeth a well-known minister in the religious Society of
Friends   They had no children   There is an autobiography
of Elizabeth Ashbridge in the fourth volume of "Friends'
Library," edited by William and Thomas Evans   It gives a
singular picture of some phases of life in her time

JOSEPH ASHBRIDGE

He was the youngest son of George Ashbridge I. and his
wife, Mary Malin Ashbridge, and was born in 1723   In 1749
he married Priscilla Davis and settled at Chester. Their children were   Aaron, Joseph, Sarah, Jane, Priscilla, Logan, Mary,
Hannah, Phebe, and George   Their eldest son, Aaron, married Ann Howell   Their children were   Israel, Joseph, Lydia,
Myers, Sarah, Gildersleeve, Elizabeth, and George W.

JOSHUA ASHBRIDGE

He was the fourth son of George Ashbridge II , and was born
in 1746, married Mary Davis, 1773, at Springfield Meeting.
His wife was daughter of Lewis Davis, of Haverford, and was
born in 1746   They lived at the old homestead in Goshen.
Their children were: Daniel, John, Joseph, Rebecca, Thomas,
Hannah, and Lydia. Joshua Ashbridge deceased in 1820; his
wife in 1798.

THOMAS ASHBRIDGE

He was the fourth son of Joshua and Mary Ashbridge, and
was born in 1781   He married Phebe, daughter of Jesse and

22

Abigail Yarnall Garrett, and died in 1850   Their children
were   Phebe, Joshua, Jesse and Abigail (twins), Mary D ,
Hannah Goub, Phebe Ann, John, Thomas, Lydia, Eliza H., and
Washington.

JOSHUA ASHBRIDGE

He was the eldest son of Thomas and Phebe Ashbridge, and
was born in 1806.   He married Rebecca E , only daughter of
Peter and Rebecca E Pechin   Their children are   Mary P ,
John P , who died in 1859, Emily R , and Eliza Helen.
Joshua Ashbridge deceased in 1887, and his wife in 1891.

PARENTAGE OF JANE HOOPES, WHO WAS THE WIFE OF GEORGE ASHBRIDGE II

Joshua Hoopes, with Isabell, his wife, and their children,
Daniel, Margaret, and Christian, came from Cleveland, in Yorkshire, 1683   They settled in Bucks County, Pennsylvania

About 1696 their son Daniel removed to Westtown, in
Chester County, and married, near the end of that year, Jane
Worrilow, of Edgemont   Daniel and Jane Hoopes had seventeen children ; their sixth child, Jane, was born Fifth month
14, 1706, and married George Ashbridge, Eighth month 21,
1730

PARENTAGE OF REBEKAH GARRETT, WHO MARRIED GEORGE ASHBRIDGE III

John and Mary Garat were the parents of the children whose
names are recorded in a Bible printed in 1634, from which the
following notes have been copied ·

" John Garat was borne the 10 day Januari 1631 and baptized
forteanth "

" —— Garat was borne the 30 day of Aprill 1640, baptized
the third of May "

" Mari Garat was baptized the 15th of May 1642 "

" William Garat borne 21 of August and baptized the third
of September 1643."

" Catnn Garatt baptized May 26 in the year of our Lord God 1646 "

"Thomas Ganat, the sonne of John Garrat and Mary his wife was baptized in May the 17th 1649 "

WILLIAM GARRATT

He was the son of John and Mary Garat, as given above. He married Anne Kirke Second month 19, 1668, in England, probably at a Friends' meeting

They lived in the parish of Harby, Leicestershire, until 1684, when they came to Pennsylvania and their seven children with them   William Garratt, Samuel Levis, John Smith, and Robert Cliffe brought a joint certificate from their Monthly Meeting in England, which they presented to a meeting of Friends held at "the Governor's House," in Philadelphia, "the 4th of 9th month 1684 "

Before leaving England, William Garratt, jointly with Samuel Levis, had purchased one thousand acres of land in Pennsylvania   Early in 1685 William Ganatt located his share, two hundred and twenty-five acres, in Darby, now Upper Darby, Delaware County, at which place he and his family resided. William Garratt took an active part in public affairs, being a member of the Pennsylvania Assembly for Chester County in 1707

Both he and his wife were consistent members of the religious Society of Friends, and were confided in by the Meeting. In his old age he removed to Philadelphia, having the following certificate from his Monthly Meeting :

"To ffriends at Philadelphia Monthly Meeting Greeting Whereas our ffriend William Garratt, a member of our Monthly Meeting having lived amongst us Thirty and seven years, and is now in his old age removed to Philadelphia within the verge of your meeting we was willing to give this short account concerning him, and this may certifie that he is a man that has lived in Love and Unity amongst us and beene servissable amongst ffriends here and is cleared from cumber in this world

desiring his preservation to the end and his satisfaction in his
removal we remain your ffriends

in the Truth	DAVID THOMAS
ffrom our Monthly meeting	JOSIAH HIBARD
at Darby the 4th day of	RICHARD PARKER
5th mo 1722	SAMUEL GARRATT
JOHN BLUNSTONE	SAMUEL SELLARS
MICHAEL BLUNSTONE	JOSIAH FEARN
THOMAS WORTH	JOB HARVEY
SAMUEL BRADSHAW"	

William Garratt died about 1724, Anne Garratt, his wife,
died in Philadelphia in 1731.

THOMAS GARRATT

Thomas, son of William and Anne Garratt, married Lydia
Lewis Their daughter Rebekah married George Ashbridge
III.*

* For the account of John and Mary Garat and their descendants as far as
Rebekah Ashbridge, I am indebted to Joseph R Rhoads's " Memorials of our
Ancestors," and to notes given me by Mary T Zook   M R H.

EVANS LINEAGE.

The genealogy of this family between Conan, King of all Wales, and his daughter, Essylt, who married Mervyn Frych, King of Anglesey, 843, and David Goch, of Penllech, and his wife Maud, is taken from "Americans of Royal Descent," by Charles H. Browning.

1.   Conan, King of all Wales.

2. Essylt, or Esselt, *m.* Mervyn Frych, King of Anglesey.

3. Rhodri-Mawr, King of all Wales, *d.* 876, *m.* Lady Angharad, dau. Melriz, son of Arthur ap Seissyllt, Prince of Cardigan.

4. Cadell, Prince of South Wales, *m.* Reingar, daughter of Tudor Trevor, Earl of Haverfod.

5. Howell-dda, King of all Wales, *m.* Lady Jane, daughter of Earl of Cornwall.

6. Owen, Prince of South Wales, *m.* Lady Angharad, daughter of Llewellyn ap Mervyn, Prince of Powis.

7. Einion, eldest son, *m.* Lady Nesta, daughter of Earl of Devonshire.

8. Tudor-Mawr, Prince of South Wales, *m.* Gwenlian, daughter of Gwyr ap Rhyddrch, Lord of Dyfet.

9. Rhys ap Tudor-Mawr, Prince of South Wales, *m.* Lady Gwladys, daughter of Rhiwallon, Prince of Powis.

10. Griffith ap Rhys, Prince of South Wales, *m.* Lady Gwenlian, daughter of Griffith ap Cynan, Prince of North Wales.

11. Rhys ap Griffith, Prince of South Wales, Lord Rhys, Chief-Justice of South Wales, *d.* 1197, *m.* Lady Gwenlian, daughter of Madoc, Lord of Bromfield.

12. Rhys Gryd, Lord of Yestradtywy, *m.* Lady Joan, daughter of Richard de Clare, Earl of Hertford.

13. Rhys Mechyllt, Lord of Llandovery Castle, *d.* 1242-43.

14. Rhys Vaughn, of Yestradtywy, *m.* Lady Gwladys, daughter of Griffith, Lord of Cymcydmaen.

15. Rhys-Gloff, Lord of Cymcydmaen, *m.* Lady Gwyril, daughter of Maclywn ap Cadwalader.

16. Madoc ap Rhys *m.* Lady Tanglwyst, daughter of Gronowy ap Einion.

17. Trahairn-Goch, of Llyn, Grainianoc and Penlech, *m.* Lady Gwyrvyl, daughter of Madoc ap Meirig.

18. David-Goch, of Penllech, 1314, *m.* Lady Maud, daughter of David Lloyd.

19. Ievan ap David-Goch, of Grainoc and Penllech, *m.* Lady Eva.

20. Madoc ap Ievan, of Grainoc; wife's name unknown.

21. Deikws-ddu *m.* Gwen, daughter of Ievan-ddu.

22. Einion ap Deikws *m.* Morvydd, daughter of Matw ap Llowarch.

23. Howel ap Einion, *m.* Mali, daughter of Llewllyn ap Ievan.

24. Griffith ap Howel *m.* Gwenlian, daughter of Einion ap Ievan Lloyd

25. Lewis ap Griffith, of Yshute, *m.* Ethll, or Ellin, daughter of Edward ap Ievan Llanoddyn.

26. Robert ap Lewis *m.* Gwryl, daughter of Llewllyn ap David, of Llan Rwst, Denbighshire.

27. Ievan ap Robert ap Lewis, of Rhiwlas and Vron Goch, *m.* Jane ——.

28. Evan ap Evan, of Vron Goch; his wife's name not on our records.

29. Thomas ap Evan, came from Wales to Gwynedd, Penna., 1698, *m.* Ann, who died 1716.

30. Evan Evans, born in Wales 1684, *d.* 1747; came to Gwynedd 1698, with his parents, *m.* 1713, Elizabeth Musgrave.

31. Jonathan Evans, *b.* 1714, *d.* 1795, *m.* 1740, Hannah Walton, *d.* 1801.

32. Jonathan Evans, *b.* 1759, *d.* 1839, *m.* 1786, Hannah Bacon, *b.* 1765, *d.* 1829, and had:

Evans Lineage—*Continued*

JONATHAN and HANNAH (BACON) EVANS had:

I. William, *b.* 1787; *d.* 1867; *m* first, 1811, Deborah
Musgrave, *b.* 1788, *d* 1815, and had   *322 Union St (now Dela.*

    1 Abigail, *m.* Horatio C Wood, and had:
       William Evans.

    2 Jonathan, who deceased 1841.

He *m* secondly, 1824, Elizabeth Barton, and had ·

    3 Rebecca, 4 √Hannah; 5 ⬦Elizabeth R.

    6 √William, *m* ⬦Rebecca Carter, and had:
       John C , Charles, Alice C ; Grace, William , Ruth.

II Joseph, *b* 1789, *d* 1871, *m* 1814 Grace Trimble, and had

    1. Ann, *m* Isaac C. Evans, and had
       Mary L , Joseph, Isaac, Anne, Lydia, Rowland;
       William

    2. William; and 3. Hannah, who deceased in child-
    hood

    4. Mary, *m* William Mickle, and had
       √Anne, √Mary; Sarah ; √Joseph , √William

    5. √Thomas, *m.* √Agnes Shay, and had:
       Mary, Charles, Grace

    6 John, *d.* near his twentieth year

III. Mary, *b.* 1791; *d.* 1859; lived unmarried, faithful in
her love and helpfulness to her parents and all their
family

IV. HANNAH, *b.* 1793, *d* 1865; *m.* 1818 Joseph Rhoads, of
Marple, Delaware County, Pennsylvania, *b* 1787, *d* 1861,
and had

    1 √MARY, *m* 1841 William Ellis Haines, and had
       HANNAH RHOADS, *m.* 1866 John Biddle Garrett, and
       had
         MARY RHOADS and FRANCES BIDDLE

    2 √Deborah, *b.* 1821 ; *d.* 1892.

    3. √Joseph, *m* 1862 Elizabeth Snowdon, and had   *× d. at Springfield 9.9.18,*
i. 1910 √Hannah , √Jane, √Joseph Snowdon , James

    4 Hannah, *b* 1824, lived here two years and eight
months.

5 √Elizabeth

6 √James E , *m* 1860√Margaret W Ely, and had .

   Anna Ely ; Caroline Newbold , Charles James.

7 √Charles, *m* first, 1856, Anna H Nicholson, and
   had ·

   Mary Nicholson , √Katharine E , √Eleanor , √Anna
   Nicholson , √Samuel Nicholson

He *m* secondly, 1870,√Beulah Sansom Morris, and had :
   Mary Morris, *d.* in infancy.

   Eleanor R , daughter of Charles and Anna N Rhoads.
   m 1886√William T Elkinton, and had
   √Anna Nicholson , √Thomas William.

   Anna N , daughter of Charles and Anna N Rhoads,
   m 1891√George G Williams, and had
   √Charles Rhoads

8 √Jonathan Evans, *m* 1856 √Rebecca C Garrett, and
   had :

   √Joseph ; Thomas G , *d* 1872 , √George Ashbridge ,
   √Edward G , √John Biddle ,√Frances , √William E ,
   √Elizabeth

   √Joseph, son of Jonathan E and Rebecca G Rhoads,
   m 1882√Harriet E Masters, and had .
   √Joseph Edgar

   √George Ashbridge, son of Jonathan E and Rebecca
   G Rhoads, *m.* 1890 √Frances Canby Tatum, and
   had

   Thomas G. ,√Elizabeth Tatum

   √Edward G , son of Jonathan E and Rebecca G
   Rhoads, *m* 1892 Margaret Ely Paxson

V Joel, *b* 1796, *d* 1865 , *m.* Hannah, daughter of Owen and
Mary (Hall) Rhoads, and had

   1 Mary R , *m* 1849√William Rhoads, Jr , and had
   Mary.

   2 William, *d* in early life

   3 Owen, *m* Lydia Thompson, and had
   Mary , Beulah , Edwin , William

   4 Elizabeth , 5 Elizabeth , 6 Joel , all three died in infancy

7. Charles, *m* first, Jane Lawrence, secondly, Anne Belle Kirby, and had
   Charles Wistar
8 Hannah R , *d.* 1892
9 Susan
10 Samuel, *m.* Anne Taylor, and had :
   Mary, Ella; Caroline, Albert, Bertha.
11. Joel, *m* Emma Stokely, and had
   Mary, William, Stokely; Laura
VI Thomas, *b* 1798, *d* 1868, *m* 1834 Catharine, daughter of John and Charlotte Wistar, *b* 1802, *d* 1871, and had. *house 517 Arch St. Phila*
   1 John Wistar, *m* 1867 Eleanor Tyson Stokes, and had · *d in 38*
      I Elizabeth W., *m* 1892 Francis Goodhue, Jr, and had
         Mary Brooks Goodhue, Jr.
      II Thomas, III John Wistar; IV Eleanor
   2 Thomas Wistar
   3 Hannah Bacon
   4 Katharine W , *m* 1865 Francis Stokes, and had :
      I Katharine E, *m* 1886 Samuel Mason, and had :
         Samuel, Henry Stokes, Katharine Wistar.
      II. Henry W. Stokes; III Esther Newlin Stokes, IV.
         Edith Wistar Stokes, V. Francis Joseph Stokes
   5. Jonathan, *m* 1873 Rachel R , daughter of Francis R. and Anna S Cope, and had ·
      I Anna Cope, II Francis Algernon, III Edward Wyatt, IV Ernest Mervyn, V Harold.
VII Charles, *b* 1802, on Christmas-day, *d* 1879, *m* 1836 Mary Lownes Smith, daughter of Robert and Mary Bacon Smith

----

Copy of a record in a quarto edition of the Bible printed in London, 1722, by John Baskett. The record of the births is in the handwriting of the father, Jonathan Evans. The record of deaths in the margin partly by his son Jonathan and one by his granddaughter, Hannah Rhoads .

" Elizabeth Evans Daughter of Jonathan Evans and Hannah his wife was born the third day of March 1740–41 at four o'clock in the afternoon, the third day of the week

" Died Aug⁺ 26th, 1746.

" Samuel Evans Son of Jonathan Evans and Hannah his wife was Born the twenty sixth day of Octoʳ 1742 at four o'clock in the morning, the third day of the week.

" Died Aug⁺ 22, 1744

" Joel Evans Son of Jonathan Evans and Hannah his wife was Born the twenty fourth day of February 1743-4, at ten o'clock in the morning the Sixth day of the week.

" Died in Jamaica West Indies.

" Mary Evans Daughter of Jonathan Evans and Hannah his wife was Born the Seventh Day of December 1746, the First day of the week at six o'clock in the morning

" Died the 14th of the 6 month 1794, about half past seven o'clock in the morning

" William Evans Son of Jonathan Evans and Hannah his wife was Born the fourth day of May 1749, the Fifth day of the week at five o'clock in the morning.

" Benjamin Evans Son of Jonathan Evans and Hannah his wife was Born the Sixteenth day of November 1751, the Seventh day of the week at half past three in the morning

" Died the 3rd of the 1st month 1793 at ¼ past 9 o'clock in the evening

" John Evans Son of Jonathan Evans and Hannah his wife was Born the thirtieth day of May 1753, the Seventh day of the week at five o'clock in the morning.

" Jonathan Evans Son of Jonathan Evans and Hannah his Wife was born the 25ᵗʰ January 1759 between three and four o'clock in the morning, Fifth day of week.

" Died the 8th of the 2nd month 1839 between 7 and 8 o'clock in the morning

"My father Jonathan Evans deceased the 3rd of 2nd month 1795 at his dwelling house in Dock street.

"My mother Hannah Evans deceased at my house the 23rd of 4th month 1801" *

COPY OF AN ORIGINAL RECORD OF THE DAVID BACON FAMILY

"David Bacon Son of John and Elizabeth Bacon was Born the 14th day of the First month old stile in the year 1729

"Mary Bacon, wife of David Bacon, was born the 23rd of the Eleventh month old stile 1727 Daughter of Joseph and Dinah Trotter.

"Elizabeth Bacon Daughter of David Bacon and Mary Bacon was Born the 17th of the Eighth month 1752: old stile, 3 o'clock in ye morning

"Rebecca Bacon, Daughter of David and Mary Bacon was Born the 23rd of the First month 1754 10 o'clock in the morning

"Joseph Bacon Son of David and Mary Bacon was Born the 31st of First month 1756, 10 o'clock in the morning

"John Bacon Son of David and Mary Bacon, was Born the 24th of the Tenth month 1757, 8 in the morning

"Mary Bacon Daughter of David and Mary Bacon was Born the 23rd of the Fifth month 1759, 3 in ye morning

"John Bacon Son of David and Mary Bacon, was Born the 13th of the Fourth month 1761, 7 o'clock in ye morning.

"David Bacon Son of David and Mary Bacon was Born the 10th of the Fourth month 1763, 10 in ye Evening

* These last two records are in the handwriting of my grandfather, Jonathan Evans. M R. H.

"Hannah Bacon Daughter of David and Mary Bacon was Born the 5th of the Third month 1765, 5 o'clock in ye morning.

"David Bacon Son of David and Mary Bacon was Born the 16th of ye Tenth month 1766, 8 o'clock in ye evening.

"Rachel Bacon Daughter of David and Mary Bacon was Born the 11th of the Eleventh month 1767, 2 o'clock in the morning

"Mary Bacon Wife of David Bacon Departed this life the 15th of the Tenth month 1793 aged near 66 years"

To the above record may be added the following memorandum:
"David and Mary Bacon's eldest daughter Elizabeth married Thomas Scattergood, Tenth mo 22nd 1772
"Their children were
Joseph, born 1 mo 7. 1774, deceased 6 mo 28 1824
Martha " 4 mo 1775 " 8 mo 1775
David " 7 mo 1779 " 6 mo. 1780
"Elizabeth Scattergood deceased 10 mo 11 1780"

Joseph Scattergood, elder son of Thomas and Elizabeth Scattergood, married Ann Rogers Their children were
Thomas, William, David, Joseph, Elizabeth, and Sarah

Joseph Scattergood, the fourth son of Joseph and Ann Scattergood, married Mary McCollin. They had seven children
Rachel, Anna, George Jones, Joseph, Thomas, William, and Henry Anna and Henry died in infancy, Joseph in mature life. He was a valued minister among Friends.
There are numerous descendants of David and Mary Bacon now living in Pennsylvania and New Jersey Those of their daughter Hannah, who married Jonathan Evans, are given in the genealogy of the Evans family

INDEX.

(References to individual names are generally limited to the main portion of the volume In the Appendix these may be found by reference to families, as "Ashbridge Family, genealogy of ")

339

THE END

9782

CPSIA information can be obtained
at www.ICGtesting.com
Printed in the USA
BVHW041005160620
581365BV00003B/46

9 781341 593703